Mastering IoT for Industrial Environments

Unlock the IoT Landscape for Industrial Environments with Industry 4.0, Covering Architecture, Protocols like MQTT, and Advancements with ESP-IDF

Shrey Sharma

www.orangeava.com

First published: March 2024

Published by: Orange Education Pvt Ltd, AVA™

Address: 9, Daryaganj, Delhi, 110002

ISBN: 978-81-97081-97-2

www.orangeava.com

Dedicated To

My beloved Grandparents:

Late Sh. Tara Chand Sharma and Late Smt. Vidya Devi

My Strength and Support System

About the Author

Shrey Sharma, a graduate in Electronics and Communication from M.D. University, Rohtak, Haryana, has been passionate about Internet of Things (IoT) technology since his pre-final year of engineering. His journey began with an internship in the domain and culminated in the creation of SmarDen, an IoT-based startup focused on transforming homes, hotels, and enterprises into smart spaces.

SmarDen not only automates these spaces but also provides an IoT platform for developers. This cloud-based solution empowers them with an MQTT server, back-end, dashboard, and mobile application, fostering innovation within the IoT ecosystem.

Starting with no clients, products, or team, SmarDen has grown into a thriving Start-up and now registered under Start-up India and MSME. Up till now, SmarDen has automated homes for more than thousands of people across India and Nigeria. Starting from home automation to builder projects, SmarDen is now providing IoT Solutions for homes, offices, buildings, data centers and custom IoT projects.

Driven by his passion for education, Shrey has delivered lectures and hosted seminars, webinars, and workshops on IoT at prestigious institutions like VIT (Vellore), Amity University, Thakur College (Mumbai), BKBIET (Pilani), and VCE (Rohtak). He even conducted webinars for MNCs like Adani Transmission and did workshops for in-house Indian Railway officers at the National Academy of Indian Railways, contributing his expertise to national development.

Shrey's mission is to make IoT accessible and affordable, from product development and implementation to services and learning. His dedication to democratizing this transformative technology positions him as a leader in the IoT space.

About the Technical Reviewer

Julien Bertolini has been a part of the Internet of Things (IoT) market since its early days, dating back to 2008 when he started working with Machine-to-Machine (M2M) technology. With a strong technical background in electronics, development (embedded, mobile, web, server), and teams/projects management as a director, Julien has worked across various industries, including automotive and telecommunications, to develop customized IoT solutions that cater to business needs.

Currently, he is an IoT expert at Volvo, where he primarily focuses on creating and implementing IoT solutions in factories worldwide. Additionally, he is actively involved in devising strategies aimed at achieving Industry 4.0 objectives. Julien firmly believes in the philosophy of *Think big, start small.*

Acknowledgements

As I reflect on this journey, I am filled with profound gratitude towards those who have played pivotal roles in shaping the course of this book.

First, to the Arduino and Espressif, a heartfelt bow. You gifted me, and countless others, the physical tools and digital playgrounds to sculpt our dreams into reality. Like a child given a box of paints, you set alight an explosion of creativity, empowering millions to become not just consumers but inventors. Your visionary contributions have empowered millions, including myself, to explore new realms of possibility and bring our ideas to life.

To my Mom and Dad, my eyes well up with a love deeper than words can express. You never once clipped my wings, but instead, held them aloft, urging me to soar as high as I dared. You fueled my curiosity with tireless support, providing the resources I needed not just to survive, but to thrive. This book, in many ways, is a testament to your boundless faith in me, and for that, I am eternally grateful.

My dearest wife, your belief in me has been the lighthouse in my stormiest seas. You've seen me at my most lost and frustrated, and yet, you never wavered. You pushed me gently and relentlessly, reminding me of the potential I sometimes forget. This book, my love, is as much yours as it is mine, a tangible expression of the strength you ignited within me.

To my esteemed co-founder, a silent understanding hums between us. You trusted my vision and my decisions, even when they veered off the beaten path. Your partnership isn't just a professional one; it's a bond forged in the crucible of shared ambition and mutual respect. Thank you for being the rock that steadied my hand when doubt threatened to pull me under.

To the students who filled my workshops and lectures, your eager faces were a constant source of inspiration. You reminded me of the power of sharing knowledge. Your thirst for learning fueled my own, pushing me to explore the academic side of this field. Thank you for being the wind beneath my wings, propelling me forward on this incredible journey.

And finally, to you, the reader. You chose this book, entrusted me with the responsibility of sharing my knowledge, and in doing so, you became part of this incredible story. May the pages within unlock doors to new possibilities, ignite your own creative fire, and empower you to build something extraordinary.

This book is a love letter, a testament to the invisible threads that bind us together. Thank you, from the depths of my being, for playing your part.

Preface

Welcome to the exciting journey into the world of IoT for industrial environments! As industries evolve in the era of Industry 4.0, the Internet of Things (IoT) emerges as a transformative force, reshaping traditional practices and revolutionizing data collection and operational processes.

In this book, we delve deep into the core principles, technologies, and applications driving the IoT revolution within industrial settings. Each chapter is meticulously crafted to offer a blend of theoretical insights and practical knowledge, equipping readers with the skills needed to navigate the complexities of IoT integration and implementation.

Chapter 1: Industrial Revolution with IoT

We kickstart our exploration by tracing the historical context of industrial revolutions and delving into the principles underpinning Industry 4.0. Through this foundational chapter, readers gain insights into the pivotal role of IoT in driving the transformative changes reshaping industries worldwide.

Chapter 2: The Architecture of IoT

Our journey into IoT architecture unveils the intricate layers that power the seamless exchange of data and information. From perception to application layers, readers gain a comprehensive understanding of the underlying infrastructure driving IoT ecosystems.

Chapter 3: Micro-controllers - The Brain behind IoT Devices

We unravel the world of microcontrollers, exploring their functionalities, applications, and significance in modern technology. From Arduino to ESP32, readers gain practical insights into leveraging microcontrollers to build innovative IoT solutions.

Chapter 4: Communication Protocols in IoT

Efficient communication lies at the heart of IoT systems. This chapter delves into the diverse communication protocols underpinning IoT networks, empowering readers to make informed decisions in selecting the most suitable protocol for their applications.

Chapter 5: Introduction to Interfacing Protocols

We explore the critical role of interfacing protocols in enabling seamless communication between microcontrollers and external devices. Through practical examples and applications, readers gain hands-on experience in configuring and programming interfacing protocols for IoT projects.

Chapter 6: MQTT - The Protocol for Internet of Things

We delve into the lightweight messaging protocol of MQTT, exploring its principles, features, and applications in IoT deployments. Readers gain insights into establishing secure and efficient communication networks using MQTT.

Chapter 7: Machine to Machine Communication

Explore the fascinating realm of Machine to Machine (M2M) communication, unlocking the potential of connected devices to collaborate and perform tasks seamlessly.

Chapter 8: Shifting to ESP-IDF

A comprehensive overview of the ESP-IDF framework equips readers with the tools and knowledge needed to develop IoT applications on Espressif's ESP32 microcontrollers.

Chapter 9: IoT in Industry 4.0

We conclude our exploration by examining the transformative impact of IoT on industrial processes, paving the way for smart factories, predictive maintenance, and intelligent decision-making in the fourth industrial revolution.

This book is designed to be a practical companion for both seasoned professionals and aspiring enthusiasts seeking to harness the power of IoT in industrial environments. Through a blend of theoretical frameworks, real-world examples, and hands-on tutorials, we aim to empower readers to unleash innovation and drive meaningful change in their respective fields.

Embark on this journey with us as we navigate the dynamic landscape of IoT for industrial environments, from theory to reality.

Downloading the code bundles and colored images

Please follow the links or scan the QR codes to download the ***Code Bundles and Images*** of the book:

https://github.com/ava-orange-education/Mastering-IoT-For-Industrial-Environments

The code bundles and images of the book are also hosted on ***https://rebrand.ly/724e15***

In case there's an update to the code, it will be updated on the existing GitHub repository.

Errata

We take immense pride in our work at **Orange Education Pvt Ltd,** and follow best practices to ensure the accuracy of our content to provide an indulging reading experience to our subscribers. Our readers are our mirrors, and we use their inputs to reflect and improve upon human errors, if any, that may have occurred during the publishing processes involved. To let us maintain the quality and help us reach out to any readers who might be having difficulties due to any unforeseen errors, please write to us at :

errata@orangeava.com

Your support, suggestions, and feedback are highly appreciated.

DID YOU KNOW

Did you know that Orange Education Pvt Ltd offers eBook versions of every book published, with PDF and ePub files available? You can upgrade to the eBook version at **www.orangeava.com** and as a print book customer, you are entitled to a discount on the eBook copy. Get in touch with us at: **info@orangeava.com** for more details.

At **www.orangeava.com**, you can also read a collection of free technical articles, sign up for a range of free newsletters, and receive exclusive discounts and offers on AVA™ Books and eBooks.

PIRACY

If you come across any illegal copies of our works in any form on the internet, we would be grateful if you would provide us with the location address or website name. Please contact us at **info@orangeava.com** with a link to the material.

ARE YOU INTERESTED IN AUTHORING WITH US?

If there is a topic that you have expertise in, and you are interested in either writing or contributing to a book, please write to us at **business@orangeava.com**. We are on a journey to help developers and tech professionals to gain insights on the present technological advancements and innovations happening across the globe and build a community that believes Knowledge is best acquired by sharing and learning with others. Please reach out to us to learn what our audience demands and how you can be part of this educational reform. We also welcome ideas from tech experts and help them build learning and development content for their domains.

REVIEWS

Please leave a review. Once you have read and used this book, why not leave a review on the site that you purchased it from? Potential readers can then see and use your unbiased opinion to make purchase decisions. We at Orange Education would love to know what you think about our products, and our authors can learn from your feedback. Thank you!

For more information about Orange Education, please visit **www.orangeava.com**.

Table of Contents

CHAPTER 1
Industrial Revolution with IoT

Introduction

The Industrial Revolution was a turning point in human history. It marked a big change from societies based on farming to ones based on factories and machines. It happened in three waves, and each one caused huge changes in markets, societies, and how people lived and worked. In this chapter, we'll talk about the first, second, and third Industrial Revolutions. We'll look at what made them different and how they changed the world.

Structure

In this chapter, the following topics will be covered:

- Brief History of the Industrial Revolution
- What is Industry 4.0
- Elements of Industry 4.0
- The Internet of Things - 1st element of IoT
- Growth of IoT

- Applications of IoT
- Future Trends of IoT

Brief History of the Industrial Revolution

This section explains the history of the Industrial Revolution.

The First Industrial Revolution

The First Industrial Revolution happened mostly in Britain at the end of the 18th century. It started because of changes in farming, like the enclosure movement, which combined farms and made more workers than needed. This extra labor force was put to work in industries that were growing quickly thanks to new technologies like the steam engine and the automation of cloth production.

During this time, output moved from small shops and homes to factories. The steam engine changed the way people and things were moved, making it easier to get from one place to another. With the help of machines like the spinning wheel and the power loom, the textile industry was changed. This led to more work being done and the growth of cities.

The Second Industrial Revolution

The Second Industrial Revolution happened from the middle of the 19th century to the beginning of the 20th century. It was marked by big scientific advances. During this time, steel production, electricity, and the growth of railroad networks all started. These new ideas took manufacturing to new heights and changed markets all over the world.

Steel was the key to civilization because it made it possible to build bridges, buildings, and railroads. Electricity changed many fields, from industry to transportation to communication. People could talk to each other across long distances once telegraphs and phones were invented. This made it easier for businesses to talk to each other.

The Third Industrial Revolution

The broad use of digital tools in the late 20th century was the start of the Third Industrial Revolution, which is also called the Digital Revolution. This wave brought in computers, the internet, and other information technology systems that changed businesses around the world and paved the way for the digital age we live in now.

Computers and improvements in microelectronics have led to automation, which has increased efficiency and productivity. People, companies, and information from all over the world can now link through the internet. This made it easy to talk to each other, do business online, and share information quickly.

The Industrial Revolution had a huge effect on societies and businesses all over the world. They changed rural societies into urbanized, industrialized countries. People moving from rural places to cities helped cities grow and changed the way people interact with each other. Even though these changes brought a lot of good things, they also brought problems, such as abuse of workers, overcrowding in cities, and damage to the environment.

Industrialization helped the economy grow and made way for capitalism systems. It changed the way things were made, making mass production possible and making items cheaper. The rise of workplaces and the division of labor changed the way people worked, which led to the rise of labor organizations that fought for workers' rights and better working conditions.

The Industrial Revolution made it possible for technological advances that are still changing our world today. They made it possible for robotics, artificial intelligence, and the Internet of Things (IoT) to grow in the future. We are on the verge of the Fourth Industrial Revolution, which will be driven by the combination of digital, biological, and physical technologies. This will bring more changes and possibilities.

The Industrial Revolutions are important parts of human history because they show how societies went from being based on farming to being based on machines. Each wave brought scientific advances that had never been seen before. These transformations changed markets, societies, and our way of life. By learning about changes in the past, we can learn important lessons about the present and get ready for the challenges and chances of the future.

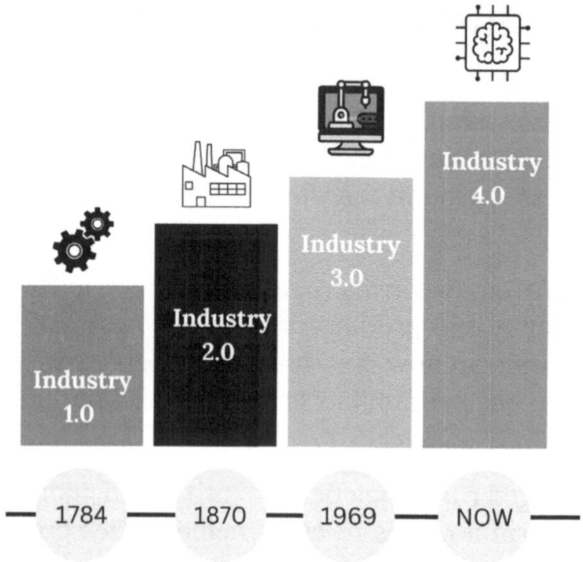

***Figure 1.1**: Industrial Revolution*

The Industry 4.0

Industry 4.0 is a brand-new industrial revolution that has emerged in the era of quick technological advancements. Modern industrial practices are being integrated with cutting-edge technologies during this transformational phase, completely changing how goods are produced. The concept of Industry 4.0 will be examined in this article in a human-written and understandable manner, with an emphasis on its importance, key technologies, and the exciting future it holds.

Recognizing Industry 4.0

The term "Industry 4.0" refers to the fourth industrial revolution, which is based on earlier waves of industrialization. It uses the power of digital technologies to build a manufacturing ecosystem that is smarter, more connected, and more effective. Fundamentally, Industry 4.0 seeks to improve the productivity, quality, and agility of industrial processes by utilizing developments in automation, data analytics, artificial intelligence, the Internet of Things (IoT), and cloud computing.

Industry 4.0's key technologies include:

- **Internet of Things(IoT):** The Internet of Things(IoT), which involves tying together physical objects and machinery in order to collect and exchange data, is one of the core components of Industry 4.0. Real-time monitoring, preventative maintenance, and improved control over manufacturing operations are made possible by this interconnectedness.

- **Artificial intelligence (AI)**: By giving machines intelligence akin to that of a human, AI enables them to analyze massive amounts of data, make independent decisions, and carry out difficult tasks. AI is essential to Industry 4.0 because it helps to enhance quality assurance, optimize production processes, and enable predictive analytics.
- **Data analytics**: Manufacturers now have access to an unprecedented amount of data thanks to Industry 4.0. Data analytics tools take advantage of this wealth of data to generate insightful conclusions, spot patterns, and reach informed choices. These insights contribute to efficiency improvement, downtime reduction, and optimization of operations.
- **Robotics and Automation**: Industry 4.0 uses cutting-edge automation and robotics to optimize production processes, boost output, and enhance safety. Robots with AI capabilities work alongside humans, handling dangerous or repetitive tasks while people concentrate on complex problem-solving and creativity.

The advantages of Industry 4.0 include:

The fourth industrial revolution, known as Industry 4.0, has completely changed the production environment because of its numerous benefits. Industry 4.0 encourages increased manufacturing flexibility and agility, enabling quick response to shifting market demands. Since IoT-enabled sensors and AI-driven analytics ensure improved monitoring and control throughout the manufacturing process, this technological advancement also improves product quality and customization. Predictive maintenance and intelligent monitoring systems also encourage sustainable and economical practices by lowering operational expenses and preventing expensive equipment failures. Overall, the benefits of Industry 4.0 go beyond particular companies and contribute to the development of robust, interconnected industrial ecosystems:

- **Increased Effectiveness**: Industry 4.0 boosts manufacturing efficiency by integrating technologies and streamlining processes. Predictive maintenance, real-time data analysis, and automated systems minimize downtime, cut waste, and maximize resource efficiency.
- **Better Quality**: Industry 4.0 ensures consistent product quality with data analytics and AI-powered quality control systems. Early detection and correction of flaws improves customer satisfaction and lowers the price of recalls and rework while also improving quality.

- **Flexibility and Customization**: Mass customization is made possible by Industry 4.0, allowing products to be tailored to specific customer preferences without sacrificing efficiency. Faster time-to-market is made possible by smart factories with adaptable production systems that can quickly change to meet changing market demands.
- **Empowering the Workforce**: Industry 4.0 empowers human workers with cutting-edge technologies rather than replacing them. Because automation and AI free up workers to concentrate on complex problem-solving, creativity, and innovation, the workplace becomes more satisfying.

Taking the Future on:

Adopting Industry 4.0 is crucial for the manufacturing industry's future. However, a thorough strategy is necessary for its adoption to be successful. To protect data and operations, manufacturers must upskill their workforce, invest in technology infrastructure, and put strong cybersecurity measures in place.

A paradigm shift in the manufacturing sector is represented by Industry 4.0, which uses digital technologies to build smarter, more productive, and customer-focused factories. Manufacturers can achieve previously unattainable levels of productivity, quality, and agility by leveraging the power of IoT, AI, data analytics, and automation. Adopting Industry 4.0 means embracing a future in which innovation, sustainability, and competitiveness converge rather than merely keeping up with the times.

The Internet of Things

The Internet of Things (IoT) is a technology of interconnected devices, as the name suggests, it is a network of multiple things. In IoT all the things/devices are connected within a network and share the data and information or upload it to the cloud network or internet from where it is easily remotely accessible via smart-phone, laptop or any other device connected to the internet. In the network of connected devices or an IoT network, all the devices have their unique addresses or IPs, which makes it easy for the users to track down the data coming from a specific device or thing.

IoT is not a single technology that is designed over a period, the Internet of Things is a stack of multiple technologies, including hardware and software technologies. It is a combination of both hardware and software that has evolved in the last few decades and is evolving very rapidly nowadays. The fusion of numerous technological developments over the years is where the Internet of

Things got its start. The idea originated from the desire to connect and converse with physical objects, allowing them to autonomously gather and share data. Let's examine the significant turning points in IoT history.

Figure 1.2: *Internet of Things*

A Brief History of IoT

IoT hasn't been around for very long. Kevin Ashton came up with the phrase "Internet of Things" in 1999. He used the phrase as the title of his talk about a new sensor project he was working on, and it stuck after that.

Even though the term "connected devices" didn't come into use until 1999, the idea has been around since 1832. When the first electromagnetic telegraph was made, it made it possible for two machines to talk directly to each other by sending and receiving electrical messages. However, the real history of the Internet of Things started when the Internet was created in the late 1960s.

The first IoT gadget was made at Carnegie Mellon University in the early 1980s. A group of university students came up with a way for the Coca-Cola machine on campus to let them know if it was out of Coke through a network. This would save them the trip if the machine was empty. They put microswitches in the machine so that it could tell how many Coke cans were there and if they were cold.

John Romkey was the first person to hook up a toaster to the internet. This was in the year 1990. A year later, a group of the University of Cambridge students reported on coffee using a web camera. They had the idea of using the first web camera device to check how much coffee was in the coffee pot in their computer lab. They did this by setting up the web camera to take a picture of the coffee pot three times a minute. The pictures were then sent to computers in the area so that everyone could check if there was coffee.

Currently, we are living in a time where we first need to collect the data, deploy multiple sensors, get all the information and analyze it. This process needs to be done at a nuclear level to truly understand the functionality of a particular system. Once the data is collected from the environment, it will be easy to integrate multiple machines and devices to control the outcome and hence the process of automation will be achieved.

Pillars of IoT

The IoT is an idea that is changing the way we connect with devices and the world around us. It is a game-changer in a field that is always changing: technology. IoT is the network of physical devices, cars, appliances, and other things that are linked to each other and have sensors, software, and network connections that let them collect and share data.

Since its start, IoT has grown and been used in many industries in a way that has changed how companies work and how people live their daily lives.

IoT's success can be attributed to its fundamental pillars, which enable seamless integration and communication between devices:

- **Connectivity**: It enables device communication and data transfer at the heart of IoT. This information exchange is made possible by a number of communication protocols, including Wi-Fi, Bluetooth, Zigbee, and cellular networks. Newer, more effective networking solutions are developing as technology progresses, expanding the possibilities of IoT.
- **Data Collection and Analysis**: One of the biggest advantages of IoT is its capacity to collect enormous amounts of data from linked devices. IoT device sensors can gather information on anything from user behavior and preferences to location and temperature. This data is then processed and analyzed to yield insightful knowledge that supports predictive analytics and data-driven decision-making.

- **Control, Monitoring and Automation**: IoT makes automation possible by allowing devices to function independently based on the data they gather. For instance, smart houses can modify lighting and temperature settings based on user preferences and occupancy. Automation of manufacturing processes with Industrial IoT (IIoT) applications increases productivity and lowers costs. Controlling of devices and monitoring of multiple data parameters and automation of various processes based on the collected data is all possible with the help of the Internet of Things.

Growth of IoT

As early as the 1980s, the concept of tying devices together to exchange data was being discussed. Visionaries saw a future in which computing would be seamlessly integrated into our surroundings. Since then, a wave of connected devices has started and with this growing wave, we see huge business potential and the growth of IoT markets.

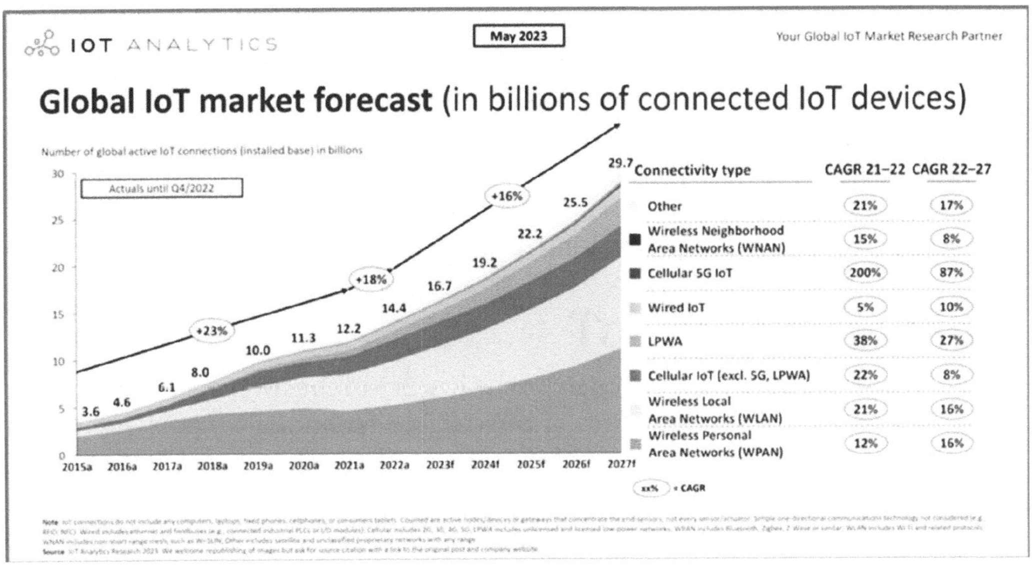

Figure 1.3: *The growth of the IoT market*

- **The use of RFID and sensors**: IoT's foundation was greatly aided by the advancement of sensor technology and Radio Frequency Identification (RFID) technology. It has a total of three components: RFID tags, RFID reader and RFID antennas. RFID, which uses radio waves to uniquely identify objects, has found use in asset tracking and supply chain management, toll collection, access control systems, livestock tracking and medical applications.

- **M2M (Machine-to-Machine) Communication**: The development of machine-to-machine communication accelerated in the late 1990s and early 2000s. M2M enabled automated data exchange between devices. This innovation made it easier to automate, monitor, and control various processes remotely. M2M communication began to be used in industrial applications, such as SCADA(Supervisory Control and Data Acquisition) where it is used to collect the telemetry data and then transfer the information to a central hub or central control station. The growth of M2M communication is increased as there is an increase in wireless technologies, a decrease in the cost of sensors and actuators, a growing demand for real-time data and the requirement to increase the efficiency of the system. Today M2M Communication is used in multiple areas such as Asset tracking, Smart Metering, Fleet Management, Healthcare, and so on, and it will continue to grow due to the increasing demand for connected devices and the growth of advanced technologies like 5G.
- **Wireless connectivity and IPv6**: The address space required to accommodate a large number of connected devices was made available by the widespread adoption of IPv6, the next-generation internet protocol. IPv6 uses a 128-bit address as compared to IPv4 which uses only a 32-bit address, which allows a much larger number of possible addresses. Furthermore, the development of wireless connectivity technologies like Wi-Fi and cellular networks made it possible for devices to communicate without interruption over long distances.

Applications of IoT

- **Wearables and Smart Homes**: In the history of the Internet of Things, the emergence of smart homes and wearable technology was a significant turning point. This massive shift in technology made it easily accessible to everyone. These consumer-focused gadgets, which ranged from connected thermostats and lighting systems to fitness trackers and smartwatches, demonstrated the potential of IoT in enhancing daily life.
- **Industry 4. 0 and Industrial IoT (IIoT)**: The Industrial Internet of Things (IIoT) and Industry 4.0 were created as a result of the convergence of IoT with industrial applications. Through real-time data collection and analysis, these developments aimed to optimize industrial processes, boost productivity, and enable predictive maintenance.
- **Infrastructure in smart cities**: With the help of IoT, the idea of "smart cities" has gained popularity and improved urban living. The development

of interconnected systems has improved productivity, sustainability, and quality of life in the areas of transportation, energy management, waste management, and public safety.

- **Connected Cars**: IoT has also found its way into the automotive industry, giving rise to connected cars equipped with advanced driver assistance systems (ADAS). These technologies enhance safety, improve navigation, and enable real-time diagnostics, making driving more efficient and secure.
- **Healthcare**: In the healthcare sector, IoT applications are revolutionizing patient care. Remote patient monitoring devices allow healthcare professionals to track patients' health metrics from afar, leading to better disease management and reducing the need for frequent hospital visits.
- **Agriculture and Smart Farming:** IoT's presence in agriculture, known as smart farming, has brought significant improvements to the industry. Smart sensors can monitor soil moisture, temperature, and crop health, enabling precision farming techniques that conserve resources and maximize yields.
- **Retail sector**: Retailers have embraced IoT to enhance customer experiences. IoT-enabled beacons can provide personalized promotions and product recommendations to shoppers based on their preferences and location within a store, leading to increased customer engagement and loyalty.
- **Smart Logistics and Fleet Management:** IoT plays a vital role in improving the overall efficiency of the complete logistics sector, with the help of IoT it is now very easy to track assets, manage the critical parameters, maintain the temperature, and provide the condition monitoring of the assets.
- **Smart Warehousing:** IoT is rapidly transforming the warehousing industry. IoT devices can collect and exchange data in real-time, providing businesses with a wealth of information that can be used to improve efficiency, optimize operations, and reduce costs. It provides real-time tracking of the material, automated guided vehicles (AGVs) are used to move goods, central warehouse temperature and lighting control and smart shelves to monitor and manage the inventory. These are some of the use cases with which IoT is transforming the warehousing industry.
- **Military Applications**: Battlefield simulation awareness, target identification, remote healthcare monitoring and surveillance are a few

of the major areas where IoT is revolutionizing the current operations and increasing overall efficiency for the military.

Future Trends in IoT

The Internet of Things (IoT) has emerged as one of the most transformative technologies of the 21st century. With the seamless integration of devices, sensors, and software, IoT has opened up a world of possibilities across industries, redefining how we interact with technology. Looking ahead, IoT is all set for continuous growth with several new trends on the horizon.

- **IoT Empowerment via Edge Computing**

  The IoT environment will undergo a change thanks to edge computing. IoT devices produce enormous amounts of data, which can cause latency and bandwidth problems when processed by centralized cloud servers. Edge computing eliminates the need for far-off data centers by bringing computation closer to the data source. This improves data processing speed and effectiveness while also putting less stress on cloud infrastructures.

- **Integration of AI and machine learning**

  There is tremendous potential in combining IoT with AI and ML. We may gain important insights, perform predictive analyses, and streamline processes by using AI algorithms to analyze data from IoT devices. Our lives can be made easier and more effective by smart gadgets powered by AI that can learn from user behavior, adjust to preferences, and give a highly personalized experience.

- **The Growth of IoT and 5G Connectivity**

  The introduction of 5G technology is revolutionary for IoT. More connected devices and apps are made possible by its ultra-fast and low-latency communication. Real-time applications like driverless vehicles, remote surgery, and smart city infrastructure are now possible thanks to 5G networks, which enable IoT devices to connect effortlessly and respond instantly.

- **Increased Security Measures**

  The worry for security grows along with IoT application development. Strong security measures that secure sensitive data and guarantee user privacy are essential for the IoT's future. IoT security will be strengthened and consumer confidence in these technologies will increase thanks to improvements in encryption methods, secure booting procedures, and multi-factor authentication.

- **Use of Blockchain Technology**

  IoT is embracing blockchain, the technology that underpins cryptocurrency. IoT networks' security and transparency can be improved by their decentralized and irreversible characteristics. Blockchain can prevent unauthorized access and offer a more dependable IoT environment by producing a tamper-proof record of device interactions and data exchanges.

The future of IoT is brimming with innovation and potential. As IoT continues to evolve, we can expect even more interconnected, intelligent, and sustainable systems that enhance our lives and redefine industries. From edge computing and AI integration to environmental sustainability and smart cities, the possibilities are boundless. Embracing these future trends in IoT will undoubtedly pave the way for a brighter and more connected world.

Security Concerns in IoT

Although the technology of IoT is incredibly efficient and convenient, it also presents serious security risks. With billions of networked devices, from industrial systems to smart home appliances, cybercriminals' potential attack surface has drastically increased. A few of the major concerns are:

- **Insufficient Device Security:**

  The ineffective security measures used in many devices are one of the main issues with IoT technology. Manufacturers frequently place more emphasis on utility and affordability than strong security, leaving holes that can be used by criminals. Common problems that raise the possibility of unauthorized access and data breaches include default passwords with weak encryption, outdated firmware, and a lack of encryption during data transmission.

- **A lack of Standardization** :

  Because there are no standardized security procedures in the IoT sector, it is challenging to guarantee uniform protection across all platforms and devices. As a result, the security environment may be uneven, with some devices having robust security protections while others are still exposed. The lack of standard security controls also makes it difficult for various IoT systems to collaborate effectively, which could cause interoperability problems and security holes.

- **Privacy Issues with Data**:

  IoT devices frequently gather enormous volumes of sensitive data, including behavioral patterns, location data, and personal information. This information could be used for identity theft, extortion, or other criminal acts if it ends up in the wrong hands. In the IoT ecosystem, data breaches can have significant repercussions that threaten not only specific persons but potentially entire businesses and sectors.

- **Distributed Denial of Service (DDoS) Attacks:**

  IoT devices are capable of being used in massive DDoS attacks due to their interconnectedness. Cybercriminals can take control of numerous devices and transform them into a botnet, which would then saturate the targeted servers or networks with traffic. Critical services may be interrupted by such attacks, resulting in losses in money and serious harm to a company's reputation.

- **Insufficient User Awareness**:

  End users frequently disregard security issues when configuring IoT devices. They might skip firmware upgrades, use default passwords instead of changing them, or unintentionally give critical data to outside applications. Without the right knowledge and training, people unintentionally expose their gadgets and data to possible dangers.

- **Vulnerabilities in Firmware and Software**:

  In order to function properly, many IoT devices depend on sophisticated software and firmware. Unfortunately, attackers can take advantage of software flaws and vulnerabilities to access restricted areas, change device functionality, or steal confidential data. Making sure that manufacturers consistently patch and update their products to fix known vulnerabilities is difficult.

- **Attacks along the Supply Chain**:

  IoT security issues go beyond the actual devices. Malicious actors may choose to target the supply chain, adding tainted parts or altering the hardware during production. Such assaults can build backdoors that permit unauthorized access in the future and are difficult to identify and stop.

The way we engage with technology has been revolutionized by the Internet of Things, which has had a huge positive impact on both our daily lives and certain businesses. However, the quick spread of IoT devices also raises a number of security issues. The IoT ecosystem has a number of difficult challenges when it comes to security, including inadequate device security, a lack of standards, data privacy concerns, DDoS attacks, user knowledge gaps, software vulnerabilities, and supply chain threats.

Collaboration between industry stakeholders, policymakers, and cybersecurity professionals is essential to properly address these issues. To make the IoT environment safer for everyone, it is crucial to implement strong security measures, frequent firmware updates, data encryption, and promote user awareness.

Conclusion

We travelled across time in the first chapter to examine the remarkable development of business and technology that gave rise to the Fourth Industrial Revolution and the Internet of Things (IoT). We saw how the three previous industrial revolutions altered the world we live in today as a result of game-changing breakthroughs.

Mechanization and steam power, which propelled the First Industrial Revolution, signaled the start of a new era in production and manufacturing. Electricity and mass production, which fueled the Second Industrial Revolution, hastened global industrialization and raised millions of people's standards of living. The digital age was ushered in by the Third Industrial Revolution, which was driven by computerization and automation and connected systems and people like never before.

The fundamental idea of Industry 4.0, or the Fourth Industrial Revolution, which unites the physical and digital worlds through cutting-edge technology, emerged as a result of our investigation. The Internet of Things, a global network of networked devices that easily exchange data and communicate, is at the center of the Industry 4.0 revolution.

Understanding the IoT pillars of connectivity, data, and processes opened our eyes to the underlying ideas that underpin the success of this technology. IoT connects objects and systems by utilizing the power of connection, opening up a world of opportunities for real-time data sharing and decision-making. Data, the lifeblood of the IoT, enables organizations to gain insightful information, streamline processes, and provide better customer experiences.

Additionally, IoT is expanding at an incredible rate. The exponential growth of the Internet of Things (IoT), which now connects billions of devices, is continuing to change sectors like healthcare, agriculture, transportation, and smart cities.

This rapid expansion is fueled by the promise of increased convenience, lower prices, and higher efficiency, which has inventors and businesspeople all around the world intrigued.

We delved into the wide range of IoT applications in this changing landscape. The possibilities range from industrial IoT solutions that will revolutionize manufacturing and supply chain management to smart homes that give unprecedented control and automation. A brighter and more sustainable future for everybody is also promised by the potential of IoT in industries like healthcare, environmental monitoring, and energy management.

However, we must not ignore the crucial issue of IoT security worries. Data breaches and cyber dangers are more likely as the network of connected devices grows. The absence of standardized security methods, firmware flaws, and limited user awareness present serious issues that need to be addressed right away.

In sum, this first chapter prepares us for our in-depth exploration of the Internet of Things' transformational world. As we move further, we will learn about the complexities of IoT applications, investigate the protocols involved in IoT, focus on developing IoT-based solutions, and develop solutions to strengthen the security of this connected environment. The Fourth Industrial Revolution will usher in a connected world that is both affluent and secure by embracing IoT's potential and solving its risks.

In the next chapter, we will focus more on the IoT ecosystem and the IoT network. We will take a look at the architecture of the technology of the Internet of Things. We will delve into the layers of IoT architecture, starting with the Perception layer that comprises various sensors, actuators, and devices. Moving up, we examine the Network layer, which encompasses different protocols and networking technologies facilitating device connectivity. Furthermore, we explore the cloud layer, where data is stored, processed, and analyzed, enabling intelligent decision-making. Additionally, we discuss the application layer, where IoT solutions and services are developed to cater to diverse industries and use cases. By the end of this chapter, readers will gain a comprehensive understanding of the underlying architecture that powers the vast ecosystem of IoT.

References

- https://www.itonlinelearning.com/history-of-the-internet-of-things-iot/#:~:text=The%20Internet%20of%20Things%20(IoT)%20has%20not%20been%20around%20that,and%20it%20stuck%20from%20there
- https://www.cisco.com/c/en/us/solutions/internet-of-things/overview.html
- https://ieeexplore.ieee.org/document/7755463
- https://www.nature.com/articles/nature14539
- Gupta, S., Kumar, N., & Sangwan, O. P. (2018). Internet of Things (IoT) Security: A Survey. Procedia Computer Science, 132, 897-905.
- Alaba, F. A., Olatinwo, M. O., & Adigun, M. O. (2020). A Comprehensive Review of Internet of Things (IoT) Security and Privacy Issues and Solutions. Journal of Ambient Intelligence and Humanized Computing, 11(11), 4301-4323.
- Figure 1.2 - https://pixabay.com/users/jeferrb-590530/?utm_source=link-attribution&utm_medium=referral&utm_campaign=image&utm_content=782707
- Figure 1.3 - https://iot-analytics.com/wp/wp-content/uploads/2023/05/Global-IoT-market-forecast-in-billions-of-connected-IoT-devices.png

CHAPTER 2
The Architecture of IoT

Introduction

IoT- a complex design of interconnected things, a network of billion devices that allows the easy flow of data and information. We will explore the architecture behind this humongous network and focus on each and every tiny part of it. We explore the IoT architecture's layers, beginning with the Hardware layer, which consists of a rangc of scnsors, actuators, and gadgcts. As wc asccnd, wc look at the communication layer, which includes various networking technologies and protocols that facilitate device connectivity. We also look at the cloud layer, which is where data is processed, stored, and analyzed to help people make smart decisions. We also talk about the application layer, where IoT services and solutions are created to serve various sectors and use cases.

Structure

In this chapter, we will focus on the following topics:

- Architecture of IoT
- Perception Layer

- Network Layer
- Application Layer

Architecture of IoT

The mobile device you are holding in your hand is a passage to the Internet where you can connect with another similar mobile which is on the other side of the world and that too in real-time. Ever wondered how this transmission of data is possible over continents without any latency? What is the architecture behind the data collection and data transmission? How does any device collect information from the environment and how all of this is happening in real time? The architecture of IoT explains the flow of data transmission in real-time from the IoT edge device to the cloud.

The architecture of IoT is divided into three major parts, the first part is the perception layer which consists of all the IoT edge devices and the hardware part, the second layer is the network layer which is responsible for transferring the data from the perception layer to the cloud and the third part is the application layer where we design the IoT applications based on that data.

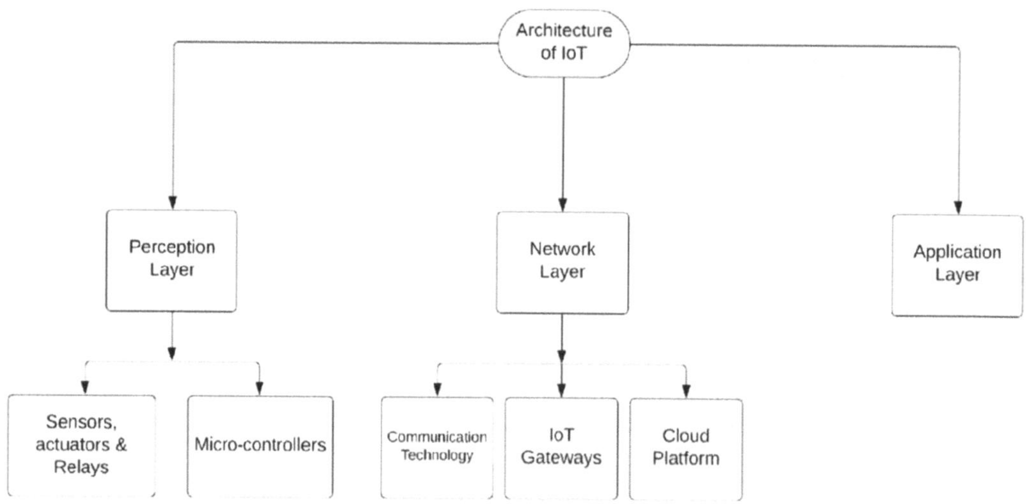

***Figure 2.1**: Architecture of IoT*

Perception Layer

Imagine IoT as a giant network of interconnected devices, such as smart home gadgets, wearable fitness trackers, industrial sensors, and more. These devices collect and share data with each other and with the internet. But how do they understand the world around them and make sense of all the information they gather?

That's where the perception layer comes into play. The perception layer is the first part of the IoT architecture and it is like the eyes, ears, and senses of the IoT system. It is responsible for gathering data from the physical world. Just like our eyes and ears help us see and hear things, the perception layer's sensors and devices do the same for IoT devices.

For instance, think about a smart thermostat in your home. It needs to know the temperature in the room to adjust the heating or cooling. It has a sensor as part of its perception layer that can "feel" the temperature and send that information to the brain of the device (the processing layer).

Similarly, in a smart factory, there could be sensors on machines that monitor their performance and detect any potential issues. These sensors are part of the perception layer and provide valuable data to the system.

The data collected by the perception layer is then sent to the next layer in the IoT system, known as the network layer.

Hence, it is clear that the perception layer is divided further into two parts: sensors, actuators, relays and another one is microcontrollers. The sensors, the actuators or the relays are used along with the micro-controllers to build an IoT edge device and all these IoT edge devices are considered under the perception layer.

Sensors

Devices called sensors serve as the "senses" of contemporary technology. Sensors allow electrical devices and machines to perceive and engage with their surroundings in a similar way to how our human senses allow us to see, hear, taste, touch, and smell things in the world around us. These tools are made to recognize particular occurrences or changes in the real world and translate them into electrical signals or data that computers or other electronic systems can use. There are many distinct types of sensors, each designed to detect a particular component of the environment.

For instance, there are sensors for temperature and motion that measure a location's warmth or coldness, light, and pressure sensors that measure the force or weight exerted on an object, and sensors for light and motion that detect movement. Gas sensors, proximity sensors, humidity sensors, and more are additional types of sensors.

From commonplace gadgets like smartphones, smartwatches, and home automation systems to more complicated systems used in industrial processes, healthcare, transportation, and environmental monitoring, sensors play a key role in various applications.

When developing any IoT project, prototype, or product, we must first choose the kind of parameters we must track. Then, the appropriate sensors are attached to the IoT device.

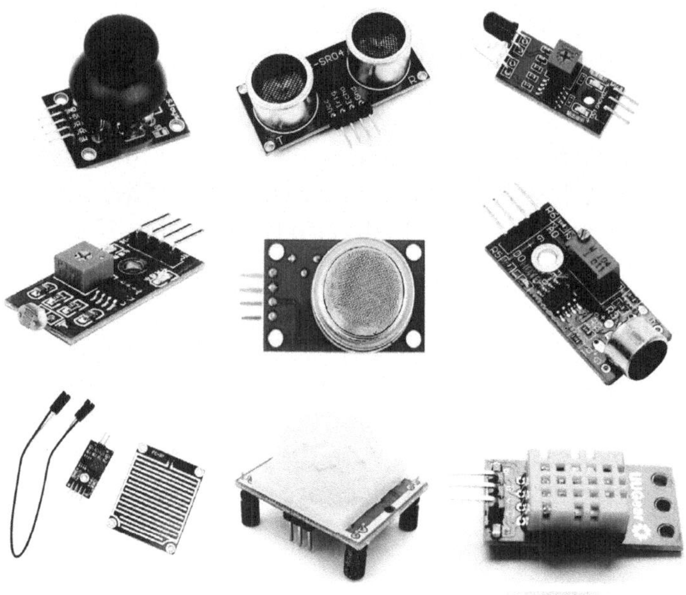

Figure 2.2: *Sensors*

Actuators

The IoT and the technology industry depend heavily on actuators. They are devices in charge of acting or doing physical duties in accordance with the directives received from the IoT system or the information gathered by sensors.

To put it simply, if sensors serve as the "senses" of IoT devices, actuators serve as the "muscles" that allow these devices to communicate with the actual world.

They transform electrical impulses or data coming from an Internet of Things system into actual actions or alterations in the environment.

The use of actuators in IoT edge devices is particularly crucial because edge devices are the devices that are situated close to the data source or the point where data is generated. These devices perform data processing and decision-making at or near the source, which reduces the need for constant communication with cloud servers and enhances real-time responsiveness.

***Figure* 2.3:** *Actuators*

Relays

A relay is an electrical switch that is controlled by an external signal to open or close the circuit, thereby regulating the passage of electricity to a connected device or component. It functions as a link between the low-power control circuit and the high-power circuit it regulates.

In simple terms, a relay serves as a remote-controlled switch that can turn on or off electrical devices or systems without direct physical contact. It is commonly used in situations where a low-power control signal, such as one from an IoT edge device, needs to control a higher-power electrical load.

The use of relays in IoT edge devices provides a level of separation between the low-power control circuit (handled by the IoT device) and the higher-power load, ensuring safety and efficiency. By integrating relays into IoT edge devices, users can remotely control and automate a wide range of electrical devices and systems, making them more efficient, convenient, and responsive to real-time data.

Figure 2.4: *Relays*

Micro-Controllers

Small integrated circuits (ICs), sometimes known as chips, called microcontrollers serve as the brains of numerous electronic gadgets. They are specialized computers created to manage and carry out particular functions in embedded systems, which are electronic systems integrated into other objects to give them "smart" and functional capabilities.

Following are some crucial details about microcontrollers:

- **Small Size**: Small and available in a variety of sizes, microcontrollers are frequently between a few millimeters and a few centimeters in length. They may be quickly and readily integrated into electronic products because of their compact form factor.
- **Built-in components:** The central processing unit (CPU), memory (RAM and ROM), input/output (I/O) pins, timers, and occasionally analog-to-digital converters (ADCs) are all present on these devices. These parts give the microcontroller the ability to communicate with other parts of the device and perform particular functions.
- **Programmability**: The programmability of microcontrollers is one of its fundamental characteristics. They can be programmed to carry out a set of instructions utilizing particular software languages. These instructions control the microcontroller's behavior and how it reacts to various inputs and circumstances.
- **Embedded systems**: In embedded systems, microcontrollers are frequently employed. An embedded system is a set of hardware and software created specifically for a given device or application. Microcontrollers, for instance, are used in a variety of products, including household appliances, automobile systems, industrial machinery, consumer electronics, and medical equipment.

- **Specific Task**: Each microcontroller was created with a particular function in mind. While some microcontrollers are designed specifically for controlling motors, others might be especially suited for processing sensor data or performing communications duties. They can be effective and economical for their intended applications thanks to their specialization.
- **Real-time operations**: Many microcontrollers can operate in real-time, which enables them to react quickly to inputs and carry out tasks with little latency. They are therefore appropriate for applications that call for quick and accurate answers.
- **Low Energy Consumption**: Microcontrollers are suitable for battery-powered devices since they are frequently made to be energy-efficient. They use very little power, which is crucial for increasing the life of portable devices' batteries.

  Consider a standard light bulb; if it needs to be connected to the Internet to monitor its brightness and control its state, an IoT edge device composed of an LDR sensor, a relay to control the bulb, and a micro-controller is used to convert it into an IoT-based light bulb; this combination of devices is part of the perception layer.

Figure 2.5: *Micro-controller*

Network Layer

The network layer in the Internet of Things (IoT) plays a crucial role in enabling communication and data exchange among connected devices. It serves as an intermediary between the physical devices and the cloud, ensuring seamless connectivity and efficient data transmission. At its core, the network layer is responsible for addressing, routing, and forwarding data packets between IoT devices within a network. Each IoT device is assigned a unique identifier, known as an IP address, which facilitates the identification and communication with other devices. The network layer utilizes various protocols, such as IPv4 or IPv6, to manage the addressing and routing of data packets. These protocols ensure that data is directed to the intended recipient device, even if the devices are interconnected through different networks.

One of the key challenges in the network layer of IoT is the diverse nature of IoT devices, ranging from resource-constrained sensors to more powerful gateways. To accommodate this diversity, the network layer employs different communication technologies, such as Wi-Fi, Bluetooth, Zigbee, LoRaWAN, and cellular networks, based on the specific requirements of each IoT device. Hence, the network layer is further divided into three parts - Communication technology, gateways, and Cloud.

Additionally, the network layer is responsible for ensuring data security and privacy during transmission. Encryption and authentication mechanisms are often employed to safeguard sensitive data from unauthorized access or tampering.

In summary, the network layer forms the backbone of IoT communication, facilitating seamless connectivity, efficient data transfer, and robust security measures to enable the vast ecosystem of interconnected IoT devices to function harmoniously.

Communication Technology

Consider a laptop or desktop computer; if you need to connect it to the internet, what are the most prevalent methods currently available? These are the three fundamental communication technologies used to connect any device to the internet: Wi-Fi, Ethernet, and GSM. However, when it comes to the IoT, there are numerous other communication technologies used to construct IoT Edge devices. It is dependent on the requirements of the IoT edge to determine which communication technology must be used to accomplish the objective. BLE

(Bluetooth Low Energy), Lo-Ra, Zigbee, Z-wave, nRF, NB-IoT, and so on, are a few of the most prevalent communication technologies.

The right communication technology can determine the success or failure of an IoT project, making it essential to carefully evaluate various factors before deciding. Here are the key considerations that play a crucial role in choosing the right communication technology for IoT applications.

- **Data Transmission Speed and Bandwidth**: One of the primary factors to consider while choosing communication technology for IoT is data transmission speed and bandwidth. Depending on the nature of the IoT application, data transmission requirements can vary significantly. Some applications, like smart home devices, may require low bandwidth and moderate transmission speeds, while industrial applications, such as remote monitoring and control systems, may demand high bandwidth and ultra-fast data transmission capabilities.
- **Range and Coverage**: The range and coverage of the communication technology are essential aspects to evaluate. IoT devices can be scattered across vast geographical areas, and the communication technology should provide seamless connectivity even in remote locations. For instance, cellular networks offer extensive coverage but might not be suitable for applications in remote rural areas. On the other hand, technologies like LoRaWAN and Sigfox are designed to cover large distances with minimal power consumption, making them ideal for certain IoT applications.
- **Power Consumption**: IoT devices are often battery-powered or rely on low-power sources, and optimizing power consumption is critical for ensuring extended device lifespans and reducing maintenance efforts. Choosing a communication technology with low power requirements can significantly impact the efficiency and longevity of IoT deployments. Technologies like Bluetooth Low Energy (BLE) and Narrowband IoT (NB-IoT) are designed to operate with minimal power consumption, making them suitable for energy-efficient IoT devices.
- **Security and Privacy**: Security is a top concern in IoT applications, as compromised devices can lead to severe consequences. When selecting a communication technology, it is vital to assess its security features and protocols. Look for encryption, authentication, and data integrity mechanisms to safeguard data from unauthorized access and cyber threats. Additionally, considering the privacy implications of communication technology is crucial, especially when dealing with sensitive user data.

- **Scalability and Flexibility**: IoT applications often start with a limited number of devices but have the potential to scale rapidly as the project expands. Therefore, the chosen communication technology should be scalable to accommodate a growing number of connected devices without sacrificing performance or reliability. Moreover, flexibility in supporting various device types and use cases is essential to ensure seamless integration and adaptability to changing requirements.
- **Cost and Affordability**: Cost is a significant factor that influences technology decisions in any project. Different communication technologies come with varying costs, including hardware, network infrastructure, and data plans. It's essential to evaluate the overall cost of implementing the technology and weigh it against the expected benefits and returns on investment.
- **Interoperability**: In the diverse IoT landscape, various devices and platforms need to communicate with each other smoothly. Interoperability between devices from different manufacturers and compatibility with various software platforms are critical aspects to consider when choosing communication technology. Standards like MQTT and CoAP are popular choices that promote interoperability in IoT ecosystems.
- **Latency and Responsiveness**: Certain IoT applications require real-time data processing and instant responsiveness. For example, in autonomous vehicles, any communication delay can have dire consequences. Evaluate the latency and responsiveness offered by the communication technology to ensure it aligns with the application's requirements.
- **Environmental Conditions**: IoT devices can be deployed in a wide range of environmental conditions, from harsh industrial settings to outdoor weather conditions. The chosen communication technology should be resilient enough to withstand environmental challenges like extreme temperatures, humidity, and dust.
- **Regulatory Compliance**: Compliance with regional regulations and industry standards is a vital consideration for IoT deployments. Ensure that the chosen communication technology adheres to relevant regulatory requirements to avoid legal issues and penalties.
- **Data Throughput and Payload Size**: Different IoT applications generate varying amounts of data, and the communication technology should be able to handle the required data throughput and payload size. Analyze the data flow requirements of your application and select a technology that can meet those demands effectively.

- **Network Topology:** The network topology plays a significant role in determining the efficiency and performance of IoT applications. Depending on whether your application requires a star, mesh, or hybrid network topology, choose a communication technology that supports the desired configuration.
- **Reliability and Redundancy**: For mission-critical IoT applications, reliability and redundancy are of utmost importance. Evaluate the communication technology's track record and explore its built-in redundancy features to ensure uninterrupted connectivity and data transfer.
- **Longevity and Future-proofing**: IoT deployments are typically long-term projects, and it is essential to consider the longevity of the chosen communication technology. Additionally, opting for a future-proof technology can save you from costly upgrades as the IoT landscape evolves.
- **Support and Maintenance:** Lastly, assess the level of support and maintenance offered by the communication technology provider. A robust support system ensures timely assistance in case of issues or updates, ensuring smooth operations throughout the IoT deployment.

Choosing the right communication technology for IoT is a critical decision that can significantly impact the success of your project. By carefully evaluating factors such as data transmission speed, range, power consumption, security, scalability, and cost, you can make an informed choice that aligns with your specific IoT application. Additionally, considering factors like regulatory compliance, network topology, and support will contribute to the seamless operation and longevity of your IoT deployment.

Gateways

Internet of Things gateways are essential elements in IoT architectures. They act as a bridge between Internet of Things (IoT) gadgets and sensors, and the cloud or centralized data processing platforms. IoT gateways' primary function is to provide seamless data transfer between the various and frequently heterogeneous IoT devices and the centralized network or cloud architecture. IoT gateways play a vital role in optimizing data transmission and reducing latency. Apart from the three fundamental communication technologies, that is, Wi-Fi, Ethernet and GSM that provide direct internet access, all the other communication technologies use transceiver modules, which enables them to transfer and receive data from a similar communication tech and hence they are not able to upload the data directly to the Internet. Here comes the IoT gateway which acts as an intermediate device that supports these transceiver modules as well as the other fundamental communication technologies, which makes it capable of connecting multiple IoT devices based on multiple communication technologies to the internet.

Key Components of IoT Gateways

- **Protocols and Communication Standards**: IoT devices often use different communication protocols to transmit data. IoT gateways must support multiple protocols like Wi-Fi, Bluetooth, Zigbee, MQTT, and more to establish connections with diverse devices.
- **Data Processing Capabilities**: IoT gateways have the ability to pre-process data locally before sending it to the cloud. This feature not only reduces the load on cloud servers but also ensures real-time data analysis and quicker responses.
- **Security Features**: As data breaches and cyber threats become more prevalent, IoT gateways are equipped with robust security measures to safeguard sensitive information. Encryption, firewalls, and authentication protocols are essential features of a secure IoT gateway.

Benefits of IoT Gateways

- **Improved Data Transmission**: IoT gateways enable efficient data transmission by aggregating and optimizing data from multiple devices. This leads to reduced bandwidth usage and faster data transfer rates.
- **Enhanced Security and Privacy**: By processing data locally, IoT gateways minimize the risk of exposing sensitive information to external threats, ensuring enhanced security and privacy for IoT networks.
- **Localized Data Processing**: The ability to preprocess data at the edge allows IoT gateways to perform real-time analytics, making them suitable for applications where low latency is crucial.
- **Scalability and Flexibility**: IoT gateways provide a scalable and flexible architecture, accommodating a wide range of devices and applications, and making them highly adaptable to evolving IoT environments.

Once the Infrastructure is all set, that is, the IoT edge device, IoT gateway, and the IoT cloud platform, the data is collected from the perception layer and then transmitted to the IoT cloud platform using communication technologies and IoT gateways. The process of transferring the data from the IoT edge devices or IoT gateways is covered with the help of multiple protocols. There are a few protocols that are used to transfer the data. The most commonly used IoT protocol is MQTT – message queuing telemetry transport. MQTT is widely used in IoT globally. It is a very lightweight protocol designed for IoT communication and it is based on the TCP/IP communication protocol. We'll study the MQTT protocol in detail in *Chapter* 6, "MQTT- *The Protocol for Internet of Things*". Until then, MQTT is considered as a protocol for data transmission in IoT devices.

Several communication protocols, in addition to MQTT, are often used in the IoT ecosystem. These protocols include, among others:

The internet is powered by the HTTP (Hypertext Transfer Protocol), which also enables communication between web browsers and web servers. IoT devices frequently communicate with cloud-based servers or web services using HTTP. When devices must communicate with web applications or RESTful APIs, it is extremely common.

- **CoAP (Constrained Application Protocol):** CoAP was created for IoT devices with limited resources, making low-power and low-memory devices a perfect fit. It is a simple protocol that makes it possible for gadgets to interact effectively over limited networks, like those used in IoT applications.
- **AMQP (Advanced Message Queuing Protocol):** AMQP is a messaging protocol that makes it easier for messages to be reliably and securely sent between various systems. It works well in situations when numerous devices need to share a lot of data.
- **DDS (Data Distribution Service DDS):** DDS is a publish-subscribe communication protocol that focuses on data and is frequently used in real-time and industrial systems. It makes it possible for dispersed devices to share data effectively, providing real-time data transmission and effective network utilization.
- **LWM2M (Lightweight M2M)** is a protocol created especially for controlling Internet of Things (IoT) devices and the applications they run. It offers an industry-standard method for IoT devices to sign up, update, and communicate with a management server about their capabilities.
- **Extensible Messaging and Presence Protocol**, or **XMPP**, was initially created for instant messaging but has now found use in the Internet of Things (IoT) for real-time communication and data transfer between devices.

Cloud Platform

What comes to your mind when someone talks about cloud computing? Is it the storage space available at remote locations to store the data? Storage of data is merely an application of the cloud. Cloud computing is categorized into three parts, SaaS (software as a service), PaaS (platform as a service), and IaaS (Infrastructure as a service).

Software as a service: SaaS is the part of the cloud where there is no need to download or install specific software into your system. Consider an example where you need to convert a PDF file to a Word file, one option is to download and install some tool or software from the internet and use it to fulfill your requirement, another option is to search for an online service where you don't need to install or download any tool or software into your system and you can fulfill the requirement just by using a web-tool available on the internet. In this second case where you are not installing or using any software in your own system and just using the web tool over the internet to get the desired output, this part of the cloud is termed SaaS, where it provides software as a service and sometimes the service is free of any charge and sometimes the developers charge rent or subscription for the provided services.

Platform as a service: Platform as a Service (PaaS) is a cloud computing model that provides a platform and environment for developers to build, deploy, and manage applications without the complexity of managing the underlying infrastructure. In simple terms, PaaS offers a ready-to-use platform where developers can focus on creating and running their applications without worrying about server setups, operating systems, or hardware maintenance.

Imagine you want to build a house–a beautiful and functional one. Instead of starting from scratch and buying all the materials, hiring construction workers, and managing every little detail, you decide to use a pre-built construction site that already has the foundation, walls, and basic utilities in place.

Platform as a Service is like that pre-built construction site for software developers. It provides them with a set of tools, services, and resources to develop and run their applications without the need to set up the entire infrastructure from scratch.

Here's how PaaS works:

- PaaS offers a ready-made development environment that includes programming languages, frameworks, libraries, and tools needed to create applications.

- Once the application is ready, PaaS takes care of deploying it on servers and makes it available to users over the internet. PaaS platforms can automatically scale applications up or down based on demand, ensuring optimal performance.
- PaaS provides middleware services, like databases, messaging queues, and caching, which are essential for applications to function properly. These services are pre-configured, saving developers from the trouble of setting them up manually.
- PaaS providers handle security aspects such as data encryption, access control, and system updates. They ensure that the platform is secure and up-to-date, allowing developers to focus on building their applications rather than worrying about security vulnerabilities.

By following a similar fashion, IoT platforms are designed to collect the data from the IoT edge devices and to transfer the data to the devices. IoT platforms consist of all the important aspects that are required for a fully functional IoT ecosystem as they provide the device commissioning, handle the data transmission protocol, databases, security and third party services whatsoever are required by the developers to develop any IoT application.

Infrastructure as a Service: IaaS makes virtualized computing resources available online. Simply put, it provides the essential components of a conventional IT architecture, such as virtual computers, storage, and networking, but they are provided as cloud services.

Let's use a familiar comparison to describe what Infrastructure as a Service (IaaS) is:

Consider a scenario in which you require a computer to complete a project but do not want to purchase a new one. Instead, you opt to rent a computer that is fully functional and that you can use whenever and wherever you need it. The hardware and software you need are already installed on this rental computer, so you don't have to worry about upkeep or upgrades.

Technology as a Service is similar to that of the borrowed computer but for the internet. It offers as a service over the Internet all required computing resources, including virtual servers, storage space, and networking capabilities. Businesses and developers can use these resources without having to worry about maintaining physical hardware in this way.

The cloud's IaaS model is as follows:

IaaS provides virtual machines (VMs), which serve as servers in the cloud. With their own operating systems and programs, these VMs operate just like actual computers. Like configuring a new computer, users can set them up to suit their needs.

IaaS platforms offer storage services, including databases and disk space, so users may store and manage their data. It functions like a virtual hard drive that can be accessed from any location with an internet connection.

- **Infrastructure for networking**: IaaS enables customers to create virtual networks to link their virtual servers and other resources. This makes it possible for their applications' many parts to communicate seamlessly with one another.
- **Flexibility and Scalability**: One of the key benefits of IaaS is its flexibility to grow. According to demand, users can easily scale up or down their computing capacity. For instance, they can expand the number of virtual servers to accommodate more traffic during peak hours.

IaaS has a "pay-as-you-go" business model, which means customers only pay for the resources they utilize. It is comparable to paying water or energy bills based on usage.

IaaS services like Amazon Web Services (AWS) enable companies to host websites, operate applications, and store data by renting virtual servers (EC2 instances) and storage (S3 buckets). They are in complete control of their virtual infrastructure, which gives them the ability to effectively develop and manage computing resources.

In conclusion, Infrastructure as a Service (IaaS) in the cloud offers organizations and developers a flexible and affordable alternative to access virtual computing resources without having to make an investment in physical hardware. In the digital world, it's comparable to renting a fully functional computer. Users can concentrate on their applications and services while leaving the administration of the underlying infrastructure to the cloud service provider.

Application Layer

The last and final layer in the IoT architecture is the application layer, once the data is collected from the perception layer and transferred to the cloud using the network layer, the application layer comes into action where the user designs multiple IoT applications based on the data that is available at cloud platform.

It directly interacts with users and provides the final interface through which people can access and utilize IoT services and data. It is the top layer of the IoT architecture and is responsible for delivering the end-user applications and services that make IoT devices and data valuable and meaningful.

Here's a simple explanation of the application layer in the IoT architecture:

- **User Interface:** The application layer is where the user interface resides. It includes various applications, software, and web portals that allow users to interact with IoT devices and access the data generated by these devices. This user interface can be in the form of mobile apps, web apps, or dedicated software.
- **Data Visualization and Analytics:** The application layer processes and presents the data collected from IoT devices in a meaningful way. It employs data visualization techniques, charts, graphs, and dashboards to make complex data understandable to users. Additionally, it may apply data analytics to derive valuable insights from the collected data.
- **Remote Control and Management:** Through the application layer, users can remotely control and manage their IoT devices. For example, you can adjust the temperature of your smart thermostat using a mobile app or turn on/off smart lights from your smartphone.
- **Notifications and Alerts:** The application layer enables real-time notifications and alerts to be sent to users based on the data collected by IoT devices. For instance, you might receive a notification on your phone if your home security camera detects movement.
- **Integration with Other Services:** The application layer often integrates with other third-party services or platforms to enhance functionality. For example, IoT data from a weather station can be integrated with a weather forecasting service.
- **Security and Access Control:** Security is an essential aspect of the application layer. It ensures that only authorized users can access and control IoT devices and that data transmission is secure and encrypted.
- **User Authentication and Identity Management:** The application layer handles user authentication, ensuring that only authenticated users can access specific IoT services and data. It also manages user identities and permissions.
- **APIs (Application Programming Interfaces):** APIs are an important part of the application layer as they enable developers to create applications that interact with IoT devices and services. These APIs provide a

standardized way for applications to communicate with the underlying IoT infrastructure.

In summary, the application layer in the IoT architecture is the top layer responsible for delivering user-friendly interfaces, data visualization, remote control, notifications, and integration with other services. It serves as the bridge between users and the vast network of interconnected IoT devices, making the IoT ecosystem accessible, manageable, and valuable to people in their daily lives and businesses.

3V data model in IoT

The 3V data model in IoT refers to the three key characteristics that define the nature of data generated and processed within the Internet of Things (IoT) ecosystem. These three V's stand for Volume, Velocity, and Variety.

- **Volume:** Volume refers to the vast amount of data that IoT devices generate and collect. With the ever-increasing number of connected devices and sensors, the amount of data being generated has grown exponentially. This large volume of data requires efficient storage, processing, and analysis mechanisms to derive valuable insights and meaningful information.
- **Velocity:** Velocity represents the speed at which data is generated and transmitted in real-time. IoT devices continuously produce data, and this data is transmitted rapidly to centralized systems or cloud platforms. The high velocity of data flow in IoT requires responsive and efficient data processing to ensure timely actions and decisions based on the data.
- **Variety:** Variety denotes the diverse types and formats of data that IoT devices produce. IoT data can be structured (for example, sensor readings, timestamps) or unstructured (for example, images, audio, video). Moreover, data can come from various sources and devices, each with its unique characteristics. Managing this diverse range of data formats and sources requires flexible data processing and storage capabilities.

The 3V data model in IoT highlights the challenges and complexities associated with handling large volumes of data arriving at high velocities and originating from diverse sources. To effectively harness the potential of IoT data, organizations need robust data management strategies, advanced analytics tools, and scalable infrastructure that can handle the unique characteristics of IoT data. By efficiently managing the three V's of data, businesses and industries can gain valuable insights, make data-driven decisions, and fully leverage the transformative power of the Internet of Things.

Conclusion

The architecture of the Internet of Things (IoT) represents a remarkable blend of innovation, integration, and limitless possibilities. Throughout this chapter, we have embarked on a journey into the intricate world of IoT architecture, exploring its foundational layers and intricate components that enable the seamless interconnection of billions of devices.

As we delved into the foundational layers, we unraveled the significance of the perception layer, the gateway layer, and the network layer. Each layer, acting as a crucial building block, facilitates data acquisition, processing, and transmission, forming the backbone of the IoT infrastructure.

Moreover, the chapter delved into the heart of IoT architecture, the application layer. This layer embodies the essence of IoT, where end-users interact with the technology, unleashing the true potential of connected devices. Through intuitive user interfaces, real-time data visualization, and seamless integration with other services, the application layer brings IoT to life, creating a world where devices seamlessly interact with humans and each other.

As we explored the various communication protocols and data models, we witnessed how standardization plays a pivotal role in ensuring interoperability and facilitating the seamless exchange of information across diverse devices and platforms. This interoperability fosters a collaborative ecosystem that fuels innovation and drives the growth of IoT applications.

The security aspect of IoT architecture proved to be of paramount importance. We have come to recognize that as the IoT ecosystem expands, so do the potential security vulnerabilities. A comprehensive and robust security framework is vital to safeguard data, protect privacy, and instill confidence in users and stakeholders.

Throughout this chapter, we have witnessed the boundless potential of IoT, ranging from revolutionizing industries with smart manufacturing and precision agriculture to enhance daily lives with smart homes and personalized healthcare. The transformative impact of IoT is not limited to technological advancements; it extends to shaping economies, societies, and the very fabric of our interconnected world.

As we stand at the precipice of an ever-evolving digital era, the architecture of IoT continues to evolve, presenting new challenges and opportunities. Embracing this evolution requires a harmonious convergence of technological prowess, ethical considerations, and visionary leadership.

In conclusion, the architecture of IoT is more than just a technical blueprint; it symbolizes a convergence of human ingenuity and digital prowess, a gateway to a connected future where devices, data, and people intertwine to build a smarter, more sustainable, and interconnected world. It is with this understanding and collaborative spirit that we march forward into the future, driven by the promise and potential that the Internet of Things holds for us all.

In the next chapter, we will look into the world of microcontrollers, exploring their functionality, applications, and significance in modern technology. We begin by providing a comprehensive introduction to microcontrollers, explaining their role as integrated circuits that combine a microprocessor, memory, and input/output peripherals on a single chip.

We then dive into the various types of microcontrollers, discussing their architectures, instruction sets, and programming languages. Furthermore, we explore the wide range of applications where microcontrollers play a vital role, such as embedded systems, robotics, consumer electronics, automotive systems, and industrial automation.

Throughout the chapter, we examine the key features and capabilities of microcontrollers, including their low power consumption, real-time processing capabilities, and ease of integration.

References

- https://www.researchgate.net/publication/312957467_Internet_of_Things_Architectures_Protocols_and_Applications
- https://ieeexplore.ieee.org/stamp/stamp.jsp?arnumber=7888916 Figure 2.2 - https://www.robotbanao.com/cdn/shop/products/9-in-1-mini-sensor-kit-pir-ultrasonic-sensor-ir-sensor-ldr-rain-sensor-sound-sensor-mq-2-gas-sensor-dht-11-and-joystick-module-324829766-94508_1200x.jpg?v=1635000775
- Figure 2.3 - https://nerdytechy.com/wp-content/uploads/2022/05/servo-motors-vs-stepper-motors.png
- Figure 2.4 - https://www.circuitbasics.com/wp-content/uploads/2020/11/relays.png
- Figure 2.5 - Photo by Sahand Babali (on Unsplash (https://unsplash.com/photos/Oc9wZnEiamI?utm_source=unsplash&utm_medium=referral&utm_content=creditCopyText)

CHAPTER 3

Microcontrollers – The Brain Behind IoT Devices

Introduction

Microcontrollers are the essential components of many electronic devices that we use on a daily basis. These small yet highly efficient components are integrated into a variety of appliances, devices, and systems that enable them to operate with accuracy and intelligence. Microcontrollers have had a profound impact on the field of electronics and have become an integral part of the modern technology landscape. A microcontroller, commonly referred to as a microcomputing unit (MCU) or microcomputing module (μC), is a small-scale integrated circuit that houses a processor core, associated memory, and associated peripherals. It functions as the brain of a variety of devices and can be programmed to perform specific operations. Unlike a microprocessor, which is intended for general-purpose processing, a microcontroller is optimized for controlling operations and executing real-time applications.

A microcontroller comprises three main components:

- **Central Processing Unit (CPU):** This is the core of the microcontroller responsible for executing instructions and performing calculations.
- **Memory:** Microcontrollers have different types of memory, such as Read-Only Memory (ROM) to store the firmware, Random Access Memory

(RAM) for data storage, and Electrically Erasable Programmable Read-Only Memory (EEPROM) for non-volatile storage.

- **Peripherals:** These are additional features that enable the microcontroller to interact with the external world. Examples include input/output ports for connecting sensors and actuators, timers for time-sensitive operations, and communication interfaces for data exchange.

Structure

In this chapter, we'll discuss the following topics:

- Evolution and history of microcontrollers
- Components of a microcontroller
  - Processor
  - Memory
  - I/O ports
  - Analog I/O
  - Interrupts
  - Timers
- Getting Started with Arduino UNO R3
- Programming Arduino with Arduino IDE
- The Blinking of LED
- Introduction to ESP-12 and the ESP family
- Programming ESP-12 with Arduino IDE
- ESP-32
- Programming ESP-32 with Arduino IDE

Evolution and History of Microcontrollers

The term **microcontroller** has its roots in the 1960s, however, the first commercial microcontroller was introduced in 1976 with Intel's 8048. Since then, the development of microcontrollers has progressed rapidly in terms of their performance, power consumption, and capabilities. Currently, microcontrollers are available in a wide range of architectures and are widely employed in a variety of industries, including automotive and healthcare, consumer electronics, and industrial automation.

- **The Birth of Microcontrollers:** At the dawn of the computer age in the 1970s, the concept of a microcontroller was born. Engineers and scientists sought to integrate the central processing unit (CPU), memory, and input/output peripherals into a single chip. This marked the birth of the first microcontroller, a compact and self-contained computing device.
- **Early Developments and Applications:** In the early days, microcontrollers were primarily used in simple applications, such as household appliances, calculators, and industrial machinery. Their low cost and power efficiency made them ideal for embedded systems and control tasks.
- **Moore's Law and Performance Improvements:** As Moore's Law took effect, the processing power of microcontrollers doubled every couple of years, leading to significant performance improvements. This exponential growth paved the way for more sophisticated applications, including automotive control systems and consumer electronics.
- **Integration of Analog and Digital Functions:** The integration of analog and digital functions within microcontrollers was a game-changer. This convergence allowed for more complex operations, enabling microcontrollers to handle a wide array of tasks simultaneously, from reading sensor data to processing audio and video signals.
- **Real-Time Operating Systems (RTOS):** The advent of real-time operating systems (RTOS) further expanded the capabilities of microcontrollers. RTOS provided multitasking abilities, allowing microcontrollers to manage multiple tasks simultaneously while maintaining precise timing requirements. This led to their extensive use in critical applications such as medical devices and aerospace systems.
- **Internet of Things (IoT) and Connectivity:** The rise of the Internet of Things (IoT) propelled microcontrollers into the realm of interconnected devices. With built-in wireless connectivity like Wi-Fi and Bluetooth, microcontrollers became the backbone of smart home automation, wearable gadgets, and industrial IoT applications.
- **Power Efficiency and Low-Power Modes:** Efficiency has always been a crucial factor in the development of microcontrollers. Manufacturers continually improved power management, introducing low-power modes that extended battery life, making them ideal for portable and battery-operated devices.

- **32-bit and 64-bit Microcontrollers:** The shift from 8-bit to 32-bit and 64-bit microcontrollers opened up new possibilities for processing complex data and running more sophisticated algorithms. This transition made them suitable for high-performance applications, such as advanced robotics and artificial intelligence.
- **Security and Encryption:** With the growing concern over data security, microcontroller manufacturers focused on implementing robust encryption and security features. This led to their application in secure communication systems, digital payment platforms, and secure access control.
- **Machine Learning and Edge Computing:** The integration of machine learning capabilities into microcontrollers brought about the era of edge computing. Now, microcontrollers can process data locally, reducing latency and enabling real-time decision-making in various applications like autonomous vehicles and smart surveillance systems.
- **The Future: Quantum Microcontrollers:** As technology continues to push boundaries, researchers speculate about the possibility of quantum microcontrollers. These futuristic devices could leverage quantum computing principles, exponentially enhancing processing power and revolutionizing computing as we know it.

Now the question arises as to which microcontroller to select for a particular application. Given the importance of cost, it is logical to select the most cost-effective device that meets the requirements of the application. Consequently, microcontrollers tend to be tailored to specific applications. Consequently, there is a wide range of microcontrollers available. The first choice of a designer is the controller family, which defines the architecture of the controller. All controllers within a family share the same processor core, thus being code-compatible. However, they differ in additional components, such as the number of timers and memory capacity. There are numerous controller families available in the market today, which can be verified by visiting the websites of a few electronics vendors and browsing their microcontroller stock. There are a variety of controller families available, such as 8051 microcontroller, PIC microcontroller, HC microcontroller, ARM microcontroller, and more. Within a single controller family, there may be a variety of controllers available.

Controller	Flash (KB)	SRAM (Byte)	EEPROM (Byte)	I/O-Pins	A/D (Channels)	Interfaces
AT90C8534	8	288	512	7	8	
AT90LS2323	2	128	128	3		
AT90LS2343	2	160	128	5		
AT90LS8535	8	512	512	32	8	UART, SPI
AT90S1200	1	64		15		
AT90S2313	2	160	128	15		
ATmega128	128	4096	4096	53	8	JTAG, SPI, IIC
ATmega162	16	1024	512	35		JTAG, SPI
ATmega169	16	1024	512	53	8	JTAG, SPI, IIC
ATmega16	16	1024	512	32	8	JTAG, SPI, IIC
ATtiny11	1		64	5+1 In		
ATtiny12	1		64	6		SPI
ATtiny15L	1		64	6	4	SPI
ATtiny26	2	128	128		16	SPI
ATtiny28L	2	128		11+8 In		

Figure 3.1: *Comparison of AVR microcontrollers*

Figure 3.1 shows a selection of microcontrollers of Atmel's AVR family. The one thing all these controllers have in common is their AVR processor core, which contains 32 general-purpose registers and executes most instructions within one clock cycle.

Once you've chosen the controller family, it's time to pick the right one for the job. There are a lot of different controllers out there, and they all have different memory configurations and different I/O types. Of course, the controller you choose should meet your hardware requirements, but it's also important to figure out how fast your application will run and how much memory you'll need, and make sure you're picking a controller that'll give you enough performance.

When it comes to memory, there's a general rule of thumb you'll want to stick with. You don't want your application to take up more than 80%, which gives you a bit of a buffer for later on. I think this rule can be applied to all controllers in general, and it's always a good idea to have some extra buffer in case of unexpected issues or extra features.

In the case of complex applications, a priori estimation is not simple. In addition, in 32-bit microcontrollers, you usually include an operating system that supports the application and the application development, which further increases the performance requirements. In the case of a small 8-bit controller, only the application needs to be taken into account. Here, for example, you can make rough estimates based on prior and/or comparable projects.

Microcontrollers have similar basic internal designs. The block diagram in *Figure* 3.2. illustrates the typical microcontroller design. Each component is connected to the external world using an internal bus. Each component is integrated on a single chip. Modules connect to the external world via an I/O pin.

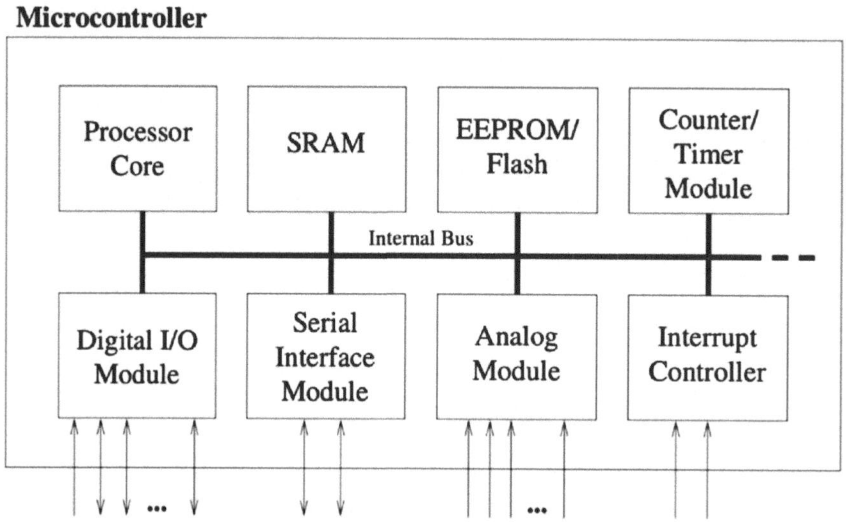

***Figure* 3.2:** *Layout of a microcontroller*

The following is a list of commonly used microcontroller modules.

- **The Processor Core** of a controller is composed of the Arithmetic Logic Unit (ALU), the Control Unit, and the Registers (Stack pointer, Program Counter, Accumulator Register, Register File, and so on).
- Memory is sometimes divided into Program Memory and Data Memory, and in larger controllers, a **Data Memory Access Controller (DMA)** is responsible for transferring data between peripheral components.
- **Interrupt Controller** is a feature of the controller that is used to interrupt normal program flow when an important external or internal event occurs. Interrupts can be combined with sleep modes to conserve power.
- **Timer/Counter** is a feature of most controllers that can be used for timestamping events, measuring intervals, or counting events. PWM (Pulse Width Modulation) outputs are also present in many controllers and may be used to drive motors or to achieve safe breaking (such as with an Antilock Brake System, ABS, or an External Filter).
- **Digital I/O** Ports are a key feature of the controller family, with the number varying from 3 to more than 90.

- **Analog I/O:** Most microcontrollers (with the exception of a few tiny controllers) have built-in analog/digital converters. These converters vary in number of channels from 2 to 16 and resolution from 8 to 12 bits. The analog module usually includes an analog comparator, in some cases the microcontroller also includes digital/analog converters.
- **Interfaces:** Most microcontrollers are equipped with a minimum of one serial interface, which is capable of downloading the program and communicating with the development PC generally. As serial interfaces are also capable of connecting to external peripheral devices, the majority of controllers offer a wide range of interfaces, such as SPI, SCI, and more. Additionally, many microcontrollers also include integrated bus controllers, which are used for the most commonly used (field) bus types. The leading controllers in this area are IIC and CAN. Additionally, larger microcontrollers may include a variety of other interfaces, such as PCI, USB, and Ethernet.
- The **watchdog timer** is a device used to reset a microcontroller in the event of software "crashes" due to program and/or hardware errors, as safety-critical systems are a major application area for microcontrollers.
- **Debugging unit**: Some controllers have extra hardware that allows you to debug the chip remotely from your PC. So you don't have to download any extra debugging software. One of the advantages of this is that bad application code can't overwrite the debug unit.

A microcontroller is a stripped-down processor that includes memory, timers, I/O (parallel) pins and other peripherals. The main reason for this is cost. By integrating all elements on a single chip, space is saved, manufacturing costs are reduced, development time is shortened, and time is a key factor in embedded systems. Other benefits of integration are easy upgradeability, low power consumption, and improved reliability.

On the other hand, if a microcontroller is used to solve a problem in software that can also be solved by a hardware solution, it will not achieve the same speed as the hardware solution. Therefore, applications that have very short reaction times may still require a hardware solution. However, most applications, especially those that require some kind of human interaction (such as microwaves, mobile phones, and so on), do not have such fast reaction times. Therefore, microcontrollers are suitable for these applications.

Components in a Microcontroller

A microcontroller contains the following components:

Processor

The processor, which is also referred to as the CPU, is the microcontroller's **brain**. It is responsible for executing instructions, executing calculations, and managing the overall performance of the processor. The processor's capabilities define the performance and types of tasks that a microcontroller is capable of performing.

Here are the key aspects of a processor:

- **CPU**: The CPU core is made up of the Arithmetic logic unit (ALU), the Control Unit, and the registers. The Arithmetic Logic Unit (ALU) carries out the mathematical operations and logical operations. The Control Unit carries out the execution of instructions. The Control Unit coordinates the data flow between different components.
- **Instruction Set Architecture**: The instruction set architecture (ISA) is the collection of instructions that a processor is capable of recognizing and executing. Each instruction is associated with a particular operation, for example, adding, subtracting, or branching. The programming and capabilities of a microcontroller are determined by its instruction set architecture.
- **Clock Generator**: The processor needs a clock signal to keep everything running smoothly. The clock generator creates a constant clock signal that tells the processor when to execute instructions. The clock speed, which is usually measured in Hertz, tells how quickly the processor can run instructions.
- **Registers**: Registers are a type of high-speed memory located within the processor. These memory locations are used to temporarily store data during instruction execution. Common types of registers include a Program Counter (PC) which stores the memory address for the following instruction to be received, and an Accumulator which is used for intermediate calculations.
- **Memory Management Unit (MMU):** The memory management unit (MMU) is a feature of certain microcontrollers, particularly those with more sophisticated features. The MMU facilitates the conversion

between the virtual memory addresses utilized by the software and the physical memory addresses employed by the hardware.

- **Pipeline architecture**: In some microcontrollers, a pipeline architecture is used to increase instruction throughput. A pipeline is a processor in which multiple instructions are executed in different stages at the same time. This enables more efficient utilization of the processor's resources and faster execution overall.
- **Interrupt Controllers:** Microcontrollers need to be able to respond quickly to outside events or signals. This is what the interrupt controller does. It stops the normal execution of the program and jumps to a pre-defined part of the code (called an interrupt service routine). This is especially important for applications that run in real-time.
- **Peripherals interface**: A microcontroller has a processor component that provides interfaces (commonly called GPIO pins) to various external devices or sensors.
- **Power Management**: A lot of microcontrollers today have power management functions to control power consumption. The power management function of the processor component is responsible for controlling the power modes that the microcontroller can enter into when specific conditions are met.

In short, the Processor is the part of a microcontroller that executes instructions, manages data, manages interrupt handling, and manages the interactions between different parts of a microcontroller. Processor performance, capabilities and efficiency have a significant impact on the overall performance and usability of a microcontroller in different applications.

Memory

The memory component of a microcontroller refers to the storage elements within the microcontroller that hold data and instructions for the processor to operate on. Memory plays a vital role in storing the program code, data, and temporary values during the execution of tasks.

Therefore, an obvious distinction of memory types can be made according to their function:

- **Register File:** A (usually) relatively small memory embedded in the CPU. It is used as a scratchpad for temporary storage of values the CPU is working with - you could call it the CPU's short-term memory.

- **Data Memory:** For longer-term storage, generic CPUs usually employ an external memory that is much larger than the register file. Data that is stored there may be short-lived, but may also be valid for as long as the CPU is running. Of course, attaching external memory to a CPU requires some hardware effort and thus incurs some cost. For that reason, microcontrollers usually sport on-chip data memory.
- **Instruction Memory**: Like the data memory, the instruction memory is usually a relatively large external memory (at least with general CPUs). Actually, with von Neumann architectures, it may even be the same physical memory as the data memory. With microcontrollers, the instruction memory, too, is usually integrated right into the MCU.

The memory in semiconductor devices is divided into two different categories: one is volatile memory and another one is non-volatile memory. These volatile and non-volatile memories are further divided into multiple parts such as RAM and ROM, and so on.

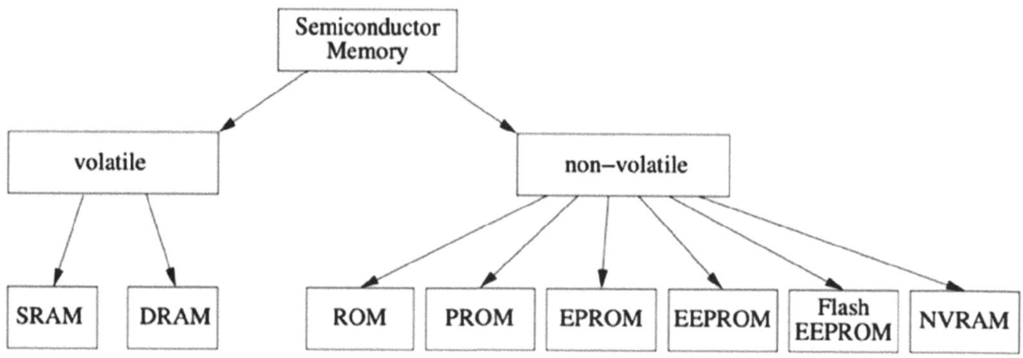

Figure 3.3: *Type of memory in Microcontrollers*

Volatile Memory

In the world of Embedded Systems, Volatile Memory plays an important role in Microcontrollers. Microcontrollers are the brains behind many electronic devices, from consumer gadgets to industrial machines. In this article, we explore the complex nature of Volatile Memory in Microcontrollers and its importance and influence on overall system performance.

The term **volatile memory** is often used interchangeably with "temporary memory" or "dynamic memory". Volatile memory stores data that is essential for the day-to-day operation of the microcontroller.

Unlike regular memory, which stores information even when the power is knocked out, volatile memory, on the other hand, loses its data as soon as the power is turned off. This means that volatile memory can be used to store temporary data like variables and registers that are needed for instant processing and calculations.

Types of volatile memory

- **Static Random Access Memory (SRAM):** SRAM is a high-speed volatile memory that provides rapid access times and low power consumption. It is commonly used in microcontrollers for cache memory and registers due to its quick read and write operations. However, its drawback lies in its higher cost per bit compared to other memory types.
- **Dynamic Random Access Memory (DRAM):** DRAM, known for its higher density compared to SRAM, is another vital volatile memory component in microcontrollers. It requires periodic refreshing to maintain data integrity, which can introduce delays in read and write operations. Nevertheless, its cost-effectiveness and compactness make it an ideal choice for certain applications.

The speed and responsiveness of the microcontroller are directly related to volatile memory management. Rapid access to volatile memory variables and instructions improves the performance of the system. Developers often optimize the memory allocation strategies to reduce memory access times and improve the overall execution speed. Due to the short-term nature of volatile memory, careful memory management is required to avoid loss of data. Developers implement fault-tolerant mechanisms and use non-vault memory for important data backup so that even power outages do not affect system performance.

Non-volatile Memory

Non-volatile memory is a memory that stores data even when power is off. Volatile memory, on the other hand, loses data when the power is off. Non-volatile memory keeps important information intact, so the microcontroller can continue to run smoothly when the power is back on.

Non-volatile memory is important for storing long-term data, like firmware, configuration, and user information that must be kept even when there is no power.

- **ROM**: ROMs were the first non-volatile memories. Did we just say that write access is more important in non-volatile memory than in volatile memory? In the case of ROMs, we were a bit wrong. As the name suggests, you simply can't write to a ROM. You need to hand over the data to the chip manufacturer where a specific chip containing your data is made. A Mask-ROM is a common type of ROM. Like any IC chip, an MROM is composed of several layers.

Geometrically, the geometrical arrangement of the layers determines the function of the chip. Just like RAM, the MROM contains a matrix of memory cells, but on one layer, fixed connections are made between rows and columns, reflecting the data to be stored in the MROM. Mask-ROM is named after the single mask that defines the row and column connections.

- **PROM**: PROM stands for programmable read-only memory. Unlike other types of memory chips, a PROM chip can be programmed during manufacturing with a specific set of data or code. This means that the stored information can be read several times, but not changed. Unlike other memory chips, the cells of a PROM chip are fused during the programming process, resulting in a fixed binary pattern representing the programmed information.

  Once programmed, the contents of the PROM cannot be changed. This means that it can be used to store fixed data, such as firmware and calibration values, in a variety of electronic devices. PROMs are not as flexible as newer memory technologies, however.

- **EPROM**: EPROM is an erasable programmable read-only memory technology. It is used in electronic devices to store data. It allows you to write, store, and read data multiple times. The most important feature of EPROM is that it can be erasable through UV light exposure.

  EPROM chips are made up of memory cells with a floating-gate transistor that you can charge or un-charge to represent binary information. To erase data, you need to expose the chip to UV light. UV light will reset the memory cells so that they can be reprogrammed. Although EPROM was historically important, it has largely been replaced by faster erasable technologies such as EEPROM or Flash memory.

- **EEPROM**: Electrically erasable programmable read-only memory (EEPROM), is a non-electromagnetic memory technology that allows you to write and erase data electronically. Unlike Read-Only Memory, which relies on UV light exposure, EEPROM allows you to selectively program and erase individual memory cells using electrical signals.

EEPROM is perfect for storing configuration settings and small amounts of data in electronic devices as well as firmware updates. It is a convenient and flexible way to store and modify data.

- **Flash:** Flash, also known as flash EEPROM or flash electrically erasing programmable read-only memory, is a portable memory technology that offers the advantages of both flash memory and EEPROM. Flash allows for the electronic writing, erasure and reprogramming of data without the use of UV light. Flash offers fast and convenient storage and retrieval of data, making it one of the most popular solutions for applications that require frequent upgrades or firmware updates in different electronic devices.
- **NVRAM:** NVRAM is a form of memory that combines the features of random access memory (RAM) with the features of non-random access memory. NVRAM allows data to be stored even when there is no power supply. In most cases, NVRAM uses battery backup or capacitor-based energy storage or other means to retain data, even when power is lost or the system is shut down.

  NVRAM provides a dependable way to store important data and settings in a variety of electronic devices and operating systems.

I/O Ports

I/O ports are an integral part of a microcontroller. They act as gateways for communication between a microcontroller and an external device or system. The I/O ports allow the microcontroller to accept inputs from sensors, switches, and other peripherals as well as output signals from actuators, displays, and other components.

I/O ports can be configured as single pins that can be either input or output, depending on the application's requirements. Input pins detect voltage changes or logical states from external devices and convert these into digital signals that can be processed by the microcontroller.

Output pins, on the other hand, send control signals or data directly to external components, changing their behavior or showing information. The I/O ports in a microcontroller play an essential role in allowing interaction and control within a microcontroller-based system.

Analog I/O

An analog I/O pin is a specialized pin on a microcontroller that enables the microcontroller to communicate with analog signals. This allows the microcontroller to measure and produce continuous voltage levels instead of discrete digital values.

Analog I/O pins are essential for analog sensing, actuators, and other devices that operate on variable voltages and analog signals.

- **Analog Input:** Analog input pins are used to measure external analog signals. They convert continuous analog voltage levels into digital values that the microcontroller can process. The conversion process, known as analog-to-digital conversion (ADC), involves sampling the analog signal at specific intervals and quantizing it into discrete digital steps. The microcontroller's ADC module converts these steps into binary values that represent the amplitude of the analog signal. The resolution of the ADC determines the precision of the conversion, and it's often expressed in bits (for example, 10-bit ADC provides 2^10 = 1024 possible digital values). Analog input pins are employed for various applications, such as reading values from temperature sensors, light sensors, potentiometers, and more.
- **Analog Output:** Analog output pins enable the microcontroller to generate analog voltage levels. The digital-to-analog conversion (DAC) process is used to transform digital values from the microcontroller into corresponding analog voltage levels. By varying the output voltage, microcontrollers can control analog devices like motors, LEDs, speakers, and more. DAC modules in microcontrollers follow similar principles as ADCs but work in the opposite direction, converting digital signals into varying voltage levels.

Use Cases and Considerations:

- **Sensor Interface:** Analog input pins are essential for interfacing with various analog sensors, providing valuable information about real-world quantities such as temperature, humidity, pressure, and more.
- **Actuator Control:** Analog output pins are crucial for driving actuators like motors, controlling their speed, direction, or position based on the analog voltage level.
- **Waveform Generation:** Analog output pins can be used to generate analog waveforms for audio synthesis, waveform modulation, and other signal generation applications.

- **Precision and Noise:** The quality of analog I/O depends on factors like ADC/DAC resolution, signal-to-noise ratio, and noise reduction techniques to ensure accurate and reliable readings.
- **Calibration:** Analog I/O pins may require calibration to ensure accurate conversion between analog and digital values, compensating for any inaccuracies.

Interrupts

Microcontrollers are typically used in systems that need to respond to events. Events represent changes in the state of the controlled system and typically require some kind of response from the microcontroller.

These reactions can be as simple as incrementing a counter when a workpiece passes a photoelectric barrier along the conveyor belt or they can be more time-critical, such as turning off the system when someone reaches into the machine's working area. If the controller can observe an event, such as an input line changing its state to indicate an event, then the next question is how the controller should track the input line to provide a correct and timely response.

Of course, it is possible to poll the input signal to check for state changes on a regular basis. However, this method has several disadvantages:

Of course, it is possible to poll only the input signal to check periodically for state changes. But this is a waste of processor time: not only does the event occur infrequently, but it is also difficult to change or extend. A microcontroller usually has much more work to do than waiting for one event. So, the event is polled regularly so that the whole program can be run. However, the signal might need to be polled for a maximum period to prevent missing events. This means that the polling code might have to be called from multiple places in the master program. It already takes a lot of time to figure out which positions in code the signal needs to be polled first, and those positions need to be re-evaluated every time the master code changes. So, the idea of a poll soon loses its appeal and the software developer starts looking for alternative ways to deal with those infrequent events.

Timers

Timers in microcontrollers are essential hardware components designed to measure and manage time intervals, synchronization, and various time-related functions within the microcontroller's operation. These timers play a crucial role in a wide range of applications, including precise timing, event generation, signal modulation, and more.

Timer Types:

Microcontrollers typically feature different types of timers, each serving specific purposes:

- **Basic Timers**: These are simple timers that generate basic timing intervals or delays. They often have limited functionality and are commonly used for generating delays in software loops.
- **General-Purpose Timers**: These timers provide more advanced features, such as generating pulses, measuring time intervals, and triggering events. They offer multiple operating modes, allowing for versatile time-related tasks.
- **Capture/Compare Timers**: These timers are used for measuring time intervals between external events or generating precise PWM (Pulse Width Modulation) signals. They can capture the time of an external event occurrence or compare it with predefined values.
- **Watchdog Timers**: While not exclusively timers, watchdog timers are often integrated into microcontrollers. They act as a safety mechanism, resetting the microcontroller if a software glitch or malfunction occurs within a specified time interval.

Timer Modes:

Timers in microcontrollers can be configured in various modes to suit specific applications:

- **Timer Mode**: In this mode, the timer counts up from an initial value to a maximum value, generating an interrupt or event when it overflows. This mode is commonly used for generating precise time delays or periodic events.
- **Capture Mode**: Capture timers can measure the time between external events (rising/falling edges of signals). They are useful for tasks like measuring pulse widths, frequency measurements, and event time-stamping.
- **Compare Mode**: Compare timers are employed for generating PWM signals, where the duty cycle of the signal can be controlled by comparing the timer's value with a preset value. They're used in applications like motor control, LED dimming, and audio generation.

Applications:

Timers are integral to many microcontroller-based systems and applications:

- **Real-Time Clocks**: Timers can be configured to keep track of real-world time, allowing microcontrollers to manage tasks at specific intervals or time events.
- **Motor Control**: Timers play a key role in generating precise PWM signals for controlling motor speed and direction.
- **Communication Protocols**: Timers are often used to generate clock signals for serial communication protocols like UART, SPI, and I2C.
- **Sensor Reading**: Timers can be utilized to trigger periodic readings from sensors, ensuring data is collected at specific intervals.
- **Event Sequencing**: Timers can help sequence events in time-critical applications, ensuring tasks occur in a synchronized manner.

Getting Started with Arduino UNO R3

When it comes to the Internet of Things, there has to be a starting point to the world of IoT and Arduino Uno is that starting block for any IoT enthusiast. Arduino UNO R3 is a basic development board which is used in most IoT projects nowadays. It is the entry point to the world of embedded systems.

The Arduino Uno R3 is a popular and versatile microcontroller board that has become synonymous with accessible and user-friendly electronics prototyping. Developed by the Arduino company, this board has empowered countless individuals, from beginners to experienced makers, to bring their electronic projects to life. The Arduino Uno R3 embodies the essence of simplicity and innovation, serving as a gateway for learning, experimentation, and creativity in the world of embedded systems and electronics.

At its core, the Arduino Uno R3 is built around the versatile ATmega328P microcontroller chip, which boasts ample processing power and a generous array of input/output pins. This microcontroller serves as the brain of the board, allowing users to program and control a wide range of sensors, actuators, displays, and communication modules to create interactive projects of various complexities.

What truly sets the Arduino Uno R3 apart is its accessibility to both newcomers and experts. Its user-friendly design, paired with the Arduino Integrated Development Environment (IDE), simplifies the programming process. This allows individuals with limited coding experience to quickly grasp the concepts of coding and start writing programs to control their projects. Meanwhile, seasoned programmers appreciate the flexibility to dive deep into more intricate coding, custom libraries, and advanced projects.

Figure 3.4: *Arduino Uno*

The board's layout features a collection of digital and analog input/output pins, each clearly labeled, making it straightforward to connect various components and peripherals. This encourages rapid prototyping without the need for extensive soldering or intricate circuitry.

With built-in USB connectivity, the Arduino Uno R3 eliminates the need for additional programming hardware, allowing users to upload their code directly from a computer. This seamless integration streamlines the development process and encourages experimentation without the hassle of complex setup procedures.

Take a closer look at Figure 3.4 – Arduino Uno and you'll find that the pins on the Arduino development board are divided into 4 different parts.

- Power Pins
- Digital GPIO
- Analog Pins
- PWM

Apart from that a few GPIO pins can be used for communication purposes as well and we'll study about them later in this book.

Power Pins

Power pins are important parts of the Arduino board. They are responsible for powering the board and any connected parts or peripherals. They make sure that the board runs smoothly and that any external devices get the power they need to work. There are usually several power pins on an Arduino board, each of which has a different purpose.

- **Vin (Voltage In):** This pin allows the connection of an external power source, such as a battery or an external power adapter. The voltage supplied through this pin should be within a specified range (usually around 7V to 12V for the Arduino Uno) to ensure proper operation of the board's voltage regulator.
- **5V**: The 5V pin provides a regulated 5-volt supply generated by the board's voltage regulator. It is used to power external components that require a stable 5V input, such as sensors, modules, and peripherals.
- **3.3V:** This pin supplies a regulated 3.3-volt power output. It is useful for powering devices that operate at 3.3V logic levels, which may include certain sensors and communication modules.
- **GND (Ground):** The ground pins serve as the reference point for electrical circuits. They provide a common ground reference for the board and connected components, ensuring proper electrical connectivity and reducing noise interference.

It's important to note that proper power supply connections are essential for the safe and dependable functioning of the Arduino and all connected components. Incorrect power pins, voltage sources outside recommended limits, or insufficient power can cause board failure or damage.

When planning your projects with the Arduino, power requirements are an important factor to consider. Selecting the right voltage source, controlling voltage levels when needed, and making sure the board is properly grounded all help to keep the board and components stable and long-lasting.

Digital GPIOs

In the context of Arduino boards, Digital General-Purpose Input/Output (GPIO) pins are fundamental components that serve as versatile interfaces between the microcontroller and external devices. These pins can be configured as either input or output, enabling communication, control, and interaction with various electronic components. Each digital GPIO pin can have one of two logic states: HIGH (1) or LOW (0), representing binary values that correspond to voltage levels.

Digital Input:

Digital input GPIO pins are used to read external signals or states. When configured as inputs, these pins detect the voltage level applied to them and translate it into a digital signal that the microcontroller can process. For instance, they can detect the state of a switch (pressed or un-pressed), the presence of a sensor signal, or the logic level from another device. The microcontroller can then respond to these inputs by executing specific code or triggering appropriate actions.

Digital Output:

Digital output GPIO pins enable the microcontroller to send signals to external devices. By setting the pin to HIGH (5V or 3.3V) or LOW (0V), the microcontroller can control the behavior of connected components. This could involve illuminating LEDs, activating relays, driving motors, or communicating with other microcontrollers and modules. Digital outputs allow the microcontroller to exert control and influence over the external world.

Use Cases and Considerations:

- **LED Control**: Digital outputs are often used to control LEDs, turning them on or off to indicate states, events, or conditions.
- **Button/Switch Input**: Digital inputs can be connected to buttons or switches to detect user actions and initiate responses.
- **Sensor Interface**: Digital inputs are suitable for reading the output of digital sensors, which generate signals in the form of discrete levels.
- **Communication**: Digital GPIO pins can be used for basic communication protocols like UART, SPI, and I2C by toggling the pin states in specific patterns.
- **Logic Control**: Digital outputs can be used to control logic gates and flip-flops in more complex digital circuits.

GPIO pins in Arduino boards provide a versatile means of interaction between the microcontroller and external components. They enable input reading, output control, and communication, forming the foundation for countless electronic projects by allowing the microcontroller to sense and influence its environment.

Analog Pins

Analog pins in an Arduino UNO are special input pins that enable the microcontroller to communicate with analog signals. A0 to A5 are 6 analog pins on the Arduino board. These pins enable continuous voltage levels to be measured instead of binary digital values. The analog pins are specially designed to facilitate the analog-to-digital conversion, enabling the user to interact with a broad range of analog sensors, actuators, and devices.

An analog pin's main job is to convert an analog voltage signal into a digital value that can be interpreted and processed by the microcontroller. The precision of the conversion is determined by the number of bits (or bits of resolution) of each analog pin. A 10-bit ADC, for example, provides 2^10= 1024 discrete steps, which represent the range of possible analog voltage values to be measured.

Analog pins are used to communicate with various analog sensors that output voltage signals that correspond to real-world values such as temperature, intensity of light, humidity, and so on. By connecting the output of the sensor to an analog pin, the ADC capabilities of the Arduino UNO enable accurate measurement and interpretation of these analog signals.

Most of the time, the voltage on the analog pins of an Arduino UNO is between 0 and 5 volts. The values of the analog pins correspond to the values of the digital pins (0 to 1023) in the ADC configuration (10-bit) of the UNO. Some of the Arduino boards may have a built-in reference voltage that you can set. This allows you to measure a lower voltage range or more accurate values.

PWM Pins

PWM pins in the Arduino are special output pins that allow the generation of analog-like signals with digital components. PWM is a process by which the duty cycle of the square wave signal (the difference between high time and total time) is changed to create analog voltage levels with digital signals.

The square wave signal produced by the PWM pins of the Arduino is fixed frequency and has a duty cycle. The duty cycle can be changed. For example, the duty cycle of the Arduino PWM can be changed to 50%. The average voltage output of the PWM pins can be changed to about half the supply voltage of the Arduino. For example, if the supply voltage is set to 5V and the duty cycle changes to 50%, the voltage output can be changed to simulate an analog voltage (2.5V) (provided the supply voltage is 5V).

Applications:

PWM pins are widely used for controlling devices that require analog-like control, such as dimming LEDs, controlling motor speeds, generating audio tones, and more. Some common applications include:

- **LED Dimming**: By varying the duty cycle of a PWM signal sent to an LED, you can control its brightness smoothly.
- **Motor Speed Control**: PWM pins are often used to control the speed of DC motors or servos by adjusting the duty cycle to vary the power applied.
- **Audio Generation**: PWM pins can generate audio tones by rapidly switching the signal at different frequencies to produce different pitches.
- **Analog Voltage Simulation**: By using PWM, you can simulate analog voltage levels needed for some applications without using dedicated digital-to-analog converters (DACs).

The PWM signal frequency varies depending on the type of Arduino board and the type of PWM pin you have chosen. The resolution of the PWM pins is usually based on the number of bits used in the timer to generate the PWM signal, and this resolution affects the accuracy of your PWM signal as well as the granularity of the analog voltage levels you can simulate.

With the help of these digital GPIOs, Analog Pins, and PWM pins, there are 4 basic functions that we can perform on an Arduino board and those are:

- **Digital Read**: The digital read function is used to read the digital values, that is, 0 and 1 from the digital GPIO pins - 0 to 13.
- **Digital Write**: The digital write function is used to write the digital values, that is, 0 and 1 on the digital GPIOs.
- **Analog Read**: Analog read is used to read the analog voltages with the help of analog pins, that is, A0 to A5.
- **Analog Write**: PWM pins are used to perform the analog write function where the variable voltage level can be provided to the PIN - 3,5,6,9,10 and 11 as these 6 pins are defined as the PWM pins and there is '~' mark beside these pins which defines them as PWM pins.

Pin description of Arduino UNO

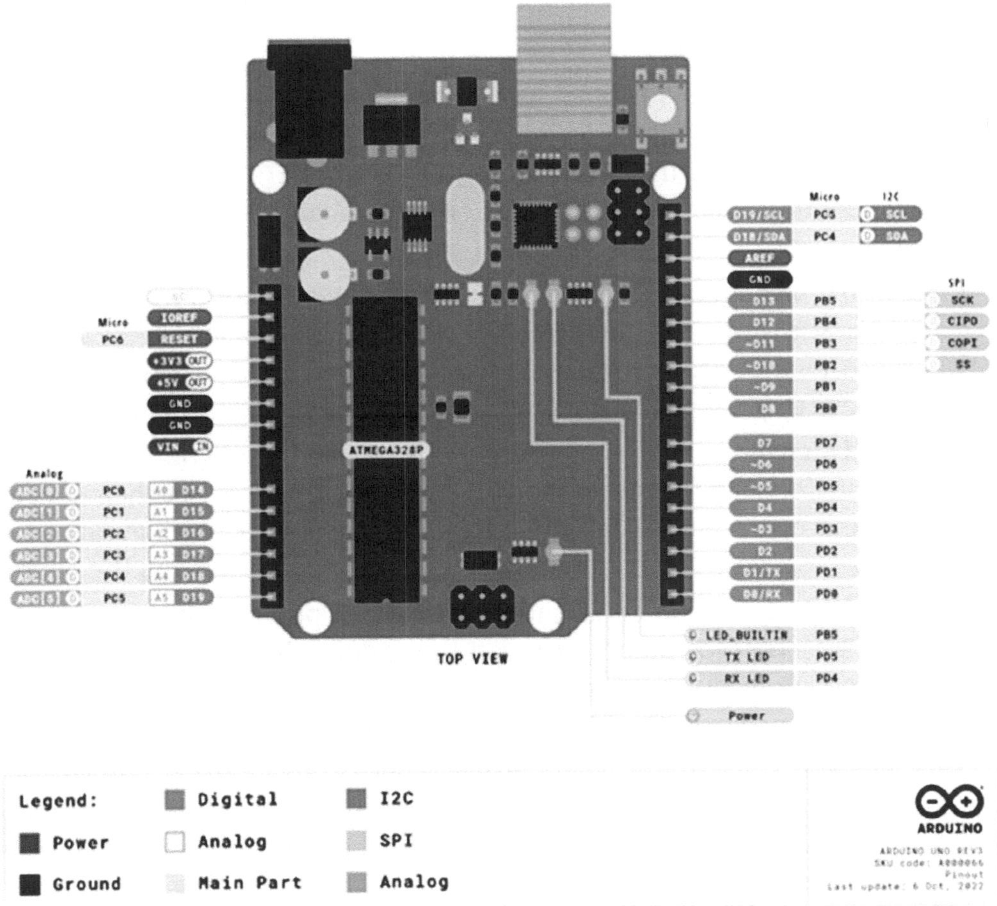

***Figure 3.5**: Pin description of Arduino UNO*

To use the Arduino board in IoT projects and prototypes, an IDE called the – Arduino IDE is used which helps in writing and uploading the Arduino program to the Arduino board. Let's take a look at the Arduino IDE and see it in action.

Programming the Arduino board with Arduino IDE

The Arduino IDE stands for "Arduino Integrated Development Environment". It is a complete software platform that makes it easy to program, develop, and deploy code for the Arduino microcontroller board. The IDE is used as the main tool to create, edit, compile, and upload code to the board. It makes working with the microcontrollers straightforward for both beginner and expert programmers.

Key Features and Functions:

- **Code Editor:** The Arduino IDE provides a user-friendly code editor where users can write, edit, and organize their code. It supports popular programming languages like C and C++ and offers features like syntax highlighting and auto-completion, which enhance code readability and efficiency.
- **Library Manager:** The IDE comes with a built-in library manager that allows users to easily integrate pre-written libraries into their projects. These libraries provide ready-to-use functions for various tasks, reducing the need to reinvent the wheel and accelerating the development process.
- **Board Manager:** Arduino supports a wide range of microcontroller boards. The board manager within the IDE enables users to select their specific Arduino board and install the necessary drivers and configurations to ensure seamless communication between the computer and the board.
- **Serial Monitor:** The serial monitor is a tool provided by the IDE that allows users to communicate with the Arduino board through the USB connection. It displays data sent by the Arduino and enables real-time interaction, debugging, and data visualization.
- **Code Verification and Compilation:** The IDE includes a compiler that transforms human-readable code into machine-executable instructions for the Arduino board. It performs syntax checking and highlights errors and warnings, helping users identify and correct coding issues before uploading to the board.
- **Upload and Deployment:** Once the code is written and verified, the Arduino IDE facilitates the process of uploading the compiled code to the Arduino board. Users can easily program the microcontroller with a single click, making the deployment process smooth and efficient.

Designed with ease of use in mind, the Arduino IDE supports users of all levels of experience. Its intuitive user interface, comprehensive documentation, and active online community give beginners the tools they need to learn and try out microcontrollers. It also provides the flexibility and tools they need for more complex projects.

Arduino IDE is an open-source software. This means that it can be used, changed, and distributed freely. It is also compatible with many operating systems, including Windows, macOS, and Linux.

The great thing about the Arduino IDE is that it has a large and active user community. This community is made up of people who use the IDE, who make the IDE, who teach the IDE, and who use the IDE to troubleshoot, learn, and share. They contribute to the libraries, the tutorials, and the forums.

To program the Arduino board, download the Arduino IDE in your system, once installed, run the IDE and this will be the first screen you'll see.

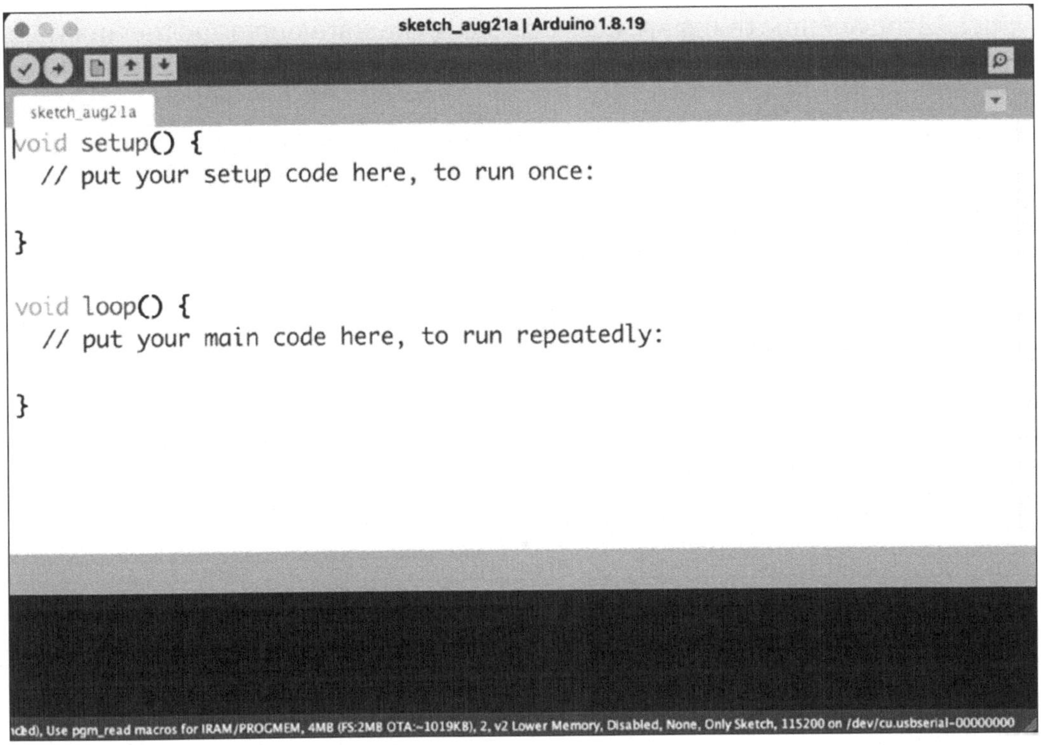

Figure 3.6: *Arduino IDE Screen*

This is the interface for the Mac users and there is a menu bar over the top that has multiple options that consist of all the settings for the IDE.

Figure 3.7: *Menu bar in the Arduino IDE*

If you are using Windows, you'll get all these menu items on the top of IDE.

On the title bar, there is a default sketch name(in Arduino a program is termed as a sketch) along with the Arduino version. Currently, as you can see, the version used here is 1.8.19 as seen in *Figure* 3.5.

There are several icons that we use for uploading, verifying, opening a new file, opening an existing file and saving the current file.

After that, there is the main window where the program is written, take a close look at the screen and you'll see two functions by the name of Setup() and Loop().

Setup and Loop are the two default functions that are included in every sketch. They are called the setup part and the loop part, the setup part is the function in which all the onetime things are defined, that is, the statements and the functions that we only need to use at the start of the microcontroller should be defined here. Inside the loop, we write the actual program or define the tasks that the microcontroller should perform in an infinite loop. Once the microcontroller is powered on, it will execute the setup part only once and after that, it will shift to the loop part where it will perform all the defined operations in an infinite loop until it is connected to the power supply.

The Blinking of LED

Hello World! This happens to be the first program whenever anyone starts learning any programming language. In the case of the Arduino, the blinking of the LED is the first program that anyone will study to start their journey in the world of embedded programming using Arduino IDE.

Once you open the Arduino IDE, you'll be introduced to the 2 default functions - setup and the loop. In the setup part, the pin number will be defined and in the loop part, the blinking of the LED operation will take place.

Code:

```
Void setup(){

   pinMode(13, OUTPUT);

}

Void loop(){

   digitalWrite(13, HIGH);

   delay(1000);
```

```
    digitalWrite(13, LOW);

    delay(1000);

}
```

This sketch will make the LED connected on the 13th pin blink every second. Let's understand the code line by line.

Inside the setup part:

The **pinMode** function in Arduino is used to configure the mode of a specific digital I/O pin on the Arduino board. It determines whether the pin will be used as an input or an output.

Here is the basic syntax of the `pinMode` function:

```
void pinMode(uint8_t pin, uint8_t mode);
```

- pin: The number of the digital pin you want to configure. This could be a number like 2, 5, 9, and so on, depending on the specific Arduino board you're using.
- mode: The mode you want to set for the pin. This can be either INPUT or OUTPUT, representing whether the pin will be used to read input from sensors or provide output to external devices.

In the example, the pinMode function is used in the setup function to configure digital pin 13 as an output.

Inside the loop part:

The `digitalWrite` function in Arduino is used to set the state of a specific digital I/O pin to either high (ON) or low (OFF). It controls the output voltage level of the pin.

Here is the basic syntax of the `digitalWrite` function:

```
void digitalWrite(uint8_t pin, uint8_t value);
```

- `pin`: The number of the digital pin you want to control. This should be a pin that has been configured as an output using the pinMode function.
- `value`: The value you want to set for the pin. This can be either HIGH (typically representing a logic level of 1 or a high voltage) or LOW (representing a logic level of 0, or a low voltage).

In the example, the **`digitalWrite`** function is used to turn an LED connected to digital pin 13 on and off by setting its state to HIGH and LOW, respectively, with a 1-second delay between each state change.

The **`delay`** function in Arduino is used to pause the execution of the program for a specified amount of time in milliseconds. It's commonly used to introduce a delay between different actions or to control timing in various applications.

Here is the basic syntax of the delay function:

```
void delay(unsigned long milliseconds);
```

- **`milliseconds`**: The amount of time in milliseconds for which you want the program to be paused. This is an unsigned long integer value, meaning it can range from 0 to 4,294,967,295 milliseconds (approximately 49.7 days).

This concludes the fundamental sketch, the blinking of an LED in Arduino, which introduces the fundamental idea of the microcontroller, helps you understand how to use the pins, defines the setup and loop part, and how to use the digitalWrite function of the digital GPIOs to send commands.

However, there is one more basic thing that one needs to understand, that is, the concept of serial output, which helps in debugging and viewing the output and eventually makes the whole coding process easy.

Uploading the sketch to the Arduino Board

Step 1: Connect Arduino Uno

- Connect your Arduino Uno board to your computer using a USB cable.
- Ensure that the board's power LED is on and that the "ON" LED is lit.

Step 2: Select Arduino Uno Board

- Go to **`Tools > Board`**.
- Select **`Arduino Uno`** from the list of available boards.

Step 3: Choose COM Port

- Go to **`Tools`** > **`Port`**.
- Select the appropriate COM port that corresponds to your Arduino Uno. If you're not sure which COM port to choose, you can check in the **`Device Manager`** (Windows) or **`System Information`** (macOS) under **`Ports`** (COM & LPT) or **`Serial-ATA`**.

Step 4: Verify and Upload Your Sketch

- Click the **Verify** button (checkmark icon) to compile your sketch and check for any errors.
- If there are no errors, click the **Upload** button (right arrow icon) to upload the sketch to the Arduino Uno.

Step 5: Observe the Upload Process

- During the upload, you'll see status messages on the Arduino IDE's console.
- The onboard LEDs (RX and TX) on the Arduino Uno might blink rapidly during the upload.

Step 8: Upload Complete

- Once the upload is complete, you'll see a **Done uploading** message in the Arduino IDE's console.
- The code is now running on your Arduino Uno board.

In Arduino, the Serial Output process refers to the act of sending data from the Arduino board to an external device, typically a computer, using a serial communication protocol. This is a crucial feature for debugging, monitoring, and exchanging information between the Arduino and a connected computer. The data sent via serial communication can include sensor readings, status updates, debug information, and more.

The main steps involved in the Serial Output process in Arduino are as follows:

- **Initialization:** To use serial communication, you need to initialize the scrial port. This is usually done in the setup function using the **Serial.begin()** function. This function sets the communication speed (baud rate) and opens the serial port for communication.

  ```
  void setup() {
  Serial.begin(9600); // Initialize serial communication at 9600 baud
  }
  ```

- **Sending Data:** You can use the **Serial.print()** and **Serial.println()** functions to send data to the computer. The print function sends data as-is, while **println** adds a new line character **("\n")** after the data, which moves the cursor to the next line.

  ```
  Void loop(){
  ```

```
digitalWrite(13,HIGH);
Serial.println("LED is ON");
delay(1000);
digitalWrite(13,LOW);
Serial.println("LED is OFF");
delay(1000);
}
```

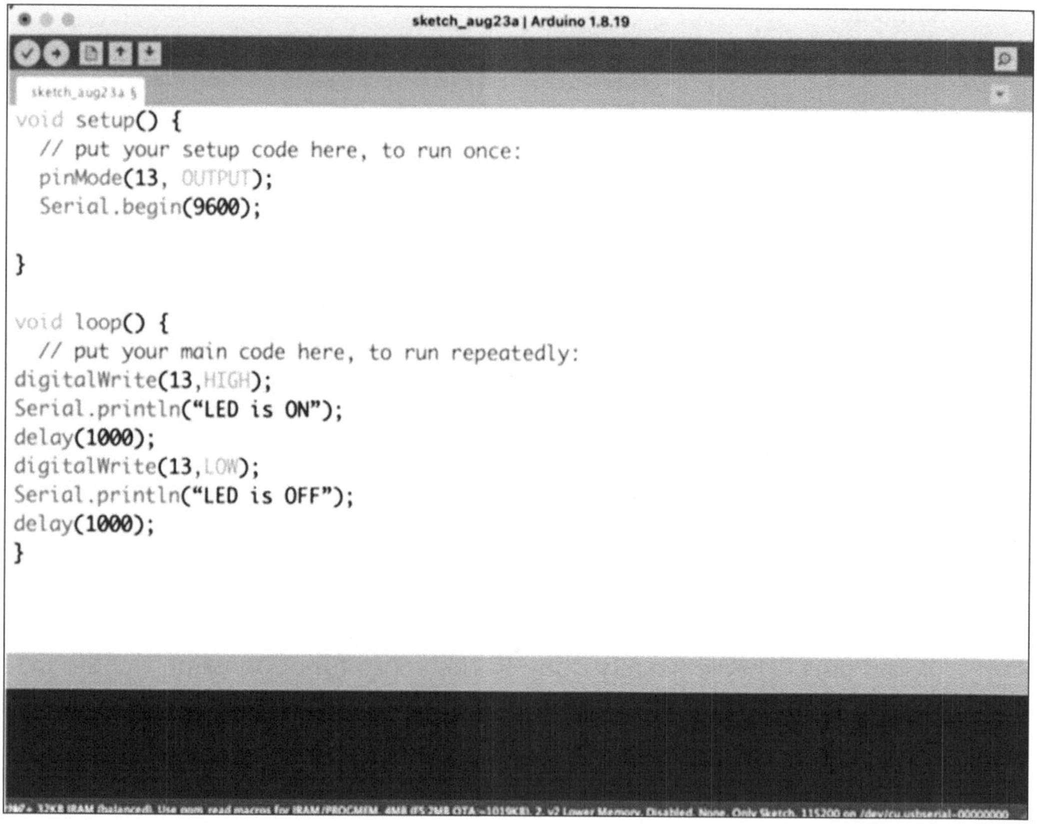

Figure 3.8: *Blinking of LED Sketch in Arduino IDE with serial output*

Viewing Data

To view the data being sent from the Arduino, you need to open a serial terminal on your computer. Most Arduino-integrated development environments (IDEs) have a built-in serial monitor that allows you to view the data received from the Arduino board.

1. Open the Arduino IDE.
2. Click on the magnifying glass icon in the upper right corner (Serial Monitor).

Figure 3.9: *Serial Monitor icon*

3. Ensure that the baud rate matches the rate set in your Arduino code (for example, 9600 baud).

You should now see the data sent from the Arduino board displayed on the serial monitor.

Introduction to ESP-12 and the ESP Family

In the world of IoT, the ESP family has emerged as a powerhouse, driving innovation and connectivity in a wide range of applications. One standout member of this family is the ESP-12 module, which has garnered significant attention for its versatility and capabilities.

The ESP-12 module, developed by Espressif Systems, has captured the imagination of developers and enthusiasts alike. Its compact size, impressive processing power, and integrated Wi-Fi capabilities make it a favored choice for Internet of Things (IoT) projects. However, to truly appreciate the ESP-12, it's essential to understand its roots within the larger ESP family.

The ESP family encompasses a range of microcontrollers designed to empower creators with seamless connectivity and computational prowess. At the heart of this family lies Espressif Systems' commitment to open-source values and community collaboration. Whether you're an electronics hobbyist, a seasoned engineer, or an educator, the ESP family offers tools to turn your concepts into tangible prototypes, and eventually, fully functional applications.

To understand the working of any microcontroller, the first step is to understand the pin description. NodeMCU is the development board that uses the ESP-12 as the basic functional chip and as a move along with our IoT journey, we'll use this Nodemcu as a go-to board for developing the IoT prototypes.

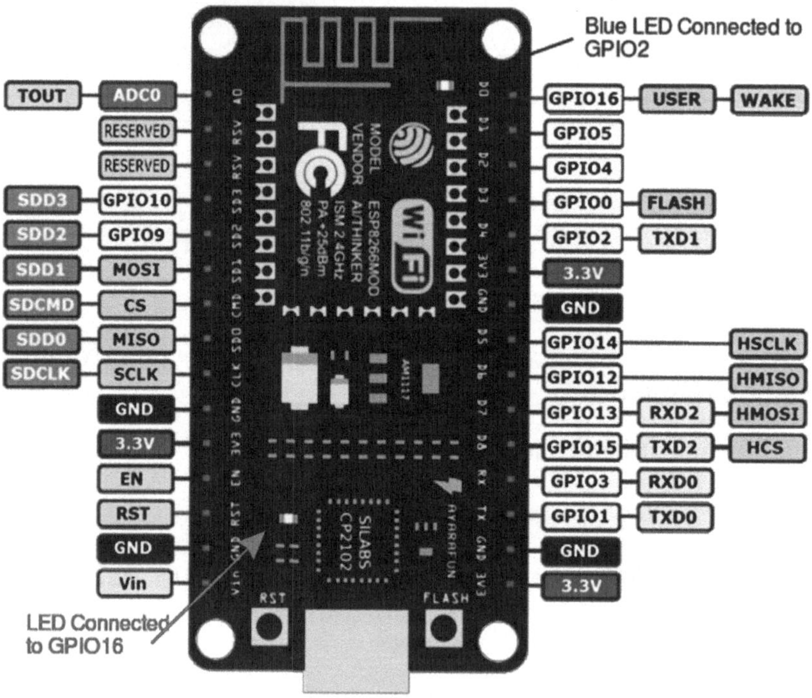

Figure 3.10: *Pin description of Nodemcu*

Programming the Nodemcu with Arduino IDE

NodeMCU is an ESP8266-based development board that provides a convenient way to use Wi-Fi for your projects. NodeMCU supports several programming environments, such as Lua and MicroPython. One of the easiest ways to program NodeMCU is to use the Arduino IDE. Let's take a look at the steps that involve programming Nodemcu with Arduino IDE.

Step 1: Set Up the Arduino IDE

a. Download and install the Arduino IDE from the official Arduino website: https://www.arduino.cc/en/software

b. Launch the Arduino IDE once the installation is complete.

Step 2: Install ESP8266 Board Package

a. Open the Arduino IDE.

b. Go to **File** > **Preferences**. Or on Mac go to **Arduino** > **Settings**

c. In the **Additional Boards Manager URLs** field, add the following URL: http://arduino.esp8266.com/stable/package_esp8266com_index.json

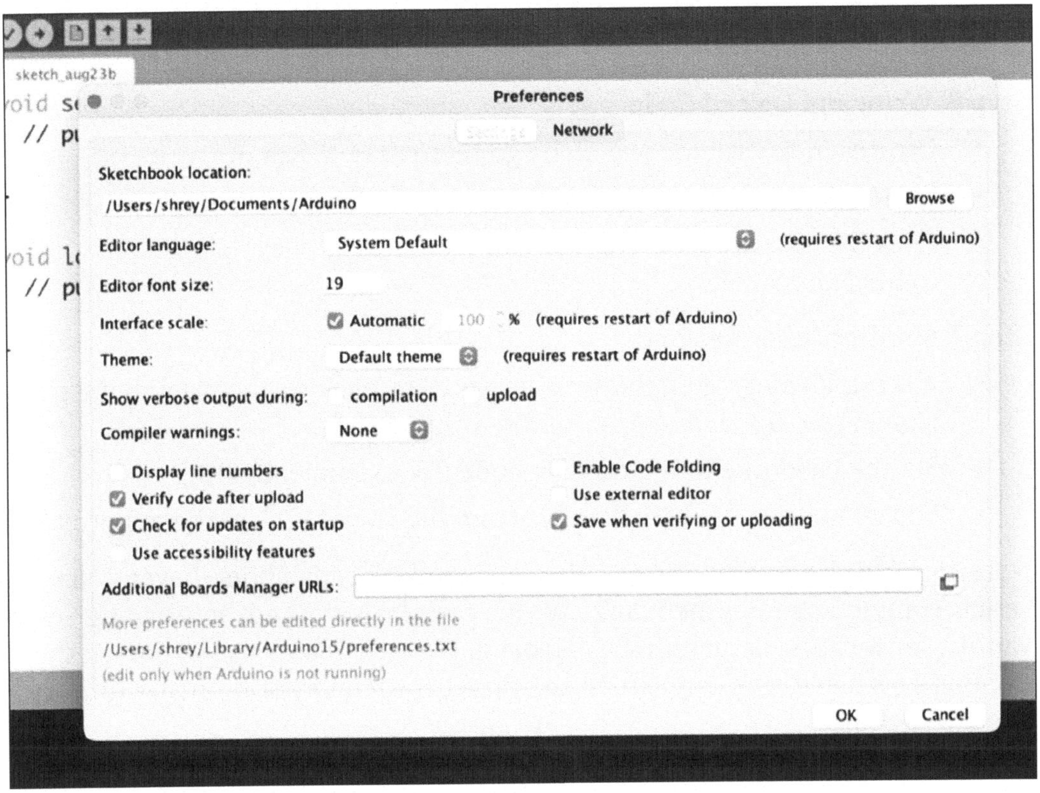

***Figure 3.11**: Preferences menu in Arduino IDE*

d. Click **OK** to close the Preferences window.

Step 3: Install ESP8266 Board Support

- Go to **Tools** > **Board** > **Boards Manager**.
- In the Boards Manager window, search for **esp8266**.
- Install the **esp8266** package by clicking the **Install** button.

Step 4: Select NodeMCU Board

- After installing the ESP8266 board package, go to **`Tools`** > **`Board`**.
- Select the appropriate NodeMCU board from the list. For example, choose **`NodeMCU 1.0 (ESP-12E Module).`**

Step 5: Choose COM Port

- Connect your NodeMCU board to your computer via USB.
- Go to **`Tools > Port`** and select the appropriate COM port that corresponds to your NodeMCU.

Step 6: Write and Upload Code

- Create a new Arduino sketch by going to **`File`** > **`New`**.
- Write your code in the Arduino IDE.
- Click the **`Upload`** button (right arrow icon) to compile and upload the code to the NodeMCU.

Step 7: Monitor Serial Output

- After uploading, open the serial monitor by clicking the magnifying glass icon in the top-right corner of the Arduino IDE.
- Set the baud rate to match your code (for example, 115200).
- You should see the serial output from the NodeMCU on the monitor.

Note that the NodeMCU offers a broad range of capabilities beyond simple serial communication, including Wi-Fi connectivity and interfacing with various sensors and actuators. By exploring the rich ecosystem of libraries and examples available, one can extend the projects to incorporate real-world data and interactions.

Conclusion

In this chapter, we delved into the fascinating world of microcontrollers, explored the capabilities of Arduino boards, and learned how to harness the power of the Arduino Integrated Development Environment (IDE). Microcontrollers have revolutionized the way we interact with and control the physical world, enabling us to create a wide array of electronic projects that range from simple blinking LEDs to complex robotic systems.

Arduino, as a widely popular and accessible microcontroller platform, offers an excellent starting point for beginners and experienced enthusiasts alike. We learned that Arduino boards are built around microcontrollers that are preprogrammed with a bootloader, allowing us to easily upload and execute custom code. This eliminates the need for dedicated programmers and lowers the entry barrier for those new to embedded systems.

Throughout the chapter, we discovered key concepts like Microcontrollers and Embedded Systems, Arduino Boards and Ecosystem, Arduino IDE Sketch Structure and Serial Communication.

As we conclude this chapter, it's clear that microcontrollers, Arduino, and the Arduino IDE have opened up a world of creative possibilities. From hobbyist projects to educational initiatives and professional applications, these tools empower individuals to turn their ideas into reality. The journey doesn't end here; the knowledge gained serves as a solid foundation for exploring more advanced topics, expanding into wireless communication, the Internet of Things (IoT), robotics, and beyond.

Remember, the world of microcontrollers is ever-evolving, with new technologies and platforms constantly emerging. Continuously learning, experimenting, and embracing innovation will keep you at the forefront of this exciting field. So, armed with your newfound knowledge, go forth and embark on your own microcontroller adventures, exploring, tinkering, and building the future, one line of code at a time.

In the next chapter, we will take a look into the realm of communication protocols within the Internet of Things (IoT) ecosystem. As IoT devices continue to proliferate and interconnect, efficient and reliable communication becomes paramount. We explore the various communication protocols employed in IoT systems, including Wi-Fi, BLE, LoRa, and Zigbee, among others. We delve into the strengths, weaknesses, and use cases of each protocol, considering factors such as data size, power consumption, scalability, and security. By understanding the nuances of different communication protocols, readers will gain insights into selecting the most suitable protocol for their IoT applications, ensuring seamless connectivity and optimal performance.

References

- Mazidi, M., McKinlay, R. H., & Causey, D. (2018). *PIC Microcontroller and Embedded Systems: Using Assembly and C for PIC18*. Pearson.
- Singh, M., & Kaur, J. (2019). *IoT Enabled Smart Home Automation Using Microcontroller*. 2019 International Conference on Inventive Research in Computing Applications (ICIRCA). IEEE.

- Uwe, M., & James, C. (2016). *Real-Time Operating Systems for ARM Cortex-M Microcontrollers.* Springer.
- Orfanidis, C. (2018). *Introduction to Signal Processing.* Pearson.
- Jacob, B. (2011). *Embedded Systems: A Contemporary Design Tool.* Cengage Learning.
- Yaghmour, K., Masters, C., Ben-Yossef, G., & Anderson, J. (2013). *Embedded Android: Porting, Extending, and Customizing.* "O'Reilly Media, Inc."
- Mazieres, D., & Shasha, D. (2017). *Introduction to Algorithms.* MIT Press.
- Filho, P. V. M. (2016). *Security and Privacy in Communication Networks.* CRC Press.
- Fernández-Caramés, T. M., & Fraga-Lamas, P. (2018). A *Review on the Use of Blockchain for the Internet of Things.* IEEE Access, 6, 32979-33001.
- Alippi, C., & Galperti, C. (2016). A *Practical Guide to the Internet of Things (IoT): How Every Consumer and Business Can Benefit From IoT.* Springer.
- Gupta, S. S., & Lehal, G. S. (2016). *Machine Learning Techniques for Big Data.* Springer.
- Ray, A., Talathi, S. S., & Sakar, C. K. (2017). *Edge computing*: A *survey.* ACM Computing Surveys (CSUR), 49(4), 58.
- https://www.arduino.cc/
- Figure 3.5 - https://docs.arduino.cc/static/2b141eb1cfe-6f465a949c203e4af1b5f/A000066-pinout.png
- Espressif Systems. (2021). ESP8266 Datasheet. Retrieved from https://www.espressif.com/sites/default/files/documentation/esp8266_datasheet_en.pdf
- Espressif Systems. (2021). ESP32 Datasheet. Retrieved from https://www.espressif.com/sites/default/files/documentation/esp32_datasheet_en.pdf
- Espressif Systems. (2021). ESP-IDF Programming Guide. Retrieved from https://docs.espressif.com/projects/esp-idf/en/latest/

CHAPTER 4
Communication Protocols in IoT

Introduction

In the era of connected devices, the Internet of Things (IoT) has taken the world by storm, connecting a wide range of devices and allowing them to communicate and work together seamlessly. Communication within IoT networks relies on a variety of communication protocols. Communication protocols are the language that devices use to communicate, exchange data, execute orders, and work together. These protocols form the foundation of IoT. They determine how devices connect, transmit data, and interpret commands. Just like humans speaking different languages need a common medium to converse, IoT devices rely on protocols to communicate effectively.

There are two major points while defining the communication protocols. One can define the communication protocols as multiple technologies that enable the transmission of data from one device to another device and the other one can be the set of rules or the language that defines how the data must be transmitted from one device to another device. To make it clear, we'll define communication technologies as the hardware technologies that enable communication, such as Wi-Fi, Zigbee, BLE, and so on. On the other hand, communication protocols are the set of necessary rules for data transmission, such as MQTT, HTTP, and so on.

Structure

In this chapter, we will study about the following topics:

- Significance of communication technologies
- Common communication technologies in IoT
  - o Wi-Fi
  - o GSM
  - o Zigbee
  - o Z-wave
  - o BLE
  - o LoRa
  - o RF
  - o NB-IoT
- Factors to consider before choosing any communication technology
- Communication protocols in IoT
- Commonly used communication protocols in IoT

Significance of Communication Technologies

In the world of IoT, communication technologies are the backbone that supports the connected fabric of devices. Communication technologies are the invisible fibers that allow devices to share information, communicate, and work together seamlessly, turning mundane objects into smart ones. The importance of communication technologies in IoT cannot be understated, as they enable the realization of IoT's transformative capabilities across industries and domains of modern life.

At the heart of IoT lies the ability of devices to communicate effortlessly, regardless of their physical location or the functions they perform. Communication technologies provide the means to exchange data in real time, allowing devices to share information, insights, and instructions without human intervention. This real-time data exchange forms the basis for informed decision-making, predictive analytics, and automation, leading to enhanced efficiency and productivity across various domains.

Creating a web of Interconnected devices

Communication technologies bring together a wide variety of devices, regardless of their characteristics or manufacturers. Standardized protocols allow devices from different ecosystems to communicate with each other, creating a unified IoT environment. This connected web allows devices to work together, coordinate their actions, and react to changing conditions, creating an intelligent network beyond the reach of individual devices.

Empowering Remote Control and Monitoring

Remote monitoring and control of devices and processes is one of the fundamental principles of IoT. Communication technologies enable this by providing real-time visibility of device information and controls from any location with an internet connection. Remote monitoring is a game-changer for industries like healthcare, manufacturing, and agriculture, as it enables early intervention, maintenance, and optimization of operations.

Driving Innovation and Industry Transformation

IoT communication technologies drive innovation by allowing new applications and solutions to be developed. IoT's communication capabilities enable the collection, real-time processing, and action of data from sensors. As a result, new business models are created, new customer experiences are created, and new disruptive technologies are introduced. Industries such as intelligent cities, intelligent homes, and intelligent precision agriculture have all undergone major transformations as a result of IoT communication.

Enhancing Efficiency and Resource Management

Communication technologies allow for predictive maintenance. Predictive maintenance refers to the process of monitoring device health and anticipating maintenance needs before an issue arises. By analyzing sensor and device data, IoT systems are able to detect patterns that indicate potential problems and perform maintenance as soon as possible. This reduces downtime, increases device lifetime, and improves operational reliability.

Common Communication Technologies in IoT

Apart from all the traditional communication technologies that we generally use in our daily lives, there are a few more that are very popular in IoT network. Here are some of the common communication technologies in IoT:

Wi-Fi

Wireless Fidelity, or Wi-Fi, is one of the most important communication technologies in the complex Internet of Things ecosystem. Communication technologies are the threads that connect IoT devices and create a smooth and connected environment. Wi-Fi is the backbone of the IoT ecosystem, enabling IoT devices to talk to each other, exchange data, and carry out commands. Its ubiquity, high speed, and flexibility make Wi-Fi one of the most versatile and essential technologies in the IoT ecosystem.

The recent emergence of Wi-Fi 6 (802.11ax) represents a significant advancement in wireless networking technology, offering a multitude of improvements over its predecessor, Wi-Fi 5 (802.11ac). This next-generation standard boasts significantly higher data transfer rates, particularly in environments populated by numerous connected devices. This translates to enhanced user experiences for various applications, including seamless streaming, rapid downloads, and lag-free online gaming. Furthermore, Wi-Fi 6 exhibits increased efficiency in managing simultaneous device connections, mitigating congestion and guaranteeing improved performance for all users within the network. Its wider channel utilization and access to the novel 6 GHz band (exclusive to Wi-Fi 6E) contribute to a stronger and more extensive signal coverage, eliminating connectivity issues in larger spaces. Notably, Wi-Fi 6 also promises reduced latency, which minimizes data transmission delays critical for real-time applications like video conferencing and online gaming.

Wi-Fi is a wireless technology that allows devices to access the internet and communicate with each other within a range of a router (or access point). Although Wi-Fi is most well-known for its use in laptops, mobile phones, and other personal gadgets, it also plays an important role in IoT as follows:

- **High Data Rates:** Wi-Fi's ability to offer high data rates makes it suitable for IoT devices that require rapid data exchange. Applications like video streaming from security cameras or real-time sensor data transmission benefit from Wi-Fi's speed.

- **Home and Office Connectivity:** In a smart home or office environment, Wi-Fi serves as the backbone for connecting various IoT devices. From smart thermostats and doorbell cameras to voice-activated assistants, Wi-Fi enables seamless communication.
- **Local Area Coverage:** Wi-Fi's range covers a significant area, allowing devices in proximity to connect efficiently. This is particularly advantageous in environments where devices are located within a confined space.
- **Ease of Integration:** Many consumer electronics are already equipped with Wi-Fi capabilities, making it easier to integrate them into IoT ecosystems. This widespread adoption simplifies the process of connecting devices.
- **Compatibility:** Wi-Fi-enabled IoT devices can seamlessly integrate with other networked devices, such as laptops, smartphones, and smart TVs. This compatibility fosters a cohesive user experience.
- **Cloud Connectivity:** Wi-Fi enables IoT devices to connect to cloud services for data storage, analysis, and remote management. This connectivity enhances the functionality of IoT applications.
- **Scalability:** Wi-Fi networks can support multiple devices simultaneously, making them suitable for scenarios where numerous IoT devices need to connect to the network.
- **Security Features:** Wi-Fi networks can implement encryption and authentication mechanisms to ensure secure data transmission, which is crucial in IoT environments where data privacy is paramount.

GSM

GSM, or Global System for Mobile Communications, is a digital cellular communications technology that has changed the way people communicate around the world. Initially created for voice communications, GSM's versatility has allowed it to be incorporated into the IoT ecosystem, allowing data-driven interaction between devices.

Technical Specifications of GSM Communication Technology are as follows:

- **Frequency Bands:** GSM operates within various frequency bands, including 850 MHz, 900 MHz, 1800 MHz, and 1900 MHz. These bands are divided into paired frequency slots, allowing for duplex communication (simultaneous transmission and reception).

- **Modulation Techniques:** GSM employs Gaussian Minimum Shift Keying (GMSK) modulation, which encodes digital data onto carrier signals. This modulation technique optimizes signal robustness and data integrity.
- **Data Rate:** In its traditional form, GSM offers data rates of up to 9.6 kbps. However, for IoT applications, data rates are often lower, providing an optimal balance between power efficiency and communication speed.
- **Cellular Architecture:** GSM networks are organized into cells, each served by a base station or cell tower. Cells are grouped into Location Areas (LAs), which are further organized into Routing Areas (RAs). This hierarchical structure enhances network efficiency.
- **Multiple Access:** GSM employs Time Division Multiple Access (TDMA), where each frequency channel is divided into time slots, allowing multiple users to share the same frequency without interference.
- **Security Measures:** GSM incorporates security mechanisms such as encryption and authentication to protect voice and data communications from eavesdropping and unauthorized access.
- **Roaming and Handovers:** GSM supports seamless roaming between different cellular networks and geographical areas. Mobile devices can transition between cells (micro-cells to macro-cells) without interrupting communication, ensuring continuous connectivity.
- **SMS and Data Services:** In addition to voice calls, GSM introduced Short Message Service (SMS), allowing the exchange of text messages. Data services like General Packet Radio Service (GPRS) and Enhanced Data rates for GSM Evolution (EDGE) enable basic internet connectivity.

The Rise of LTE-M: Powering the Internet of Things

LTE-M, or Long-Term Evolution Machine-Type Communication, stands as a transformative technology for the burgeoning Internet of Things (IoT) landscape. This standardized low-power wide-area network (LPWAN) technology, born from the evolution of 4G cellular networks, addresses the specific needs of IoT devices, offering a compelling blend of extended coverage, reduced power consumption, and cost-effectiveness. Unlike traditional cellular technologies, LTE-M excels in connecting resource-constrained devices that transmit smaller data packets infrequently. This is achieved through features like Power Saving Mode (PSM) and Discontinuous Reception (DRX), enabling a battery lifespan exceeding 10 years for many applications. Furthermore, LTE-M leverages existing cellular infrastructure, ensuring widespread global coverage and seamless integration with existing security protocols. Compared to competing LPWAN options, LTE-M boasts higher data rates and improved mobility, making it suitable for a wider range of IoT use cases, from smart city sensors and asset tracking to wearables and industrial automation. As the adoption of IoT devices continues to accelerate, LTE-M stands poised to play a pivotal role in connecting our increasingly intelligent world, offering a reliable, efficient, and scalable communication platform for the vast array of devices shaping the future.

Zigbee

Zigbee is a wireless communication protocol based on IEEE802.15.4. Zigbee operates in the frequency band 2.4 GHz. The design of Zigbee is focused on reducing power consumption while providing reliable data transmission in applications that need moderate data rates and long battery life. The features of Zigbee closely match the needs of IoT applications. Zigbee emerges as a significant communication technology that plays a vital role in enabling efficient and low-power communication between devices. As a wireless protocol designed specifically for low-data-rate, low-power applications, Zigbee brings distinct advantages to the IoT ecosystem, facilitating diverse applications across smart homes, and more. This section delves into the essence of Zigbee in the context of IoT, outlining its benefits and implications as follows:

- **Low-Power Operation:** Zigbee is optimized for energy efficiency, making it well-suited for battery-operated devices. This feature is particularly advantageous for IoT devices that need to operate for extended periods without frequent battery replacement.
- **Mesh Network Topology:** Zigbee supports mesh networking, where devices can act as relays to extend the network's coverage and enhance reliability. This self-healing network topology ensures that data can find alternative routes if one pathway is disrupted.
- **Scalability:** Zigbee networks can support a large number of devices, making them suitable for applications ranging from smart homes to industrial environments.
- **Short to Medium Range Communication:** Zigbee's communication range is typically shorter than that of Wi-Fi, making it ideal for applications where devices are in close proximity to each other.
- **Home Automation:** Zigbee is widely used in smart home applications, facilitating seamless communication between devices like smart bulbs, thermostats, door locks, and sensors.

- **Industrial Control:** Zigbee's reliability and low power consumption make it suitable for industrial control and monitoring applications, such as remote sensors in manufacturing plants.
- **Health Monitoring:** Zigbee can be employed in healthcare environments for applications like patient monitoring and tracking medical equipment.
- **Environmental Monitoring:** Zigbee-enabled sensors can be deployed for environmental monitoring, collecting data on factors like temperature, humidity, and air quality.
- **Interoperability:** Zigbee Alliance, a consortium of companies, ensures that Zigbee devices from different manufacturers can interoperate seamlessly. This fosters a diverse ecosystem of compatible devices.

Z-Wave

Z-Wave is an ultra-low-power, ultra-low-data-rate wireless communication protocol. It is primarily used in home automation applications. Z-Wave works in the sub-1 GHz frequency range, providing reliable and efficient communication in smart home environments. The technical features of Z-Wave closely match the needs of IoT applications in home and building automation.

Z-Wave is emerging as an important communication technology that enables seamless device-to-device communication and control. A wireless protocol designed for intelligent home automation and smart apps, Z-Wave provides the following unique capabilities that drive the development of IoT ecosystems:

- **Low-Power Operation:** Z-Wave is optimized for energy efficiency, making it suitable for battery-powered devices like sensors and actuators. This efficiency ensures prolonged device lifetimes without frequent battery replacements.
- **Mesh Network Topology:** Similar to Zigbee, Z-Wave supports mesh networking. Devices within a Z-Wave network can act as repeaters, relaying messages to extend the network's coverage and enhance reliability.
- **Reliable Communication:** Z-Wave employs a protocol optimized for reliable communication in environments with potential interference. This ensures that commands are delivered without disruption.
- **Security Features:** Z-Wave includes robust security features, including encryption and authentication, to protect data integrity and user privacy. This is crucial in smart home environments where sensitive information is exchanged.

- **Interoperability:** Z-Wave Alliance, a consortium of companies, ensures that Z-Wave devices from different manufacturers can seamlessly communicate and interoperate. This guarantees a diverse ecosystem of compatible devices.
- **Frequency Agility:** Z-Wave operates in different sub-1 GHz frequency bands depending on regional regulations. This frequency agility minimizes interference and enhances reliability.
- **Scalability:** Z-Wave networks can accommodate a significant number of devices, enabling comprehensive home automation setups with various devices such as smart lights, locks, and thermostats.
- **Home Automation Focus:** Z-Wave's technical design and features cater to the demands of home automation scenarios, allowing homeowners to create sophisticated and interconnected smart environments.

Bluetooth Low Energy (BLE)

Bluetooth Low Energy or BLE (short for Bluetooth Smart) is a low-power wireless communication protocol that enables efficient data transfer over short distances between devices. While Bluetooth is well-known for its ability to stream audio and transfer files, BLE is better suited for applications that require low power consumption, such as IoT devices like wearables, sensors, and smart home gadgets. As a wireless protocol tailored for short-range communication, BLE offers unique features that contribute to the growth of IoT ecosystems.

Technical Specifications of BLE are as follows:

- **Frequency Band**: BLE operates in the 2.4 GHz ISM (Industrial, Scientific, and Medical) frequency band, divided into 40 channels spaced 2 MHz apart. It uses frequency hopping to mitigate interference and improve communication reliability.
- **Data Rate**: BLE offers multiple data rates, with the most common being 1 Mbps (megabit per second) in its higher data rate mode and 125 kbps (kilobits per second) in its long-range mode (introduced in BLE 5.0).
- **Modulation**: BLE uses Gaussian Frequency Shift Keying (GFSK) modulation for data transmission. This modulation scheme aids in achieving reliable communication in noisy environments.
- **Transmission Range**: BLE's transmission range can vary based on factors like output power and environmental conditions. In general, BLE's range is designed for short distances, typically up to 100 meters.

- **Connection Types**: BLE offers two primary connection types:
  - **Master-Slave Topology**: BLE supports a master-slave topology. One device, the master, initiates and controls connections to one or more slave devices.
  - **Peripheral and Central Roles**: BLE devices can operate as peripherals (slaves) or centrals (masters). Peripherals advertise their presence, while centrals scan and connect to peripherals.
- **Advertising and Scanning**: BLE devices can broadcast advertising packets to announce their presence. Other devices can scan for these packets and initiate connections. Advertising is a power-efficient mechanism to establish connections quickly.
- **Generic Attribute Profile (GATT)**: BLE uses the GATT protocol to structure data exchange between devices. GATT defines services, characteristics, and descriptors that represent data and functionalities.
- **Security**: BLE offers multiple security layers, including encryption, authentication, and authorization. Security measures are implemented through pairing and bonding processes to protect data integrity and user privacy.
- **Low Power Consumption**: BLE's primary focus is energy efficiency. Devices spend most of their time in sleep mode and quickly transition to active mode for data exchange. This approach conserves battery life in IoT devices.
- **Universally Unique Identifiers (UUIDs)**: BLE devices use UUIDs to identify services, characteristics, and descriptors. UUIDs are used to establish the type and purpose of data exchange.
- **Connection Interval**: The connection interval defines the time between two consecutive data exchanges between devices. It can be adjusted to balance power consumption and data exchange frequency.
- **Beacon Technology**: BLE supports beacons, which are devices that continuously broadcast data for location-based applications. This enables proximity-based interactions, such as indoor navigation and targeted advertising.
- **Version Evolution**: BLE has undergone multiple version updates to enhance its capabilities. BLE 5.0 introduced improvements in data rate, range, and stability, while later versions have focused on refining existing features.

Long Range (LoRa)

LoRa, or Long Range, is a modulation technology and protocol that allows communication over long distances with low power consumption. It is especially useful for IoT applications that need to be able to communicate across large distances, such as smart agriculture, environmental monitoring, and industrial automation. Designed to cater to the demands of wide-area networks, LoRa technology introduces a new dimension to IoT ecosystems. This comprehensive exploration delves into the essence of LoRa, its technical underpinnings, and its transformative potential within the IoT landscape.

Technical Specifications of LoRa are as follows:

- **Chirp Spread Spectrum (CSS) Modulation:** At the heart of LoRa's exceptional range lies its unique modulation technique - Chirp Spread Spectrum. This technique enables the transmission of signals across a broad frequency range, enhancing resilience against interference and expanding communication distances.
- **Frequency Bands:** LoRa operates in the unlicensed Industrial, Scientific, and Medical (ISM) bands. It spans multiple frequency bands, including 433 MHz, 868 MHz, and 915 MHz, tailored to regional regulations. This inherent flexibility ensures global compatibility and harmonious coexistence with other wireless technologies.
- **Customizable Data Rate and Range:** LoRa offers a spectrum of data rates, ranging from a few bits per second to hundreds of kilobits per second. The choice of data rate determines the achievable communication range, enabling fine-tuning based on the specific IoT application.
- **Spreading Factors (SF):** LoRa devices can adjust their spreading factors, controlling the trade-off between data rate and range. Lower spreading factors result in extended transmission ranges, albeit at lower data rates, thus accommodating diverse communication needs.
- **Channel Bandwidth:** LoRa supports various channel bandwidths, typically ranging from 125 kHz to 500 kHz. Wider bandwidths enable higher data rates but might affect communication range. This adaptability ensures optimal performance in various scenarios.
- **Signal Sensitivity:** One of LoRa's remarkable attributes is its ability to decode weak signals, allowing communication in environments characterized by significant noise levels and challenging propagation conditions.

- **Battery Efficiency:** The core strength of LoRa lies in its low-power operation, ideal for battery-powered devices that require longevity. LoRa's energy-efficient design permits devices to operate for extended periods without frequent battery replacements, fostering sustainable IoT deployments.
- **Network Topology:** LoRa networks can be deployed in diverse topologies, including star, mesh, and point-to-point configurations. This adaptability suits an array of IoT use cases, from simple to intricate.
- **LoRaWAN Protocol:** To harness the full potential of LoRa technology, the LoRa Alliance introduced the LoRaWAN protocol. LoRaWAN defines the communication between devices and gateways, enabling efficient data exchange, security, and scalability.

NB-IoT

The Narrowband Internet of Things (NB-IoT) is a cellular communication technology specifically designed to cater to the unique connectivity requirements of IoT devices. It operates within the existing cellular infrastructure, utilizing narrowband channels to enable long-range and efficient communication with extended battery life. NB-IoT's design aligns with the requirements of IoT applications that prioritize efficient data exchange and coverage over high data rates.

Technical Specifications are as follows:

- **Frequency Bands:** NB-IoT operates in licensed cellular frequency bands, typically within the 800 MHz, 900 MHz, and 1.4 GHz ranges. It makes efficient use of spectrum resources, ensuring coexistence with other cellular technologies.
- **Modulation and Spreading:** NB-IoT employs various modulation schemes, including QPSK and BPSK, along with Orthogonal Frequency Division Multiplexing (OFDM) and Differential Quadrature Phase Shift Keying (DQPSK) for data transmission. These techniques optimize signal integrity and robustness.
- **Data Rate:** NB-IoT focuses on low data rates, typically ranging from a few bits per second to tens of kilobits per second. This approach minimizes power consumption and enhances coverage.
- **Transmit Power:** NB-IoT devices can adjust their transmit power based on the communication range requirements. Lower transmit power contributes to energy efficiency and extends battery life.

- **Coverage and Penetration:** One of NB-IoT's remarkable features is its ability to penetrate obstacles, making it suitable for applications in urban environments and indoors. It provides extensive coverage even in challenging scenarios.
- **Guard Bands:** NB-IoT utilizes guard bands between existing cellular channels, minimizing interference with legacy cellular networks. This seamless integration ensures efficient spectrum utilization.
- **Deployment Modes:** NB-IoT supports both standalone deployment and in-band deployment, allowing it to operate alongside other cellular services. This flexibility enables operators to optimize network resources.
- **Duplex Modes:** NB-IoT supports both half-duplex and full-duplex communication, accommodating diverse IoT use cases.
- **Energy Efficiency:** Designed for energy efficiency, NB-IoT devices can remain in a dormant state for extended periods and wake up only when necessary for data transmission. This feature significantly extends battery life.

Factors to Consider Before Choosing Any Communication Technology

Selecting the right communication technology for your IoT product is one of the most important decisions you will make, as it has a huge impact on the functionality, performance, and success of your product. Communication technology is the lifeblood of the entire IoT ecosystem. It determines how devices communicate, exchange data, and work together. The right communication technology ensures optimal connectivity by addressing factors that directly affect user experience, data performance, power efficiency, and scalability. Additionally, the chosen communication technology must match the specific requirements of your application, taking into account variables such as device density and latency tolerance, as well as security requirements. Selecting the right technology ensures integration with your existing infrastructure and optimizes interoperability so that your IoT product can be part of a unified and future-ready ecosystem.

In short, your communication technology is the channel through which your IoT devices communicate, and its choice can have a huge impact on your product's market viability and customer satisfaction, as well as long-term sustainability.

The following are common factors that need to be carefully considered before making this critical choice:

- **Range and Coverage:** Think about how far away your IoT application needs to be able to communicate. Some applications need to be able to talk to each other over a short distance within a small area, while others need long-distance connectivity that goes far.
- **Data Rate Requirements:** Take a look at how much data your IoT devices require to send and receive. Some types of applications, such as environmental monitoring, may only need low data rates, while others, such as video surveillance, may need higher data rates.
- **Power Consumption:** Battery-powered IoT devices are particularly energy-hungry, so it's important to choose the right communication technology that matches the power limitations of your devices. This will help them last longer and reduce the need for maintenance.
- **Device Density:** If your IoT deployment includes a lot of devices in tight proximity, look for communications technologies that can support high device density without sacrificing performance.
- **Cost:** Factor in installation and maintenance costs for the chosen communication technology, including hardware, licensing costs, network costs, and ongoing operating costs.
- **Network Topology:** Choose the right network topology for your IoT applications. From star topology to mesh networks to point-to-point connections, the communication technology you choose should support your preferred topology.
- **Scalability:** Think about the communication technology's ability to scale. Can it handle more devices as your Internet of Things (IoT) deployment grows?
- **Latency:** Some applications, such as industrial control in real-time, require low-latency communication. Consider whether the communication technology supports your latency needs.
- **Security:** To keep your IoT devices secure and secure, choose a communication technology that has strong security features, such as encryption and authentication.
- **Regularity Compliances:** Regulations and frequency bands vary from region to region. Make sure the technology you choose is compliant with your deployment location's regulations.

- **Interoperability:** Think about the interoperability of the communication technology. Interoperability allows the communication technology to connect to other devices, platforms, and existing systems to create a cohesive IoT ecosystem.
- **Longevity and Future Proofing:** Take a look at the technology's long-term vision and make sure you're picking a solution that's going to keep evolving and keep up with new technologies.
- **Development Ecosystem:** Find out what development tools are available, what software libraries are available, and what community support is available for the selected communication technology. A strong ecosystem can speed up product development.
- **Application Specific Requirement:** Take into account any specific environmental, mobility, or type of data exchange requirements of your particular IoT application.

With careful consideration of these elements, you can determine which communication technology is best suited for your IoT devices. Each element has a direct impact on the overall performance, dependability, and performance of your IoT deployment.

Communication Protocols in IoT

IoT communication protocols are a collection of rules and standards that regulate how devices and systems communicate with each other and exchange information. They are the digital language through which devices communicate with each other in an efficient and secure manner within the IoT environment. Communication protocols within IoT cover a broad range of features and specifications, as follows:

- **Data Format:** IoT communication protocols define how data is structured, encoded, and transmitted between devices. They specify data formats such as JSON, XML, or binary, ensuring compatibility among communicating devices.
- **Data Transport:** Communication protocols dictate how data is packaged and transmitted over networks.
- **Security:** Security protocols like TLS/SSL and OAuth are crucial components of IoT communication. They encrypt data to protect it from unauthorized access and ensure secure authentication and authorization between devices.

- **Message Queuing:** Many IoT applications rely on message queuing protocols like MQTT and AMQP to enable asynchronous communication, efficient data routing, and load balancing within IoT systems.
- **Network Layer:** IoT communication protocols also encompass network layer protocols like IPv4, IPv6, and 6LoWPAN, which facilitate device addressing, routing, and data transmission over various network topologies.
- **Device Management:** Some IoT protocols, such as the Lightweight Machine-to-Machine (LwM2M) protocol, address device management tasks, including firmware updates, configuration, and diagnostics.
- **Interoperability:** Protocols like RESTful APIs and standardized data models such as OCF and OneM2M enable interoperability among diverse IoT devices and platforms, fostering a cohesive ecosystem.
- **Low-Power and Lossy Networks:** For resource-constrained devices in IoT, protocols like CoAP and 6LoWPAN optimize data exchange while conserving energy and accommodating unreliable network conditions.
- **Pub/Sub Mechanisms:** Many IoT protocols, including MQTT and AMQP, support publish-subscribe (pub/sub) patterns, enabling real-time communication and event-driven architectures in IoT applications.
- **Industry-Specific Standards:** Certain industries, like industrial automation (for example, OPC UA) and healthcare (for example, HL7), have developed domain-specific communication standards to address their unique requirements.

Commonly Used Communication Protocols in IoT

Here are some of the most commonly used communication protocols in the field of IoT:

- **MQTT (Message Queuing Telemetry Transport):** A lightweight publish-subscribe protocol, MQTT is widely used for low-power and low-bandwidth IoT applications. It ensures efficient message distribution and is commonly employed in IoT platforms and applications.
- **CoAP (Constrained Application Protocol):** Designed for resource-constrained devices, CoAP is an HTTP-like protocol used for IoT communications over UDP or DTLS. It simplifies RESTful communication in IoT networks.

- **HTTP/HTTPS (Hypertext Transfer Protocol/Secure):** Familiar to web developers, HTTP and HTTPS are used for IoT applications requiring web-like interactions. They are suitable for scenarios where standard web protocols are advantageous.
- **AMQP (Advanced Message Queuing Protocol):** AMQP is a messaging protocol used for reliable, asynchronous communication in IoT systems. It ensures message integrity and delivery, making it suitable for critical applications.

Conclusion

As we conclude this chapter, it is evident that communication protocols are not mere technical details; they are the connective tissue that binds the IoT universe together. The right choice of protocol and communication technology empowers IoT solutions to thrive, ensuring efficient, secure, and reliable data exchange. In the ever-evolving landscape of IoT, understanding and harnessing the potential of these protocols is key to unlocking the full spectrum of possibilities that this transformative technology offers.

In the next chapter, we will study about the world of microcontroller interfacing protocols, exploring the crucial communication methods used to connect microcontrollers with external devices. We begin by providing an overview of the significance of interfacing protocols in enabling seamless data transfer and control between microcontrollers and peripheral devices.

We then delve into the most common interfacing protocols used in microcontrollers, such as I2C (Inter-Integrated Circuit), SPI (Serial Peripheral Interface), and UART (Universal Asynchronous Receiver-Transmitter). We examine the principles, working mechanisms, and key features of each protocol, highlighting their strengths and limitations.

Furthermore, we will explore practical examples and applications of these protocols, showcasing how they are implemented in real-world scenarios. Through code snippets and circuit diagrams, readers will gain a clear understanding of the configuration and programming required for successful communication between microcontrollers and external devices.

References

1. Kouicem, D. E., & Hadjidj, A. (2019). A survey of communication protocols for Internet of Things and related challenges of Fog and Cloud computing integration. Computers & Electrical Engineering, 74, 361-374.
2. Raza, S., Wallgren, L., & Voigt, T. (2017). A comprehensive study of Low-power Wireless Technologies: Sub-GHz Radio vs. 2.4 GHz ISM Bands. IEEE Internet of Things Journal, 3(6), 856-865.
3. Raza, S., Wallgren, L., & Voigt, T. (2017). A comprehensive study of Low-power Wireless Technologies: Sub-GHz Radio vs. 2.4 GHz ISM Bands. IEEE Internet of Things Journal, 3(6), 856-865.
4. Shen, W., & Nguyen, H. (2016). Z-Wave for Home Automation: A Survey. IEEE Access, 4, 6162-6178.
5. Bhuiyan, M. Z. A., & Wang, H. (2017). Bluetooth Low Energy: A technology primer. IEEE Access, 5, 18348-18370.
6. Alliance for Telecommunications Industry Solutions (ATIS). (2019). The LoRaWAN® Standard. Retrieved from https://www.atis.org/lora
7. Ericsson. (2021). NB-IoT: Enabling new opportunities for industries. Retrieved from https://www.ericsson.com/en/ericsson-technology-
8. MQTT - OASIS. (n.d.). Retrieved from https://www.oasis-open.org/standards/mqtt
9. IETF. (2022). Constrained Application Protocol (CoAP). Retrieved from https://datatracker.ietf.org/doc/rfc7252/
10. Fielding, R. (1999). Hypertext Transfer Protocol -- HTTP/1.1. Retrieved from https://datatracker.ietf.org/doc/html/rfc2616

CHAPTER 5

Introduction to Interfacing Protocols

Introduction

Microcontrollers are the unheralded heroes of the ever-changing world of embedded systems, and electronics. They power countless devices that we interact with every day. Microcontrollers are not isolated entities, but rather, they are intrinsically connected to each other through a network of communication interfaces (communications). Communication interfaces are the gateways through which a microcontroller communicates with a sensor, display, memory module, or other microcontroller.

Let's dive deeper into the world of communication in this chapter. We'll learn how microcontrollers communicate with each other, the different communication protocols, and the different interfaces they use. We'll also look at how these interfaces work, what they're good for, and what scenarios they're best suited for.

Interfacing protocols are the lifeline of microcontrollers, enabling them to interact with the world around us. From simple GPIO to complex CAN protocols, these communication standards empower microcontrollers to make our lives more convenient and efficient. As technology continues to advance, the role of interfacing protocols in microcontrollers will only become more prominent.

Structure

In this chapter, the following topics will be covered:

- Communication Interfaces
- Serial Communication - UART
- UART Communication in Arduino
- SPI Communication
- SPI Communication in Nodemcu
- IIC

Communication Interfaces

Microcontrollers typically have several communication interfaces, and sometimes more than one interface, such as two UART modules. The primary purpose of any communication interface is to enable the microcontroller to interact with other units, such as other microcontrollers or peripherals, or with a host PC. There are many ways to implement communication interfaces, but in general, they can be classified according to a few properties: Serial or parallel interface, Sync or asynchronous interface, bus or point-to-point (PTP) interface, full-duplex interface or half-duplex interface, master-slave interface or equal partners interface, and more. In this chapter, we will only consider wired communication.

A serial interface transfers data one by one. This method requires only one data line, making communication resource-efficient. On the other hand, throughput, which is the number of bits that can be transmitted per second, is low. A parallel interface transfers more than one bit per data line. The number of bits that are transferred in parallel depends on the number of data lines. The widths of the parallel interface are 4 and 8 bits, corresponding to half-bytes and bytes on the microcontroller, respectively. For example, parallel interfaces with this width can be found in LCD displays.

The synchronism of communication is concerned with the relationship between the receive clock and the send clock in an interface that is synchronous. In an interface that is not synchronous, the send clock is connected to the receive clock. This may be achieved by using an extra clock line that powers both the send unit and the receive unit. Alternatively, a data format can be used to enable the receiver to recover the clock signal, thus eliminating the need for the receiver to generate their own clock and reducing the risk of synchronization errors.

An asynchronous interface, on the other hand, does not have a send clock and a receive clock. The receiver must be aware of the transmission timing in advance and must set their receive clock to a frequency that is the same as the sender's. Asynchronous communications are generally not synchronized, and the receiver must oversample to synchronize with the sender. Additionally, asynchronous communication is slower due to the need for oversampling.

Bus topologies allow multiple devices to be connected to a single communication medium. This type of communication structure is also known as a multi-drop network. Selecting a specific device requires some form of addressing. On the other hand, point-to-point connections are intended for communication between only two devices. No addressing is required because it is obvious who will receive the message.

In most cases, the data communication between the controller and the peripherals will be bi-directional (that is, both the controller and the peripheral device will transmit data at some point). For point-to-point connections (and some bus connections), the question is whether two devices are able to transmit simultaneously or not. In the case of full-duplex connections, both parties can transmit simultaneously. This naturally implies the need for at least two wires (one for each node) to avoid collisions and allows for maximum overall throughput. This technique is useful when both communication partners have a lot of data to transmit at any given time.

In half-duplex communication, there is only one node that can transmit at any time. It saves on wires, as only one wire is needed for a 50-50 serial connection. The drawbacks include lower overall throughput and the need to negotiate access to a single wire. This mode is especially useful when there is a single communication partner (for example, a sensor device that has to transmit a lot of data, while its peer is mostly receiving).

It is important to note on the physical layer whether the communication interface is a single-ended or a differential interface. A single-ended interface has all wires with respect to ground, which means that the sender and receiver must share the same ground. This can be problematic if the sender and receiver are very distant from each other. Interference along the interface can also cause voltage spikes and therefore level changes. On the other hand, differential interfaces use two wires to carry a signal. Here, the signal is carried by the difference in voltage between the two wires. Of course, a differential connection requires two wires, as opposed to the single wire of a single-ended connection. However, there is no requirement for a common ground. Additionally, any noise will likely affect both wires in the same way, hence the voltage difference will remain the same. As a result, differential interfaces allow for longer transmission lines.

Serial Communication Interface – UART

UART (Universal asynchronous receiver-transmitter) communication is one of the most fundamental and commonly used serial communication protocols in the microcontroller and embedded systems. UART provides the foundation for devices to send and receive data in an asynchronous manner, making it a very useful protocol for a wide range of applications.

At the core of UART communication, there are two fundamental elements: a UART receiver and a UART transmitter. These two components work together to make data transfer easy and reliable.

Working of UART

The UART protocol is based on the concept of asynchronous communication. This means that data is transmitted without the need for a synchronous clock signal from the sender to the receiver. The data transfer rate is determined by the agreement of the two devices on a particular baud rate. The UART module utilizes two wires, a transmit (TXD) and a receive (RXD) line, for full- or half-duplex communication.

The UART transmitter translates parallel data into serial format and transmits the data bit by bit, beginning with the start bit. The data bits (typically 8 bits) are then followed by the optional parity bit to check for errors. Finally, one or several stop bits signal the termination of a data bit.

The receiving UART receives the start bit and listens for the data bits. At the receiving end of the UART, the start bit is read from, the data bits are read from, the parity bit (if enabled) is verified, and the stop bits are read from to confirm that the data has been received.

This simplicity in data structure and synchronicity makes UART communication reliable and easy to deploy, even in time-critical situations.

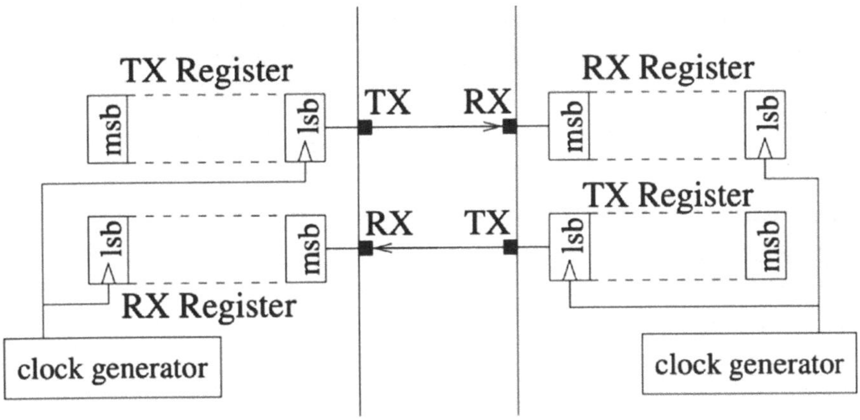

Figure 5.1: *Structure of UART*

The structure of the UART is shown in *Figure* 5.1. The UART module is composed of the transmit register and the receive register to store the data. Due to the asynchronous nature of the UART, the transmission and reception on the node are controlled by the local clock generator.

The UART isn't a communication protocol per se. It's a module that allows for asynchronous serial communication. The UART module inside a microcontroller enables the application to control most of its behavior.

Configurable parameters of UART

- **Baud Rate:** The baud rate defines the speed at which data is transmitted and received over the UART interface. It specifies the number of bits transmitted per second. Common baud rates include 9600, 115200, and others, depending on the application's requirements. Both the transmitter and receiver must agree on the same baud rate for successful communication.
- **Data Bits:** This parameter determines the number of data bits in each UART frame. It typically ranges from 5 to 9 bits, with 8 bits being the most commonly used configuration. The number of data bits represents the actual data being transmitted.

Figure 5.2: *UART Data frame*

- **Parity:** Parity is an optional error-checking mechanism. It can be set to None, Even, or Odd. When enabled, a parity bit is added to the UART frame. The receiver checks the parity bit to detect errors. Even parity ensures that the total number of set bits (1s) in the data plus the parity bit is even, while odd parity ensures an odd total.
- **Stop Bits:** Stop bits indicate the end of a UART frame and provide a small delay between characters to ensure proper synchronization. The most common choices are 1 stop bit or 2 stop bits.
- **Flow Control:** Flow control is used to manage data flow between the transmitter and receiver to prevent data overrun. Two common types of flow control are hardware (RTS/CTS) and software (XON/XOFF). Hardware flow control uses dedicated pins to signal when data can be sent, while software flow control sends specific control characters to indicate when data transmission should start or stop.
- **Data Direction:** UART communication can be configured as full-duplex (bidirectional communication) or half-duplex (communication in one direction at a time). Full-duplex UART uses separate transmit and receive lines, while half-duplex uses a single line for both transmitting and receiving, with a direction control mechanism.
- **Character Format:** This parameter defines the format of a UART character, including the order of data bits, parity bit position, and stop bit placement. Common character formats include 8-N-1 (8 data bits, no parity, 1 stop bit) and 7-E-2 (7 data bits, even parity, 2 stop bits).
- **Buffer Sizes:** UART communication often involves the use of receive and transmit buffers to store incoming and outgoing data. The sizes of these buffers can be configured to match the application's data handling requirements.
- **Error Handling:** UART modules in microcontrollers usually provide options for error handling, such as interrupt generation on framing errors, parity errors, or overrun errors. These settings help detect and manage communication errors.

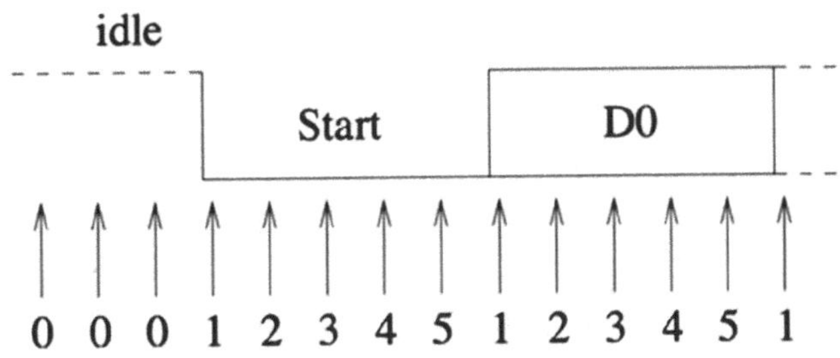

***Figure* 5.3**: *UART Bit sampling*

It is important to configure these parameters correctly in order to ensure consistent and high-performance UART communication between embedded systems and applications. Parameters are determined by the specific needs and limitations of the communication link.

Applications of UART Communication

- **Serial Data Transmission:** UART is often used for transferring data between microcontrollers, sensors, and other embedded devices, making it a go-to choice for building communication networks within electronic systems.
- **Wireless Communication:** In wireless modules and IoT devices, UART is utilized to interface with components like Bluetooth and Wi-Fi modules, enabling wireless data transmission.
- **Debugging and Programming:** UART ports are commonly found on microcontrollers and development boards, serving as a vital tool for dcbugging and programming firmware.
- **Human-Machine Interface:** UART interfaces can be used to connect microcontrollers to displays, keypads, and other human-machine interface components in appliances and industrial equipment.
- **GPS Communication:** GPS modules often communicate with microcontrollers using UART, allowing for the retrieval of location data.

The UART communication protocol is a strong and flexible protocol that serves as the foundation for communication in a wide range of electronic devices and applications. Its compactness, robustness, and broad scope make it an essential component of the Embedded Systems landscape.

USART

The universal synchronous asynchronous receiver transmitter (USART), on the other hand, adds an asynchronous transmission module to the UART. As a result, the USART has an extra third line that transmits a clock signal in synchronous mode. In this mode, a communication partner generates the clock signal, which is then used by both the UART and the communication partner to transmit and receive data. Because of the synchronous communication, there is no need for oversampling in the asynchronous module. The synchronous mode of the USART is therefore one-half of the speed of the asynchronous mode. In the case of synchronous communication, the logic of the USART module is the same for both the synchronous and the asynchronous modes. If the USART is used for asynchronous communication, then the clock line will be free and can be generally used as a standard digital input/output pin.

UART Communication in Arduino

UART communication is one of the most common communication protocols used in Arduino projects. UART communication is used to send and receive data between the microcontroller's board and various devices, including sensors, displays, and even microcontrollers themselves. Let's walk through the steps on how to use UART communication with an Arduino.

Hardware Setup

The first step is to connect the UART pins. Most of the time, the UART ports on an Arduino board are Serial pins (0 and 1), Serial 1, Serial 2, Serial 3, and more. Depending on the type of Arduino board you have, you may have more than one UART port on your board.

Connect the TX (Transmit) pin of one device to the RX (Receive) pin of the other and vice versa. Additionally, ensure that both devices share a common ground (GND) connection, as shown in *Figure* 5.4:

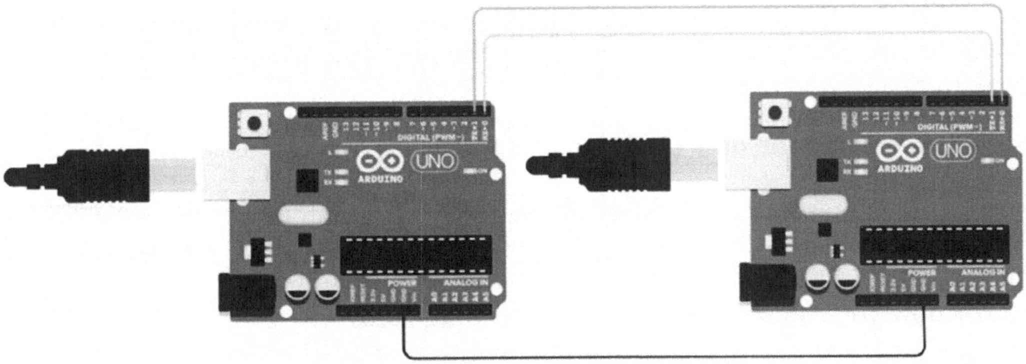

Figure 5.4: *UART connections in Arduino*

Programming

Step 1: Initializing the serial communication

To initialize Serial communication in your Arduino sketch, inside the setup part, use **`Serial.begin()`** to start the UART communication. Enter the baud rate you want to set as an argument. To set the baud rate to 9600, use:

```
Serial.begin(9600);
```

Step 2: Transmitting the data (Arduino as Transmitter)

Sending Data: To send data from the Arduino to another Arduino device, use the **`Serial.print()`** or **`Serial.println()`** functions. For example, as shown in *Figure* 5.4, the transmitter Arduino can be programmed to send the text **`"Hello, World!"`**, using:

```
Serial.println("Hello, World!");
```

Transmitter Arduino Sketch

```
Void setup () {

Serial.begin (9600);

}

Void loop () {

Serial.println("Hello world");

delay(2000);

}
```

To upload this sketch, connect the transmitter Arduinio board to the computer, open the Arduino IDE, go to Tools, select the port and Arduino board, and then click the Upload button.

Step 3: Receiving the data (Arduino as a Receiver)

Listening for Data: To receive data on the Arduino, you typically use the `Serial.available()` function to check if data is available in the UART buffer. Then, you can use the `Serial.read()` function to read the incoming data byte by byte. Here's how you can receive and print incoming data:

```
if (Serial.available() > 0) {

    char receivedChar = Serial.read();

    Serial.print("Received: ");

    Serial.println(receivedChar);

}
```

Receiver Arduino Sketch

```
Void setup () {

Serial.begin (9600);

}

Void loop () {

if (Serial.available() > 0) {

    char receivedChar = Serial.read();

    Serial.print("Received: ");

    Serial.println(receivedChar);

}

}
```

SPI

SPI stands for Serial Peripheral Interfaces. It is one of the most popular synchronous serial communications protocols in the microcontroller and digital communication industries. It is used as a reliable and efficient way to transfer data between a Microcontroller (or Main Device) and Peripheral Devices (or Slave Devices), such as Sensors, Display Modules, and Memory Chip.

SPI communication is characterized by its ease of use and high-speed data transfer, which makes it a preferred option in situations where the exchange of real-time data is essential.

Serial Peripheral Interfaces (SPIs) are synchronous point-to-point interfaces that are based on the master-slave concept. A master (typically a controller) communicates with one (or multiple) slaves (typically peripheral devices). A serial interface is composed of four single-ended lines as follows:

- **MOSI (Master Out, Slave In):** This line is used by the master to transmit data to the slave.
- **MISO (Master In, Slave Out):** This line is used by the slave to transmit data to the master.
- **SCK (System Clock):** This line is used by the master to transmit the clock signal.
- **SS (Slave Select):** This line is used by the master to select a slave.

Working of SPI Protocol

SPI communication involves a master-slave architecture, where one master device initiates and controls the data transfer, while one or more slave devices respond to the master's commands. The core components of SPI communication include:

- **Master:** The master device generates the clock signal (SCLK), controls the data transmission, and selects the slave with which it wishes to communicate.
- **Slave:** Slave devices await commands from the master and respond accordingly. Each slave is assigned a unique chip select (CS) line to enable or disable communication.
- **Data Lines:** SPI typically uses two data lines for communication:
    - **MOSI (Master Out Slave in):** The master sends data to the slave on this line.
    - **MISO (Master in Slave Out):** The slave sends data back to the master on this line.
- **Clock (SCLK):** The clock signal generated by the master synchronizes data exchange between devices. SPI can operate in different clock modes, depending on the specific requirements of the devices involved.

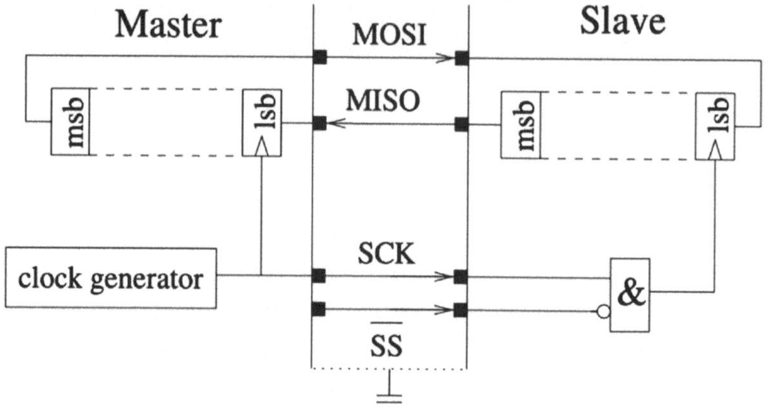

***Figure* 5.5**: *SPI Interface*

The basic principles of the SPI interface are outlined in *Figure* 5.5. The master and the slave share an internal shift register, which is controlled by SCK. Upon each clock pulse of the master's SPI register, the master's MSB (or LSB, as it is commonly configured) is moved out on the MISO line and transferred into the slave's SPI register as LSB. At the same moment, the slave's MSB is transmitted across the MISO line to the master's register as LSB. After eight such clock cycles, all 8 bits in the master and slave registers have been exchanged.

Here are the steps involved in SPI Communication:

1. **Initialization:** The microcontroller configures its SPI peripheral with parameters such as clock polarity, clock phase, data order (MSB or LSB first), and clock frequency. These parameters should match the requirements of the connected slave devices.
2. **Slave Selection:** To communicate with a specific slave device, the master first activates the SS/CS line for that device, indicating that it wants to exchange data with it.
3. **Clock Generation:** The master generates a clock signal (SCLK) and drives it on the SCLK line. The clock's polarity and phase settings determine when data is sampled and transmitted. SPI supports four combinations of clock polarity (CPOL) and clock phase (CPHA), allowing flexibility in data sampling.
4. **Data Transmission:** Data is transmitted simultaneously in both directions (full-duplex). The master places a data byte in its transmit buffer (TX buffer), which is shifted out serially on the MOSI line while simultaneously, the slave sends data on the MISO line.

5. **Synchronization:** Data is synchronized with the clock signal. The data on the MOSI line is sampled by the slave on the rising or falling edge of the clock, depending on the CPOL and CPHA settings. Simultaneously, data is sampled by the master from the MISO line.
6. **Data Transfer:** Both the master and slave shift out and receive data bit by bit. The number of bits transferred is usually 8 bits per byte, but it can vary depending on the device's configuration.
7. **Completion:** After transmitting or receiving the desired number of bits, the master and slave complete the data transfer. The master then deactivates the SS/CS line for that slave device, indicating the end of the communication.
8. **Repeat or Switch:** The master can repeat the process for the same or different slave devices by selecting the appropriate SS/CS line.

SPI Communication in Nodemcu

In this example, we'll use a Nodemcu and an Arduino UNO to demonstrate the working of SPI communication between the Nodemcu and the Arduino, where the Nodemcu will act as the master device and the Arduino will act as the slave device. The master (Nodecmu) will transfer data to the slave (Arduino), and the Arduino will use the serial monitor to print the data received from the master.

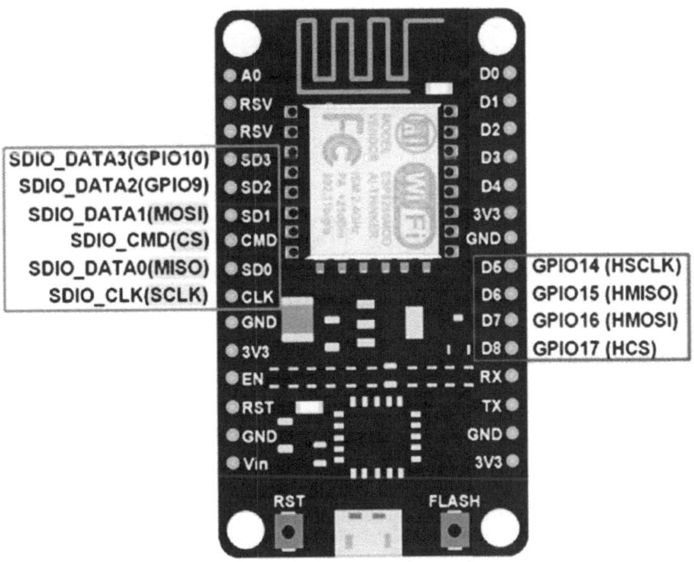

Figure 5.6: Nodemcu SPI Pins

(Source: https://www.electronicwings.com/storage/PlatformSection/TopicContent/277/description/NodeMCU_SPI_Pins.png)

Hardware Setup

In this case, we are passing the string **Hello Slave** with **\N** as the end of the string from Nodemcu master to the slave device, which prints the string on a serial monitor. Connect the pins of Nodemcu and Arduino as shown in *Figure* 5.7.

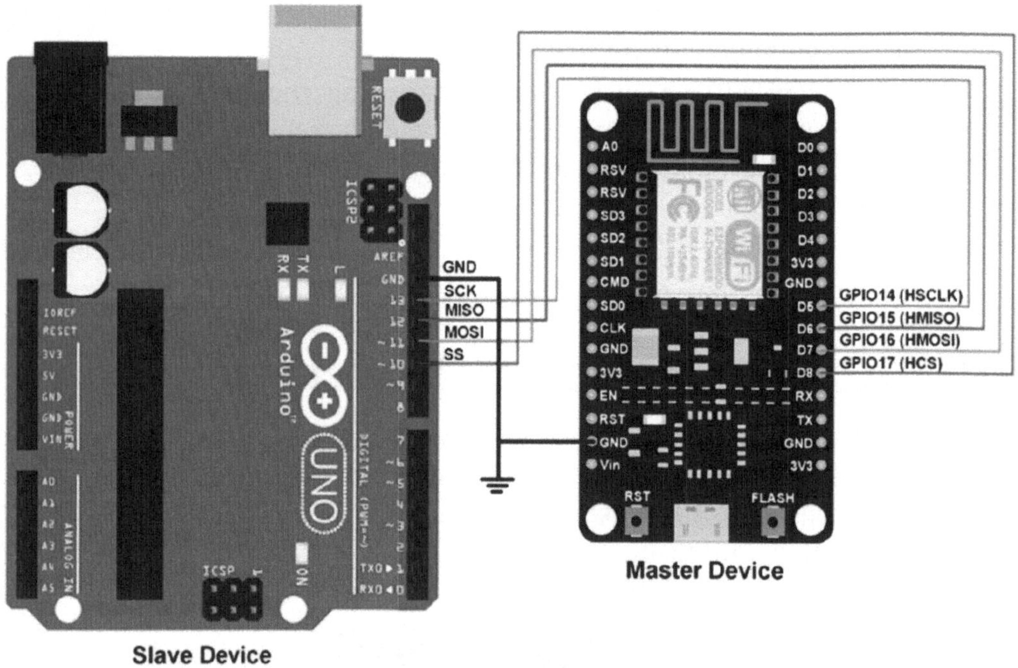

***Figure* 5.7**: *SPI Communication between Nodemcu and Arduino (Source: https://www.electronicwings.com/storage/PlatformSection/TopicContent/277/description/Arduino_NodeMCU_SPI_Interface_modified.png)*

Programming the Master (Nodemcu)

Step 1: Initializing the serial communication

To initialize Serial communication in your Arduino sketch, inside the setup part, use **`Serial.begin()`** to start the UART communication. Enter the baud rate you want to set as an argument. Additionally, include the SPI library to use the functions that are already defined in the SPI library and also define a buffer that is currently storing the dummy data. To set the baud rate to 9600, use:

```
#include<SPI.h>

char buff[]="Hello Slave\n";
```

```
void setup() {
   Serial.begin(9600);     /* begin serial with 9600 baud */
   SPI.begin();            /* begin SPI */
}
```

Step 2: Transmitting the data (Nodemcu as a master)

In the loop part, using the *transfer* function the data is being transferred from master to slave:

```
void loop() {
   for(int i=0; i<sizeof buff; i++)
   SPI.transfer(buff[i]);
   delay(1000);
}
```

The complete sketch for the Nodemcu will be:

```
#include<SPI.h>

char buff[]="Hello Slave\n";

void setup() {
   Serial.begin(9600);     /* begin serial with 9600 baud */
   SPI.begin();            /* begin SPI */
}

void loop() {
   for(int i=0; i<sizeof buff; i++)
   SPI.transfer(buff[i]);
   delay(1000);
}
```

Step 3: Programming the slave (Arduino UNO)

```
#include <SPI.h>

char buff [100];
volatile byte index;
volatile bool receivedone;  /* use reception complete flag */

void setup (void)
{
  Serial.begin (9600);
  SPCR |= bit(SPE);          /* Enable SPI */
  pinMode(MISO, OUTPUT);     /* Make MISO pin as OUTPUT */
  index = 0;
  receivedone = false;
  SPI.attachInterrupt();     /* Attach SPI interrupt */
}

void loop (void)
{
  if (receivedone)           /* Check and print received buffer if any */
  {
    buff[index] = 0;
    Serial.println(buff);
    index = 0;
    receivedone = false;
  }
}
```

```
// SPI interrupt routine
ISR (SPI_STC_vect)
{
  uint8_t oldsrg = SREG;
  cli();
  char c = SPDR;
  if (index <sizeof buff)
  {
    buff [index++] = c;
    if (c == '\n'){     /* Check for newline character as end of msg */
     receivedone = true;
    }
  }
  SREG = oldsrg;
}
```

I2C

The Inter-Integrated Circuit (I2C) protocol, also referred to as Inter Interconnected Circuit (IIC) or Two-Wire Interface (TWI), is one of the most common synchronous serial communication protocols used in electronic devices. It is used to transfer data between integrated circuits (ICs), microcontrollers (MCUs), and various peripheral devices.

The I2C protocol was first introduced in the early 80s by Philips Semiconductor (now known as NXP Semiconductor) and has since become one of the most widely used communication standards in the electronics industry.

The Inter-IC bus works as a master-slave bus. It uses two SCL (Serial clock line) wires and one SDA (Serial data line) for semi-duplex communication. The protocol specification defines three speed modes:

- Standard mode
- Fast mode
- Highspeed mode

The standard mode allows for transmission speeds of up to 100kbit/s, while the fast mode expands this range up to 400kbit/s. The highspeed mode allows for a transmission rate of 3.4Mbit/s. Because of the properties of the protocol, high-speed and fast devices can be combined. There are bus arbitration mechanisms in the protocol that allow multiple masters to co-exist. Typically, the master is the microcontroller, and all peripheral devices are simple slaves. If there are multiple microcontrollers in the system, you can select for each controller if they should be masters or slaves. The only exception is if there is a minimum number of masters in the system. One of the main advantages of the IIC bus is its easy extensibility. New devices can be added to the bus by just connecting them. There is no specific limit on the number of devices connected to the bus as long as the maximum bus capacitance of 400 pF is not exceeded.

Both the 7-bit and the 10-bit addresses are supported by the IIC bus. In the 7-bit mode, each device on the bus is identified by a single 7-bit address. Some of these addresses (for example, the highest 4 bits) are hardcoded by the manufacturer, while others are programmed by the IIC board designer. The address (0000XXX) 2 and address (1111XXX) 2 are reserved. This leaves 112 potential device addresses on the bus. The protocol was later expanded to include 10-bit addresses in order to increase addressable devices. However, due to the fact that the protocol was extended to include more devices, care was taken to maintain compatibility with 7-bit addressing modes so that 7-bit addressing devices can continue to be used under the new addressing scheme.

Data Transmission in IIC

As the IIC is a one-end bus, the voltage levels are defined in relation to the common ground. The low-level input voltages are between -0.5 and -0.3VDD voltages, and the high-level input voltages range from -0.7VDD voltages to +0.5VDD voltages. The low-level voltages on the data line correspond to logical 0, and the high voltages correspond to logical 1.

Since the wires are attached to external pull-up resistors (range 1-10k kΩ), the **high level** is never driven. It is tri-stated by the sender and the wire is pulled up externally by the pull-up resistor. The protocol depends on this behavior, so if you wish to program the protocol by hand (also known as bit-banging), you do not need to drive the high level at all. If you need to output a logical "1", you can set the controller pin directly to input. The low level is always driven as normal. To drive the low level, simply write "0" to the output pin.

This asymmetry between high and low levels results in the line having a dominant and a recessive state. If a device outputs 0 and drives the line low, it remains low even if one or more devices output 1 (that is, tri-state their output). Hence, a 0 always wins over a 1 (low is dominant, and high is recessive). This behavior is often called wired-AND (because all senders must output 1 for the line to be 1) and sometimes wired-NOR (probably because, from the point of view of an open-collector output, if one device turns on its output transistor, then the bus goes low). As we will see later, the protocol exploits this property for speed control and bus arbitration.

The general layout of an IIC packet is depicted in *Figure* 5.8.

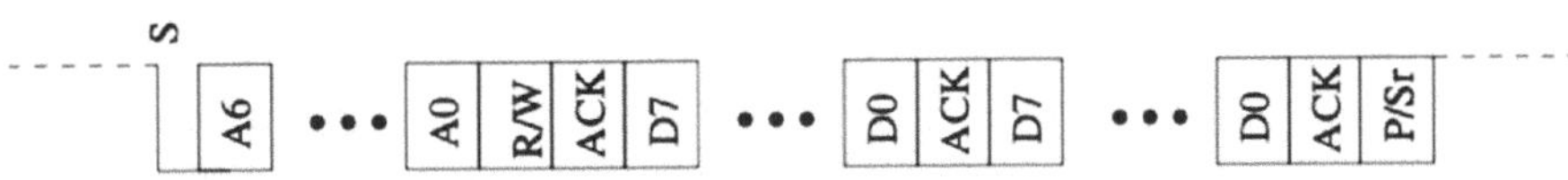

***Figure* 5.8**: *IIC data packet*

I2C is a two-way communication system between the master and the slave that uses the SDA or Serial Data line and the SCL or Serial Clock line. The SDA and SCL lines are usually pulled high by resistors, and the SCL line can be pulled low by any device on the bus. This allows multiple devices to talk to each other on the bus.

When in their idle state, both the SCL and the SDA are very high. The master initiates the transmission by sending a clock signal to the SCL and a start condition to the SDA. The master places the address on the bus and indicates whether it is a read access (the addressed device should read the data) or a write access (the master is transferring data to the address). After R/W, the slave transmits an acknowledgment to indicate that it has received its address.

The master or slave can now send any number of bytes, depending on the direction of the data. Each byte is acknowledged by the recipient (except for the last byte, which is acknowledged by the master if the receiver is the master itself). At the termination of the transfer, the master generates a stop condition (P), indicating that the bus has now become free. Alternatively, the master can continue the transfer by sending a repeat START condition (SR), which terminates the current transmission while simultaneously initiating a new one.

Here is a detailed breakdown of how the I2C protocol works:

- **Master-Initiated Communication:** In I2C, one device is called the **master**, and there can be one or more **slaves**. The master controls and initiates the communication, triggering the start of communication by pulling the SDA line low and the SCL line high.

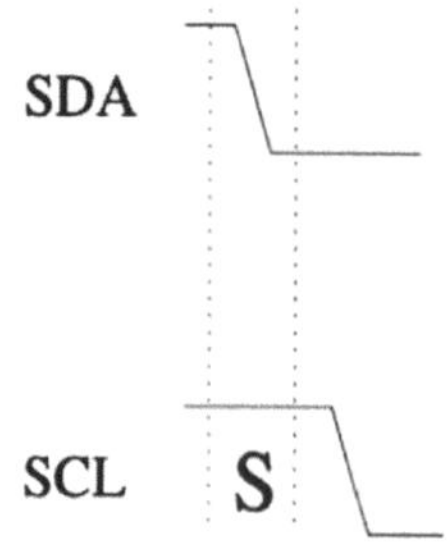

***Figure* 5.9**: *Start Condition*

- **Addressing:** After generating the start condition, the master sends the address of the slave device it wants to communicate with. Each slave device on the bus has a unique 7-bit or 10-bit address. The 7-bit address allows for up to 128 different slave devices. The 10-bit addressing mode is less common but allows for even more devices. The address byte is followed by a Read/Write (R/W) bit, indicating whether the master intends to read from or write to the slave.
- **Data Transfer:** Once the slave acknowledges its address, data transfer begins. The master and slave devices take turns sending and receiving data. The data is sent in 8-bit bytes, and each byte is acknowledged by the receiving party. If the master is writing data to the slave, it continues to send bytes until it is ready to terminate the communication.
- **Stop Condition**: To conclude the communication, the master generates a stop condition by releasing the SDA line from low to high while the SCL line is high. This signifies the end of the data transfer, and the bus is released for other devices to use.

***Figure* 5.10**: *Stop condition*

Components of IIC

Here are the components included in the IIC protocol:

- **Master Device:** The I2C communication is initiated and controlled by the master device. The master device creates the start and end conditions, sends the addresses, and manages the data transfer.
- **Slave Devices:** These are the peripherals or integrated circuits that answer to the command of the master. Every slave device has its own address that the master can read from or write to.
- **Serial Data (SDA Line):** This two-way line carries the real-time data flowing between the main and secondary devices. The high-resistance line can be pulled high by the main and low-resistance by the secondary devices on the bus.
- **Serial Clock (SCL Line):** This line supplies the clock signal used to synchronize data transmission between devices. Similar to SDA, this line is also drawn high with a resistive.
- **Start and Stop condition:** These conditions indicate the start and stop of the I2C communication. The start condition happens when SDA changes from high to low and SCL changes from low to high.
- **Address Byte:** The address is the master's 7-bit (or 10-bit) address of the destination slave device. The R/W bits indicate whether the slave is being read or written.
- **Data Bytes:** Data bytes (also known as data bits) are 8-bit bits of data that are sent between the main and slave devices. Data bytes can be used to represent commands, configurations, sensor data, or any other information.
- **Acknowledgment (ACK) Bit:** After each bit of data has been received, an acknowledgment bit is sent by the receiving device (either master or slave). A high ACK bit indicates the device has received the data successfully; a low ACK bit indicates either an error or the termination of the data transfer.
- **Pull-up Resistors:** SDA and SCL resistors are pull-up resistors that are used to hold the SDA or SCL lines high, even when no device is driving them low. Pull-up resistors keep the lines in a known condition and ready for communication.

The I2C protocol's simplicity, versatility, and support in a wide range of microcontrollers and devices make it an essential tool for connecting and communicating between various components in electronic systems. Its two-wire design and support for multi-device communication make it particularly suitable for IoT (Internet of Things) applications, sensors, and embedded systems.

I2C Communication in Nodemcu

Integrating an I²C LCD display with a Nodemcu board involves connecting the display to the NodeMCU and writing code to communicate with it using the I2C protocol. Here's a step-by-step process:

Step 1: Wiring Connections

Connect the I2C LCD display to the NodeMCU using jumper wires. The I2C LCD typically has four pins:

- **VCC**: Connect to Nodemcu 3.3V or 5V (check the display's voltage requirements).
- **GND**: Connect to Nodemcu GND.
- **SDA**: Connect to Nodemcu D2 (GPIO4) for data communication.
- **SCL**: Connect to Nodemcu D1 (GPIO5) for clock signal.

Double-check your connections to ensure they are secure and correctly wired.

Step 2: Install Required Libraries

You need to install the necessary libraries for I2C communication and the LCD display. In the Arduino IDE, go to **`Sketch > Include Library > Manage Libraries`** and search for these libraries:

- **`LiquidCrystal_I2C`** `by Marco Schwartz`
- **`Wire`** (already included with Arduino IDE)

Install these libraries if you haven't already.

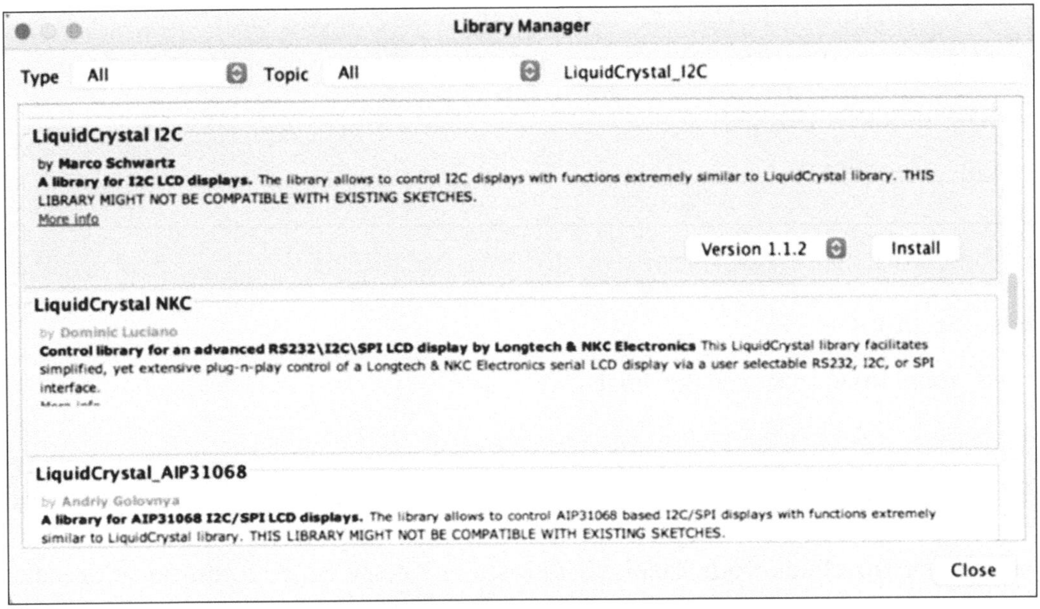

***Figure 5.11**: Liquid Crystal I²C Library*

Step 3: Upload Code

Now, you can write and upload code to the NodeMCU. Following is a simple example code to display **"`Hello, World!`"** on a 16x2 I2C LCD. Make sure to adjust the code if you have a different display size or if you've wired the I2C pins differently:

```
#include <Wire.h>
#include <LiquidCrystal_I2C.h>

// Set the LCD address (usually 0x27 or 0x3F)
LiquidCrystal_I2C lcd(0x27, 16, 2); // Change to your display's address and size

void setup() {
  // Initialize the LCD
  lcd.init();
  // Turn on the backlight (if available)
  lcd.backlight();
```

```
  // Print "Hello, World!" on the LCD
  lcd.setCursor(0, 0);
  lcd.print("Hello, World!");
}

void loop() {
  // Your main code can go here
}
```

Ensure that you've set the correct I2C address and display size when initializing the LiquidCrystal_I2C object. Some displays may have different default addresses, so check your display's datasheet or try both common addresses (0x27 or 0x3F) if you're unsure.

Step 4: Upload and Test

Connect your NodeMCU to your computer via USB, select the appropriate board and COM port in the Arduino IDE, and upload the code. Open the serial monitor to see any debugging messages.

The text **"Hello, World!"** should now appear on your I2C LCD display. You can modify the code to display different text or create more complex applications, including displaying sensor data, date, time, and more, on the LCD.

This step-by-step guide should help you integrate an I2C LCD display with your NodeMCU and get you started with displaying information on the screen. Depending on your specific project requirements, you can expand on this basic setup to create more advanced applications with the display.

***Figure 5.12**: LCD Screen with program output*

Conclusion

Microcontroller Interfaces, UART, SPI, and Inter-integrated Circuit (IICs) are the three most important communication protocols for microcontrollers. These protocols are used by microcontrollers such as Arduino, NodeMCU, and more, to communicate with various external devices, such as sensors, peripherals, and others.

In this chapter, we have explored the interesting topic of microcontroller Interfaces and how they work. We have provided detailed explanations and examples, as well as interfacing demonstrations, covering **UART Communication, SPI Communication, I2C Communication.**

In conclusion, a solid understanding of UART, SPI, and I2C protocols is indispensable for any electronics enthusiast, maker, or engineer. These protocols enable seamless communication between microcontrollers and a diverse range of peripheral devices, opening up endless possibilities for creating innovative projects. Whether you're building a weather station, IoT device, robotics project, or any electronic system, the knowledge gained from this chapter will serve as a solid foundation for your endeavors.

As you continue your exploration of microcontroller interfacing, remember that each protocol has its strengths and weaknesses, making them suitable for different applications. Mastery of these protocols empowers you to make informed decisions when selecting the most appropriate communication method for your specific project requirements.

With the knowledge and practical experience gained from this chapter, you are well-equipped to embark on exciting journeys in the world of microcontroller-based electronics, creating solutions that can make a real impact in a connected and technology-driven world.

In the next chapter, we will learn about the protocol used for the data transmission from IoT devices - MQTT (Message Queuing Telemetry Transport), MQTT is a very light weight protocol that is used in the majority of IoT devices that are deployed across the globe. We will take a closer look at the working of MQTT protocol, its application and understand about the libraries that are required by the ESP devices to transfer the data wirelessly to the cloud using MQTT protocol.

References

1. Maxim Integrated. (2001). "The Basics of UART Communication." https://www.maximintegrated.com/en/design/technical-documents/app-notes/1/129.html
2. Texas Instruments. (2008). "Universal Asynchronous Receiver/Transmitter (UART)." https://www.ti.com/lit/an/slaa363/slaa363.pdf
3. B. Wilson, J. Robertson, & L. Clark. (2007). "UART, SPI, and I2C: Communication Protocols for Designing Microcontroller-Based Embedded Systems." Pearson.
4. https://ti.tuwien.ac.at/ecs/teaching/courses/mclu/theory-material/Microcontroller.pdf
5. Microcontroller Theory and Applications with the PIC18F" by M. Rafiquzzaman
6. "Embedded Systems - Introduction to SPI (Serial Peripheral Interface)" by Bartosz Zoltak
7. Texas Instruments. (2013). Understanding the I2C Bus. https://www.ti.com/lit/an/slva704/slva704.pdf
8. NXP Semiconductors. (2007). I2C-bus specification and user manual. https://www.nxp.com/docs/en/user-guide/UM10204.pdf

CHAPTER 6

MQTT – The Protocol for Internet of Things

Introduction

MQTT is at the heart of a new breed of messaging protocols that are lightweight, efficient, and scalable for the IoT and other resource-constrained environments.

MQTT was originally developed in the late 90s by two engineers, Dr. Andrew Stanford-Clark and Arlen Nielsen, and has since grown into an open standard, which is adopted by many industries and applications. MQTT's minimalist design, publishing-subscribe communications model, and ability to scale up or down with low bandwidth, high latency, or unreliable networks are just a few of its benefits.

At the core of MQTT, clients – from IoT devices, sensors, servers, and applications – talk to each other via a central broker, also known as an MQTT server. The broker serves as a central hub, facilitating communication between clients. MQTT is best suited for situations where devices or services need to talk to each other in real-time, with different levels of dependability and limitations in real-time. This broker-mediated structure separates the publisher (device or application that generates data) from the subscriber (people who want to receive that data). This allows MQTT to provide a flexible and scalable basis for data distribution.

One of the key characteristics of MQTT is its lightweight nature. This is largely due to its minimalist header structure and TCP/IP protocol implementation. The minimal overhead allows MQTT to be very efficient in terms of bandwidth and power consumption. This is especially important for resource-poor IoT devices that often run on battery power and are limited in network connectivity. The lightweight design of MQTT makes it easy for even devices with limited computational resources to implement and use the protocol.

What's more, MQTT's publishing-subscribe model makes it even more flexible. In this model, clients (known as publishers) send messages to topics on the broker, and subscribers express interest in those topics and receive messages about them from the broker. By separating producers and consumers, MQTT allows for dynamic, high-performance, and scalable communication models. For example, a smart home can publish its temperature readings to a "temperature" topic, and thermostats, mobile apps, and other devices can subscribe to the topic to get real-time data. This flexibility allows MQTT to be used in a variety of applications outside of IoT, such as financial services, social networks, and instant messaging.

Security is another paramount concern in the IoT landscape, where devices often collect sensitive data or control critical functions. MQTT addresses these concerns by supporting various authentication and encryption mechanisms. Common security measures include the use of username/password authentication, client certificates, and Transport Layer Security (TLS) encryption. These measures help safeguard data integrity, confidentiality, and the authenticity of clients connecting to the broker, ensuring that only authorized devices and applications can participate in the MQTT communication.

The flexibility and adaptability of MQTT are further augmented by its support for retained messages and Last Will and Testament (LWT) features. Retained messages enable a broker to store the last message sent on a specific topic, ensuring that newly connected subscribers immediately receive the most recent data. LWT, on the other hand, allows clients to specify a "will" message that the broker publishes on behalf of a client in case the client unexpectedly disconnects. These features enhance the resilience and reliability of MQTT-based systems by minimizing data loss and ensuring that subscribers stay informed even when publishers or subscribers experience temporary disruptions.

As MQTT grew in popularity, it was incorporated into many open-source IoT platforms and commercial IoT services, making it available to developers all over the world. This adoption of MQTT led to the creation of MQTT client libraries in different programming languages, making it easier to implement MQTT in many applications. MQTT clients can be found in languages like Python, Java, C/C++, and JavaScript, making it possible for developers to create MQTT-enabled applications for virtually any platform.

Structure

In this chapter, we will discuss the following topics:

- Architecture of MQTT
- Features of MQTT
- MQTT packet structure
  - MQTT packet types
  - MQTT packet structure
- Using MQTT with ESP-12
- Communicating ESP-12 with MQTT Client
- MQTT broker
  - Setting up MQTT broker
  - Securing MQTT broker
- Securing MQTT communication

Architecture of MQTT

The architecture of the MQTT (Message Queuing Telemetry Transport) protocol revolves around a client-server or broker-based model, designed to facilitate efficient, lightweight, and scalable messaging in various applications, particularly in the context of the Internet of Things (IoT).

Here's an overview of the key components and their roles within the MQTT architecture:

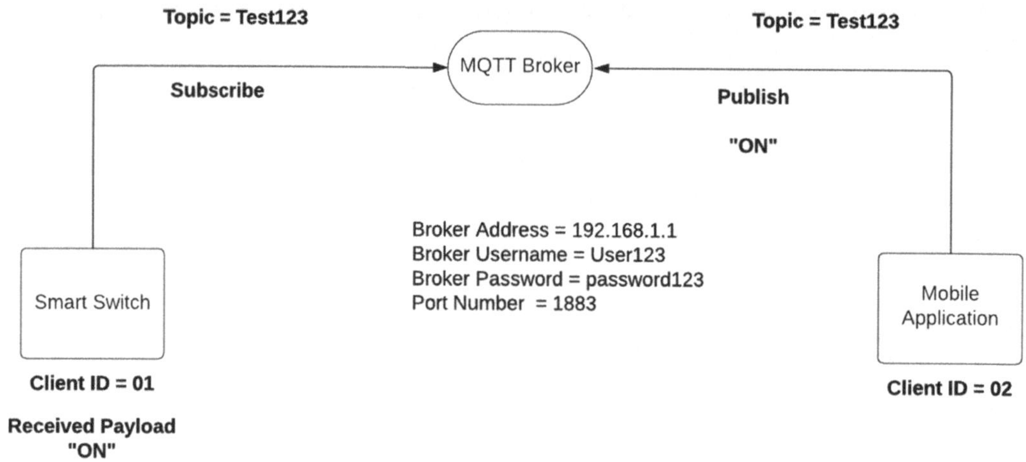

Figure 6.1: *Architecture of MQTT*

This block diagram shows the key components that are involved in any MQTT message transaction. Let's take a look at each of the components closely:

- **MQTT Clients:** MQTT clients are the endpoints that generate or consume messages in an MQTT-based system. Clients can take various forms, including IoT devices, sensors, servers, applications, and more.

  MQTT clients are responsible for connecting to an MQTT broker, publishing messages to specific topics, and subscribing to topics of interest.

  Clients can have different levels of capability, ranging from resource-constrained devices with limited processing power and memory to more powerful servers and applications. In *Figure* 6.1, there are two clients connected to the MQTT broker. One is the mobile application, which sends commands or publishes messages to the MQTT broker, and the other one is an IoT switch, which is also connected to the same broker, receiving data from the broker that was published by another client on the same topic.

- **MQTT Broker:** The MQTT broker serves as the central intermediary within the architecture, facilitating message exchange between clients. Brokers are responsible for receiving, storing, and forwarding messages from publishers to subscribers based on topic subscriptions. They manage client connections, perform message routing, and enforce security and access control policies. MQTT brokers can be standalone servers or components integrated into larger IoT platforms.

- **Topic:** Topics are hierarchical strings used to categorize messages within the MQTT system. Clients publish messages to specific topics, and other clients subscribe to topics of interest. Topics enable a flexible and dynamic way to organize and distribute messages. For example, in *Figure 6.1*, the mobile application publishes the payload "ON" to a topic 'Test123', and the client with the client ID '01' has subscribed to the same topic, and hence, receiving the same payload "ON". In addition, topics are case sensitive and can be defined with multiple levels, as 'Test123' is a single-level topic, whereas 'Home/Test123' is a two-level topic.
- **Publishers and Subscribers:** There are two main roles that MQTT clients can play: those of publishers and those of subscribers. Publishers create messages and forward them to subscribers with a specific topic. Subscribers, on the other hand, express interest in a particular topic and forward messages related to that topic to MQTT. MQTT clients can dynamically switch between these two roles for flexible communication.
- **Quality of Service (QoS) Levels**: MQTT provides three QoS levels that define the level of message delivery assurance between publishers and subscribers:
    - **QoS 0 (At Most Once)**: Messages are delivered to subscribers at most once, with no acknowledgment or confirmation.
    - **QoS 1 (At Least Once)**: Messages are delivered to subscribers at least once, with acknowledgment and possible message duplication.
    - **QoS 2 (Exactly Once)**: Messages are delivered to subscribers exactly once, ensuring no duplicates or losses.

To sum up, MQTT is built around client-server interactions, brokers, topics, and messaging paradigms. This design makes MQTT lightweight, scalable, and efficient, making it a popular choice for the IoT and other applications that require reliable and secure data exchange across resource-limited devices. The robustness and flexibility offered by MQTT-based systems are further enhanced by the use of QoS, retained messages, LWT, and security measures.

Features of MQTT

In the world of IoT, where devices and systems are becoming an integral part of our day-to-day lives, it is essential to ensure efficient and dependable communication between them. This is where MQTT comes in as a key protocol. MQTT is a lightweight and scalable protocol that can be used in a variety of ways to meet the needs of IoT and many other applications. Let's take a look at some of the key features that make MQTT so popular, along with some examples to help you understand why it has become the standard for messaging in a variety of domains:

- **Publish-Subscribe Model:**

  At its core lies MQTT's sophisticated publish-subscription communications model. In MQTT, clients communicate with each other through a central broker called the "MQTT broker." The broker serves as a central hub for the exchange of messages between clients. Publishers (clients that generate data) send messages to the broker on specific topics. Subscribers (clients that express interest in a particular topic) send messages related to that topic to the broker. This separation of producer and consumer allows for dynamic, scalable, and efficient communication patterns.

  Example:

  Imagine a smart home scenario where temperature sensors in different rooms publish their readings to respective topics like "home/living_room/temperature" and "home/bedroom/temperature." Thermostats and mobile apps can subscribe to these topics of interest. As the temperature sensors update their data, the broker ensures that the latest information is delivered to all subscribers in real-time.

- **Lightweight Design:**

  It's no secret that MQTT is lightweight. It's a protocol that's well-suited to resource-poor environments, like IoT devices with low processing power, low memory, and low bandwidth. MQTT's lightweight design is through its header structure, which minimizes the footprint of the protocol, as well as its use of TCP/IP for data transmission. All of this minimal overhead makes MQTT easy to implement and use, even for devices with limited computational resources.

  Example:

  Consider a battery-powered IoT sensor deployed in a remote location to monitor soil moisture. MQTT's lightweight design allows this sensor to communicate its readings efficiently over a low-power, low-bandwidth cellular connection without draining its battery quickly.

- **Quality of Service (QoS) Levels:**

  MQTT offers three distinct levels of QoS) to cater to varying message delivery requirements:

- **QoS 0 (At Most Once):** At this level, the broker delivers a message to subscribers at most once, without any acknowledgment or confirmation. This level prioritizes minimal latency and network usage.
- **QoS 1 (At Least Once):** At this level, the broker ensures that the message is delivered to subscribers at least once. It achieves this by requesting acknowledgment from subscribers and retransmitting the message until acknowledged. This level offers a higher degree of reliability at the cost of possible message duplication.
- **QoS 2 (Exactly Once):** The highest level of QoS, where the broker ensures that the message is delivered exactly once to subscribers. This level involves a more complex handshake process between the publisher and the broker, guaranteeing no duplicates or losses. It provides the highest level of message delivery assurance.

Example:

Imagine an industrial automation system where sensor data controls critical processes. In such scenarios, QoS 2 ensures that every message sent by a sensor reaches its destination exactly once, preventing errors that could have severe consequences.

- **Retained Messages:**

  Retained message is a feature of MQTT that allows the broker to keep the last message that was sent on a particular topic. This means that when a new client joins the network, they receive the latest message right away. This means that subscribers always get the most up-to-date information, even when they join after the last message has been sent.

  Example:

  In a weather monitoring network, the weather app keeps the most recent forecast for a particular location on a separate topic. So, when a new user joins the weather app, they get the latest forecast right away, without having to wait for a new update.

- **Last Will and Testament:**

  When establishing a connection with a broker, clients can specify a "will" message and a topic. If a client disconnects unexpectedly, such as due to a network fault or device failure, then the broker publishes the last will message on the topic specified by the client on behalf of the disconnected client. This helps to provide notifications or take action when clients unexpectedly go offline, improving system reliability.

Example:

In a remote monitoring system for industrial equipment, if a sensor device loses connectivity, it can send a "device offline" message as its "will" to a dedicated topic. This informs the monitoring system to take appropriate actions or alert maintenance personnel.

- **Security Mechanisms:**

  The security of MQTT and other IoT applications is of the utmost importance in the context of sensitive data. To address these issues, MQTT supports various types of authentications and encryptions. Some of the most common types of authentications are username/password, client certificate, and TLS encryption. All these mechanisms protect MQTT-based systems from unauthorized access and data compromise by keeping messages and clients confidential, consistent, and authentic.

  Example:

  In a healthcare IoT system, patient monitoring data is transmitted via MQTT. TLS encryption ensures that this sensitive medical data remains confidential and cannot be intercepted or tampered with during transmission.

- **Flexibility and Scalability:**

  The flexibility and adaptability of MQTT is reflected in its wide range of applications beyond the IoT. MQTT has found applications in financial services, social networks, instant messaging, and many other industries. MQTT's scalable architecture and efficient data distribution mechanism allow it to meet diverse communication needs across different industries.

  Example:

  A financial trading platform can use MQTT to send real-time stock market data to subscribers and analytics systems. This efficient message distribution allows traders to get timely updates, which is essential for making informed decisions.

- **Open Standard and Ecosystem:**

  MQTT is an open standard, fostering a vibrant ecosystem of MQTT clients, brokers, and libraries. These resources simplify the implementation of MQTT in various programming languages, making it accessible to developers across the globe. MQTT clients are available in languages like Python, Java, C/C++, and JavaScript, allowing developers to create MQTT-enabled applications for virtually any platform.

Example:

A developer creating a home automation system can leverage MQTT client libraries in Python to easily connect IoT devices, sensors, and home automation software to an MQTT broker, enabling seamless communication and control.

MQTT Packet Structure

MQTT messages are organized into packets, each serving a specific purpose within the protocol. These packets form the basis of communication between MQTT clients (devices) and the MQTT broker. Let's take a look into the structure of MQTT packets:

MQTT Packet Types

MQTT defines several packet types, each designed for a specific function within the protocol. The most common control packet types include:

- **CONNECT**: Used by a client to establish a connection to the MQTT broker. It contains information such as the client identifier, username, password, and various connection settings.
- **CONNACK**: Sent by the broker in response to a Connect packet, indicating whether the connection was accepted or refused.
- **PUBLISH**: Used to send data from a client to the broker or from the broker to a client. It includes the topic to which the message is published, the message payload, and other parameters.
- **PUBACK**: Sent by the broker in response to a Publish packet to acknowledge the receipt of a QoS (Quality of Service) 1 message.
- **PUBREC**, **PUBREL**, **PUBCOMP**: These are part of the QoS 2 message flow and are used for ensuring exactly once message delivery.
- **SUBSCRIBE**: Sent by a client to subscribe to specific topics. It includes the list of topics and their corresponding QoS levels.
- **SUBACK**: Sent by the broker to acknowledge the receipt of a Subscribe packet, indicating the maximum QoS level granted for each subscribed topic.
- **UNSUBSCRIBE**: Used by a client to unsubscribe from specific topics.
- **UNSUBACK**: Sent by the broker to acknowledge the receipt of an Unsubscribe packet.

- **PINGREQ**: Used by a client to request the broker to confirm that it is still alive.
- **PINGRESP**: Sent by the broker in response to a PingReq packet, confirming its availability.
- **DISCONNECT**: A client sends this packet to disconnect from the broker gracefully.

MQTT Packet Structure

Each MQTT packet consists of two main parts: the fixed header and the variable header/payload. The structure of these parts varies based on the packet type.

Fixed Header

The fixed header is present in every MQTT packet and contains essential information about the packet. It consists of the following fields:

<table>
<tr><th>bit</th><th>7</th><th>6</th><th>5</th><th>4</th><th>3</th><th>2</th><th>1</th><th>0</th></tr>
<tr><td>byte 1</td><td colspan="4">Message Type</td><td>DUP flag</td><td colspan="2">QoS level</td><td>RETAIN</td></tr>
<tr><td>byte 2</td><td colspan="8">Remaining Length</td></tr>
</table>

***Figure 6.2**: MQTT Fixed header*

- **Packet Type**: A 4-bit field that specifies the type of the packet (for example, Connect, Publish, Subscribe, and more).
- **Flags**: The fixed header may contain control flags that provide additional information about the packet. For example, the QoS level, the DUP (duplicate) flag, and the RETAIN flag are set in this section.
- **Remaining Length**: A variable-length field that encodes the total length of the packet, including the fixed header, variable header, and payload. The remaining length is encoded using a variable-length encoding scheme, making it efficient for messages of different sizes.

Variable Header

The structure of the variable header varies depending on the packet type. Some common fields found in the variable header include:

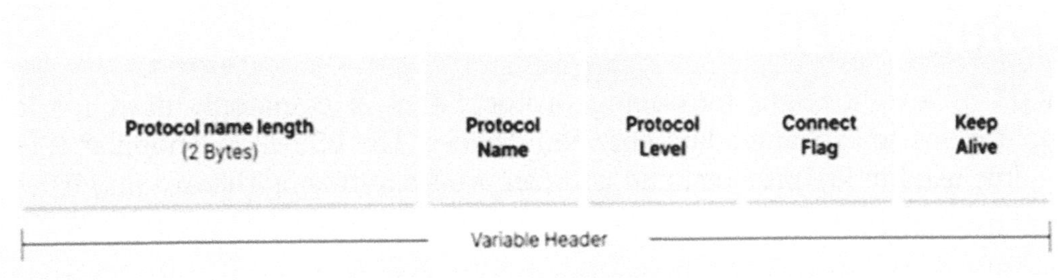

***Figure 6.3**: MQTT Variable header*

This field indicates the presence or absence of data in the payload.

bit	7	6	5	4	3	2	1	0
	User Name Flag	Password Flag	Will Retain	Will QoS		Will Flag	Clean Session	Reserved
	x	x	x	x	x	x		x

***Figure 6.4:** Connect Flag*

- **Protocol Name**: In the Connect packet, this field specifies the name of the protocol, which is typically "MQTT."
- **Protocol Version**: Indicates the version of the MQTT protocol in use (for example, 3.1.1 or 5.0).
- **Connect Flags**: In the Connect packet, these flags specify various connection parameters, such as the presence of a username and password, whether the session should be clean, and whether the broker should retain messages.
- **Keep Alive**: In the Connect packet, this field indicates the time interval (in seconds) at which the client must send PingReq packets to the broker.
- **Message ID**: For packets with QoS levels 1 and 2, this field contains a unique identifier to associate requests and acknowledgments.
- **Topic Name**: In the Subscribe, Unsubscribe, and Publish packets, this field represents the topic to which the action is related.
- **Payload**: For Publish packets, the payload is the actual message data.

Using MQTT with ESP-12

MQTT is a lightweight messaging protocol that is commonly used for IoT applications to exchange data between devices. The ESP-12 is a popular Wi-Fi module used in IoT projects, and you can program it using the Arduino IDE to work with MQTT.

The library that is used to enable the MQTT communication within ESP-12 is PubSubClient.

In Arduino IDE, Install MQTT Library:

To use MQTT with Arduino, you need to install an MQTT library. You can use the **"PubSubClient"** library, which is widely used. To install it, go to **Sketch** > **Include Library** > **Manage Libraries**, then search for **PubSubClient** and click **Install**.

Here is an example that connects the ESP-12 to your Wi-Fi network and the MQTT broker, and it publishes a message to the **"esp/test"** topic. You can customize the code to subscribe to topics and perform actions based on the received messages. This example will help us understand the multiple functions and their use throughout the sketch.

```
#include <ESP8266WiFi.h>

#include <PubSubClient.h>


// Replace with your network credentials

const char* ssid = "YourWiFiSSID";

const char* password = "YourWiFiPassword";


// MQTT broker details

const char* mqtt_server = "MQTTBrokerIPAddress";

const char* mqtt_topic = "esp/test"; // MQTT topic to subscribe to


WiFiClient espClient;

PubSubClient client(espClient);
```

```
void callback(char* topic, byte* payload, unsigned int length);

void setup() {
  Serial.begin(115200);
  WiFi.begin(ssid, password);

  while (WiFi.status() != WL_CONNECTED) {
    delay(1000);
    Serial.println("Connecting to WiFi...");
  }
  Serial.println("Connected to WiFi");

  client.setServer(mqtt_server, 1883);
  client.setCallback(callback);

  // Connect to MQTT broker
  reconnect();
}

void loop() {
  if (!client.connected()) {
    reconnect();
  }
  client.loop();
}

void callback(char* topic, byte* payload, unsigned int length) {
  Serial.println("Message received on topic: " + String(topic));
```

```
  Serial.print("Message content: ");
  for (int i = 0; i < length; i++) {
    Serial.print((char)payload[i]);
  }
  Serial.println();

  // You can add your custom logic here to handle the incoming message
}

void reconnect() {
  while (!client.connected()) {
    Serial.println("Connecting to MQTT...");
    if (client.connect("ESP-12-Client")) {
      Serial.println("Connected to MQTT");
      client.subscribe(mqtt_topic); // Subscribe to the MQTT topic
    } else {
      Serial.print("MQTT connection failed, rc=");
      Serial.print(client.state());
      Serial.println(" Retry in 5 seconds");
      delay(5000);
    }
  }
}
```

The Sketch starts by including all the important libraries:

```
#include <ESP8266WiFi.h>
#include <PubSubClient.h>
```

Defining the variables to provide the Wi-Fi credentials so that we can use these variables throughout the sketch whenever required:

```
const char* ssid = "YourWiFiSSID";

const char* password = "YourWiFiPassword";
```

Then, we need to define the MQTT broker details. If the broker is not secure, only the address is sufficient. However, if the broker is secured, we need to provide the username and password for the broker as well. We also need to provide the topic to receive or publish the messages. You can define multiple topics here as well:

```
const char* mqtt_server = "MQTTBrokerIPAddress";

const char* mqtt_topic = "esp/test"; // MQTT topic to subscribe to
```

In the setup part, we use these two functions to define the broker address and the port number. Additionally, we need to define the **callback** function, so that whenever there is a message coming to the subscribed topic, it will automatically call the **callback** function. We will use these two functions for the same:

```
client.setServer(mqtt_server, 1883);

client.setCallback(callback);
```

The **callback** function in an MQTT client is a user-defined function that gets called whenever a new message is received from the MQTT broker. Its purpose is to handle and process incoming MQTT messages. In the example provided, the callback function is defined as follows:

```
void callback(char* topic, byte* payload, unsigned int length) {

  Serial.println("Message received on topic: " + String(topic));


  Serial.print("Message content: ");

  for (int i = 0; i < length; i++) {

    Serial.print((char)payload[i]);

  }

  Serial.println();
```

```
  // You can add your custom logic here to handle the incoming message
}
```

Now, let's break down the key components of this callback function:

Function Signature:

```
void callback(char* topic, byte* payload, unsigned int length)
```

- **`char* topic`**: This parameter represents the MQTT topic on which the message was received. It's a string that contains the topic name.
- **`byte* payload`**: This parameter contains the actual message payload received from the MQTT broker. It's an array of bytes (byte data type).
- **`unsigned int length`**: This parameter indicates the length of the message payload in bytes.

Print Topic and Message Content:

The first two lines of the callback function are responsible for printing information about the received message to the serial console.

`Serial.println("Message received on topic: " + String(topic));` prints the MQTT topic on which the message was received.

It uses the String class to concatenate the topic string with a descriptive message and then prints it using **`Serial.println`**.

The following lines are responsible for printing the content of the message payload:

`Serial.print("Message content: ");` prints a label before the message content.

The for loop iterates through the payload array and prints each byte of the payload as a character using **`(char)payload[i]`**. This is useful for displaying text-based messages.

Custom Logic:

- The comment in the callback function indicates where you can add your custom logic to handle the incoming message.
- Depending on your application, you can parse and process the message payload, take actions based on the message content, or update variables or perform other tasks in response to the message.

Serial Output:

The callback function relies on the Serial object to output messages to the serial console. This is useful for debugging and monitoring the behavior of your ESP-12 and MQTT communication. You can view these messages in the Arduino IDE's Serial Monitor.

The **`reconnect()`** function in the MQTT client code is responsible for establishing and maintaining a connection to the MQTT broker. It also handles reconnection attempts in case the connection is lost. Let's break down the **`reconnect()`** function in detail:

```
void reconnect() {
  while (!client.connected()) {
    Serial.println("Connecting to MQTT...");
    if (client.connect("ESP-12-Client")) {
      Serial.println("Connected to MQTT");
      client.subscribe(mqtt_topic); // Subscribe to the MQTT topic
    } else {
      Serial.print("MQTT connection failed, rc=");
      Serial.print(client.state());
      Serial.println(" Retry in 5 seconds");
      delay(5000);
    }
  }
}
```

- **While Loop:** The **`while (!client.connected())`** loop runs as long as the MQTT client is not connected to the broker. It continuously attempts to establish a connection.
- **Connecting Message:** **`Serial.println("Connecting to MQTT...");`** It prints a message to the serial console to indicate that the MQTT client is attempting to establish a connection.
- **MQTT Connection Attempt:** **`if (client.connect("ESP-12-Client"))`** attempts to connect to the MQTT broker. The string "ESP-12-Client" is

the client identifier and can be customized to a name that identifies your ESP-12 device. It is important that each client connecting to the broker has a unique identifier.

- **Successful Connection**: If the connection attempt is successful, the code block inside the if statement is executed:
- `Serial.println("Connected to MQTT");` It indicates that the connection to the MQTT broker was successful.
- `client.subscribe(mqtt_topic);` It subscribes to a specific MQTT topic (`mqtt_topic`) after successfully connecting. This allows the client to receive messages published to that topic.
- **Failed Connection:** If the connection attempt fails, the code block inside the else statement is executed:
- `Serial.print("MQTT connection failed, rc=");` It prints an error message, indicating that the MQTT connection failed.
- `Serial.print(client.state());` It prints the MQTT client's state, which can help diagnose connection issues.
- `Serial.println(" Retry in 5 seconds");` It prints a message indicating that the code will wait for 5 seconds before attempting to reconnect.
- `delay(5000);` It introduces a 5-second delay before the next reconnection attempt. This delay prevents the client from making repeated connection attempts too rapidly.

Communicating ESP-12 with MQTT client

Communication between an ESP-12 device and a mobile MQTT client application involves the exchange of MQTT messages over a network. Here's a detailed explanation of the communication process between the ESP-12 device and the mobile MQTT client application:

1. **Setting Up the ESP-12 Device**:
    - The ESP-12 device is a Wi-Fi-enabled microcontroller often used in IoT projects. To enable MQTT communication, the ESP-12 needs to be programmed using a development environment like the Arduino IDE.
    - In the ESP-12 code, you configure Wi-Fi credentials (SSID and password) to connect to your local Wi-Fi network.

- You install an MQTT library, such as the `PubSubClient` library, to handle MQTT communication in your ESP-12 code.
- You specify the MQTT broker server's address and port to which the ESP-12 will connect. The broker server is responsible for routing messages between devices.
- The ESP-12 subscribes to one or more MQTT topics. Topics act as channels through which messages are sent. Your mobile MQTT client will publish messages to these topics, and the ESP-12 will receive and act on these messages.

2. **Setting Up the Mobile MQTT Client Application**:
    - To establish communication with the ESP-12, you need an MQTT client application on your mobile device. There are many MQTT client apps available for iOS and Android, such as MQTT Dash, MQTT Box, or IoT MQTT Dashboard.
    - In the mobile app, you configure the MQTT broker server's address, port, and any necessary security credentials (for example, username and password) to connect to the same MQTT broker used by the ESP-12.
3. **Publishing Messages from the Mobile MQTT Client**:
    - In the mobile app, you create messages that you want to send to the ESP-12. These messages could be commands, data, or requests for information.
    - You select an MQTT topic for each message. The topic should match the topic(s) to which the ESP-12 is subscribed. This ensures that the ESP-12 will receive the message.
    - You use the MQTT client app to publish the message to the specified topic. When you hit the "Publish" button, the message is sent to the MQTT broker.
4. **Receiving Messages on the ESP-12**:
    - The ESP-12, which is subscribed to the MQTT topic, continuously checks the broker for incoming messages.
    - When the ESP-12 detects a message on the subscribed topic, the MQTT client library invokes a callback function in your code. This function processes and handles the received message. You can define custom logic in this callback function to respond to the message appropriately.

- The ESP-12 can perform actions based on the received message, such as toggling GPIO pins, reading sensors, or updating its internal state.

5. **Two-Way Communication**:
   - The communication between the ESP-12 and the mobile MQTT client is not limited to one-way messaging. The mobile app can both publish messages to the ESP-12 and subscribe to topics that the ESP-12 may use to send data back to the mobile device.
6. **Security**:
   - Depending on your application's security requirements, you can implement various security measures, such as enabling SSL/TLS encryption, using secure authentication mechanisms, and restricting topic access to authorized clients.

The ESP-12 device and the mobile MQTT client application communicate via an MQTT broker, which acts as an intermediary for message exchange. This architecture allows for efficient, real-time, and bidirectional communication between the embedded device and the mobile client, making it suitable for IoT applications, home automation, and remote-control scenarios.

MQTT Broker

This guide will provide an overview of the process of configuring a Master-versus-Tunnel (MQTT) broker on a cloud operating system based on Linux, in order to ensure not only effective communication but also comprehensive security measures to safeguard confidential information.

Part 1: Setting Up an MQTT Broker

Step 1: Choose Your Cloud Provider and Server

Select a cloud provider that fits your requirements. Providers like AWS, Google Cloud, Azure, or DigitalOcean offer a variety of Linux-based virtual machines (VMs) that you can use to host your MQTT broker. Once you have chosen your cloud provider, create a VM instance with a suitable Linux distribution. For this guide, we'll use Ubuntu. Think of your MQTT broker like a mailbox. To have a mailbox, you need a physical place to put it. In this step, you're choosing a company that provides this place (the cloud provider) and then deciding on the specific spot (the server) where your mailbox (the MQTT broker) will be located.

Step 2: SSH into Your VM

Access your VM via SSH. You can use the command line in Linux or tools like PuTTY for Windows. Make sure you have the SSH key pair for authentication, as it enhances security. Imagine your server as a house with a locked door. SSH is like having the key to that door. In this step, you're using your key to open the door to your server and enter your house (your VM).

```
ssh -i path/to/your/key.pem user@your_server_ip
```

Step 3: Update Your System

Before installing any software, ensure your system is up-to-date. Run the following commands:

```
sudo apt update

sudo apt upgrade
```

- `sudo apt update`: This command updates the list of available packages and their versions.
- `sudo apt upgrade`: This command upgrades the installed packages to their latest versions.

Step 4: Install MQTT Broker (Mosquitto)

Install the Mosquitto MQTT broker, a popular choice among MQTT brokers, using the package manager:

```
sudo apt install mosquitto mosquitto-clients
```

This command installs the Mosquitto MQTT broker and client tools. The broker will be running on your VM, and the client tools allow you to interact with the broker for testing and administration.

Step 5: Test Your MQTT Broker

You can test whether your MQTT broker is working correctly by subscribing and publishing to a topic. Open two terminal windows. In one window, subscribe to a topic, and in the other, publish a message to the same topic.

In Terminal 1 (Subscriber):

```
mosquitto_sub -t test/topic
```

In Terminal 2 (Publisher):

```
mosquitto_pub -t test/topic -m "Hello, MQTT!"
```

If you see **"Hello, MQTT!"** in Terminal 1, your MQTT broker is up and running.

- You can use the **mosquitto_sub** command to subscribe to an MQTT topic.
- You can use the **mosquitto_pub** command to publish a message to the same topic.

Part 2: Securing Your MQTT Broker

Now that you have set up your MQTT broker, it's crucial to secure it to protect your data and devices. Here are some important security measures:

Step 6: Enable Password Authentication

By default, Mosquitto does not enforce authentication, allowing anyone to connect. To enable password authentication, create a password file and add user credentials.

Create the password file by using the following command:

```
sudo mosquitto_passwd -c /etc/mosquitto/passwd your_username
```

You'll be prompted to enter your password. After this, add more users without the **-c** flag by using the following command:

```
sudo mosquitto_passwd /etc/mosquitto/passwd another_username
```

- You create a password file using **mosquitto_passwd**, specifying the username and their password.
- For additional users, you can add them to the same password file.

Step 7: Configure Mosquitto

Edit the Mosquitto configuration file to enable password authentication and restrict unauthorized access.

Use a text editor to open the configuration file:

```
sudo nano /etc/mosquitto/mosquitto.conf
```

Add the following lines at the end of the file:

```
allow_anonymous false password_file /etc/mosquitto/passwd
```

Save the file and restart Mosquitto:

```
sudo systemctl restart mosquitto
```

This configuration ensures that anonymous access is disabled and points to the password file you created earlier. After saving the file, restart Mosquitto to apply the changes.

Step 8: Set Up TLS/SSL Encryption

To secure data in transit, you should enable TLS/SSL encryption. Create a directory to store your SSL certificates:

```
sudo mkdir /etc/mosquitto/certs cd /etc/mosquitto/certs
```

Generate self-signed certificates for testing. For production, consider using certificates from a trusted certificate authority (CA):

```
openssl req -new -newkey rsa:2048 -days 365 -nodes -x509 -keyout server.
key -out server.crt
```

Edit the Mosquitto configuration file again:

```
sudo nano /etc/mosquitto/mosquitto.conf
```

Add the following lines to enable TLS/SSL:

```
listener 8883

certfile /etc/mosquitto/certs/server.crt

keyfile /etc/mosquitto/certs/server.key
```

Save and exit the file. Restart Mosquitto to apply the changes:

```
sudo systemctl restart mosquitto
```

Step 9: Firewall Rules

Configure your firewall to limit access to your MQTT broker. By default, allow incoming connections on port 1883 for MQTT and port 8883 for MQTT over TLS. Deny all other incoming connections. Adjust the following rules according to your specific firewall configuration:

```
sudo ufw allow 1883

sudo ufw allow 8883

sudo ufw deny from any to any
```

Don't forget to enable the firewall:

```
sudo ufw enable
```

Step 10: Monitor and Log

Keep an eye on your MQTT broker's logs for any unusual activity. Monitor the system's resource usage and set up intrusion detection if needed. Tools like Fail2ban can help protect against brute-force attacks.

By following these steps and implementing security measures, you can set up and secure an MQTT broker on a Linux-based cloud OS. This ensures that your MQTT communication is not only efficient but also well-protected from potential threats, making it suitable for various IoT and real-time applications. Remember that security is an ongoing process, and staying vigilant is essential for maintaining a safe MQTT environment.

Securing MQTT Communication

The lightweight and efficient nature of MQTT technology makes it an appealing option for IoT devices. However, its features can also pose security risks. Due to the limited resources available to IoT devices, they may not be able to implement comprehensive security measures due to a lack of computational capacity and memory. Therefore, it is essential to ensure the security of MQTT communications, particularly when handling sensitive data or running critical applications. The following are some of the primary reasons for MQTT safety:

- **Data privacy:** The use of IoT devices often involves the handling of sensitive data, including personal information, medical data, or confidential business information. Unauthorized access to such data can result in privacy violations and legal repercussions.
- **Data Integrity:** It is essential to ensure the integrity of the data to avoid any manipulation or alteration of information during transmission. Data integrity ensures that the information remains correct and reliable.
- **Availability:** MQTT services must be available for devices to communicate without interruption. Security breaches may cause service interruptions, which may affect the functionality of IoT devices.
- **Authentication:** It is essential to verify the identity of both the publisher and the subscriber in MQTT communications. Unauthorized devices must not be permitted to access or publish data.
- **Authorization:** Even after verification, devices should be authorized to access only those resources for which they have been explicitly granted permission. Authorization mechanisms assist in restricting access to particular topics or resources.

To address these security concerns, MQTT can be secured at multiple levels. Here are some essential measures to ensure MQTT communication remains protected:

- **Implement authentication and authorization:** MQTT authentication is the process of verifying the identity of clients (physical devices) that connect to an MQTT server. Client credentials should be valid, including usernames, passwords, digital certificates, and more. Strong authentication mechanisms ensure that only authenticated devices can connect to the server.

  On the other hand, authorization defines what clients are permitted to do after they have been authenticated. This includes the ability to control which topics they are permitted to publish or subscribe to. Setting up Access Control Lists (ACLs) allows you to define who can access certain topics, thus preventing unauthorized access to confidential information.
- **Use a secure connection:** It is essential to ensure the security of data in transit to avoid interception and manipulation. TLS or SSL (Secure Sockets Layer) encryption facilitates the secure transmission of data through an MQTT channel. Clients must use certificates to authenticate themselves when establishing an MQTT connection, and the MQTT broker must support the use of TLS/SSL encryption. This guarantees that data is securely encrypted as it moves from the client to the broker.
- **Protect credentials and keys:** It is imperative to ensure the secure storage of credentials to avoid unauthorized access. It is recommended that clients store their usernames and passwords in a secure manner, and that MQTT brokers protect the private keys associated with TLS/SSL. Additional key protection can be achieved through the utilization of hardware security modules or secure enclaves.
- **Regularly update MQTT brokers and clients:** As with any software, vulnerabilities can be identified and patched over the course of time. Therefore, it is important to ensure that all software components are kept up to date to prevent them from becoming vulnerable to known security vulnerabilities. This applies to MQTT broker software and client libraries.
- **Monitor and audit MQTT traffic:** MQTT traffic monitoring is essential to identify anomalous or potentially malicious traffic patterns. Tools and services that offer real-time traffic monitoring, alerts, and traffic analysis can be utilized. Additionally, regular audits of traffic logs can assist in the detection and investigation of security incidents.

- **Secure broker configuration:** Properly configuring your MQTT broker is essential. This includes setting security-related options, such as enabling or disabling anonymous access, defining maximum connections, and specifying the location of ACL files. A well-configured broker helps prevent security misconfigurations that could lead to vulnerabilities.
- **Plan for DDoS mitigation:** Distributed Denial of Service (DDoS) attacks can disrupt MQTT services. Implementing DDoS mitigation measures, such as rate limiting, IP blocking, and load balancing, can help maintain MQTT service availability during attacks.

As the IoT ecosystem continues to grow, the need for strong MQTT security protocols increases. The implementation of authentication, encryption, and access control facilitate the safeguarding of sensitive data and ensures that only authorized devices are authorized to access MQTT. Monitoring, updates, and secure configuration are essential components of an effective MQTT security posture. Following these best practices will enable you to maximize the efficiency of MQTT while preserving the security of your IoT data.

Conclusion

In this chapter, we learned that the MQTT protocol stands as a robust and versatile solution for addressing the complex challenges of communication in today's networked world. Its lightweight design, coupled with the publish-subscribe model, enables efficient and scalable data exchange among connected devices. MQTT's inherent reliability, through its Quality-of-Service levels, ensures that messages are delivered as required, making it suitable for both telemetry and command-and-control applications. The protocol's support for bi-directional communication, security measures, and open-source ecosystem further enhance its appeal, fostering its adoption in various domains.

As IoT continues to grow and diversify, MQTT remains a critical enabler of efficient, real-time, and secure data exchange between devices and central systems. Its openness, flexibility, and resilience to network constraints make it an essential tool for developers and engineers across industries, supporting applications ranging from smart homes to smart cities and from industrial automation to environmental monitoring. MQTT's enduring relevance in the ever-expanding realm of connected devices underscores its pivotal role in shaping the future of the digital landscape.

In the upcoming chapter, we will explore the fascinating world of Machine to Machine (M2M) communication within the realm of the Internet of Things

(IoT). M2M communication refers to the seamless exchange of data between connected devices without human intervention, enabling them to collaborate and perform tasks efficiently. We will dive into the underlying principles and technologies that facilitate M2M communication, including wireless protocols, sensor networks, and data transmission methods. Additionally, we analyze real-world applications of M2M communication in various domains such as smart cities, industrial automation, healthcare, and transportation.

References

1. The MQTT Expert. "MQTT Security Fundamentals." https://www.mqtt.org/security
2. https://public.dhe.ibm.com/software/dw/webservices/ws-mqtt/MQTT_V3.1_Protocol_Specific.pdf
3. OASIS - MQTT Version 3.1.1 Specification: https://docs.oasis-open.org/mqtt/mqtt/v3.1.1/os/mqtt-v3.1.1-os.html
4. MQTT.org - MQTT Essentials: https://www.mqtt.org/qtt-essentials/
5. Eclipse IoT - MQTT: https://iot.eclipse.org/protocols/mqtt/
6. A. P. Stanford-Clark and A. R. Nipper, "Introduction to the MQTT Protocol," IBM developerWorks, 2009.
7. T. Hunkeler, S. Figi, and C. Trösch, "MQTT-S – A publish/subscribe protocol for Wireless Sensor Networks," in Proceedings of the 6th International Conference on Embedded Networked Sensor Systems, 2008.

CHAPTER 7

Machine-to-Machine Communication

Introduction

The Internet of Things (IoT) has completely changed our lives and how we work. It has connected our world to the digital one, allowing devices to communicate with each other, exchange data, and make smart decisions. At the core of this whole thing is M2M communication. In this chapter, we will discuss how M2M communication came to be in IoT, how it's changing, why it's important, and what it means for different industries.

IoT is a network of devices, sensors, and systems that communicate with each other and work together to collect, analyze and share data. The data collected often provides useful insights and enables automation in a wide range of applications, including smart homes and cities, industrial automation, healthcare, and more.

One of the most important aspects of IoT is M2M communication. M2M communication is the direct exchange of information between devices without the need for human intervention. In simple terms, it enables devices to communicate with each other, make decisions, and respond to real-time changes. This exchange of information is fundamental to IoT and allows devices to work together to accomplish specific objectives or tasks.

The term **M2M communication** has its roots in the early days of IoT. In the past, M2M communication was used in industrial automation and for remote monitoring systems. These systems had limited capabilities and required complicated, proprietary communication protocols.

It was not until the internet was introduced and standardized communication protocols were developed that M2M really took off. The growth of IP technologies and the widespread adoption of the internet made it easier for M2M to be integrated into IoT.

The significance of M2M communication stems from its ability to facilitate real-time exchange of data and automation, which reduces human intervention and improves operational efficiency across a wide range of industries.

M2M communication plays an essential role in enhancing safety, security, and scalability, as well as the user experience of IoT applications.

Whether it's in healthcare to remotely monitor patients, smart cities to manage cities more efficiently, agriculture to produce precision crops, industrial automation to streamline operations, or transportation to drive autonomous vehicles and manage logistics, IoT M2M communications are at the heart of unlocking the full promise of the Internet, ultimately transforming our way of life and work in an interconnected world.

Structure

In this chapter, we will cover the following topics:

- M2M Communication in Sensor Networking
- Significance of M2M in Sensor Network
- M2M with ESP Microcontrollers
- Wi-Fi Modes in ESP Devices
    - Key Features of ESP Microcontrollers
- Station Mode – Connecting ESP to Wi-Fi
    - Code for Connecting to Wi-Fi
- Access Point Mode
    - Code for Access Point Mode
- Client–Server Communication using ESP-12 Microcontrollers
    - Code for Server
    - Code for Client

- Wireless Sensor Network using Client-Server M2M
    - o Code for Server
    - o Code for Client
- ESP-Now
    - o Key Features of ESP-NOW
    - o Implementing ESP-NOW
    - o Sample Sketch

M2M Communication in Sensor Networking

M2M communication has become a key concept in the ever-changing technology landscape, driving sensor networking and the wider IoT ecosystem. M2M communication refers to the communication between devices and sensors that allows them to communicate and exchange information without the need for human intervention. Here, we will explore M2M communications in sensor networking, its importance, its technical foundations, and its multi-layered applications across different domains.

M2M Communication

M2M communication, often referred to as Machine-to-Machine or Machine-to-Machine Interaction, is the technology that allows machines or devices to communicate and collaborate without the need for human involvement. It is a fundamental concept within the IoT paradigm, where devices are equipped with sensors and communication modules, enabling them to collect, transmit, and receive data, as well as respond to data received from other devices. This seamless exchange of information facilitates automation, decision-making, and the execution of various tasks, ranging from routine processes to complex operations.

Sensor Networking

Sensor networking, on the other hand, is a branch of technology centered on the deployment of sensors that can monitor and collect data from the surrounding environment. Sensors, which are vital components of IoT ecosystems, come in various forms, such as temperature sensors, motion detectors, environmental sensors, and more. These sensors are interconnected through networks and are capable of relaying data to central systems for analysis or taking autonomous actions based on their observations. Sensor networks are the eyes and ears of IoT, collecting critical data that fuels decision-making and automation.

Here is the technical basis for M2M communication in sensor networking.

Sensor Nodes

Sensor nodes are the building blocks of sensor networks. These nodes are typically equipped with sensors, processing units, and communication interfaces. They can be stationary or mobile, depending on the specific application. Each sensor node is designed to sense specific parameters, such as temperature, humidity, or motion, and transmit this data to a central location or other connected nodes. Sensor nodes play a crucial role in M2M communication by providing real-time data for analysis and decision-making.

Communication Protocols

For M2M communication in sensor networking to function seamlessly, various communication protocols and standards are in place. These protocols govern how data is transmitted, received, and processed between sensor nodes and central systems. Common communication protocols used in sensor networking include Zigbee, LoRaWAN, MQTT, CoAP, and HTTP. Each protocol has its own set of advantages and trade-offs, making them suitable for different applications, whether it be low power consumption, long-range communication, or secure data transmission.

Data Aggregation and Processing

In M2M communication, the sheer volume of data generated by sensor nodes can be overwhelming. To manage this data effectively, sensor networks often employ data aggregation and processing techniques. Data aggregation involves combining data from multiple sensor nodes into a single data stream, reducing the amount of information that needs to be transmitted. Processing this aggregated data, whether on the sensor nodes themselves or in central systems, allows for the extraction of meaningful insights, enabling better decision-making.

Significance of M2M in Sensor Networking

The importance of M2M communications in sensor networking is far-reaching and encompasses many aspects of our modern lives and industries. Here are the top reasons M2M communication is essential for sensor networking:

- **Real-time monitoring and decision-making:** M2M communication allows you to monitor the environment or assets in real-time through sensor networks. Real-time data allows you to make quick decisions and act quickly when conditions change. For instance, in a smart agricultural application, sensors can track soil moisture levels and automatically turn on irrigation systems when the soil gets too dry. Not only does this conserve resources, but it also improves crop yield.
- **Enhanced efficiency and automation:** M2M communication within sensor networking is at the heart of automation. Automation of repetitive tasks and processes can significantly improve operational efficiency for businesses and industries. For example, in manufacturing, sensors on the production lines can identify defects and prompt the removal of defective products, thereby reducing waste and increasing product quality.
- **Scalability:** The advantage of M2M communication is that sensor networks can be easily scaled. You can add new sensor nodes to your existing network without having to reconfigure it. This flexibility is important for applications that need to monitor large areas or large assets, such as smart cities or logistics.
- **Improved safety and security:** M2M communication within sensor networks can enhance safety and security across a wide range of applications. For example, in the oil and gas industry, sensors can be used to detect leaks or unusual conditions, triggering real-time responses to avoid accidents. Surveillance cameras with sensors can also detect security breaches and notify authorities in real-time.
- **Consumer convenience:** In consumer-centric IoT applications, the integration of M2M communications in sensor networking improves ease of use and user experience. For instance, in smart homes, sensors automatically detect the preferences of the home's occupants and automatically adapt the lighting, temperature, and security settings to meet their needs. This degree of automation and customization improves the overall comfort and quality of life for homeowners.

M2M with ESP Microcontrollers

The ESP microcontrollers, developed by Espressif Systems, have become significant players in the world of Machine-to-Machine (M2M) communication, especially in the context of the Internet of Things. These microcontrollers, including the popular ESP8266 and ESP32 series, offer a range of features and capabilities that make them well-suited for M2M communication in various applications.

Key Features of ESP Microcontrollers

- **Wireless Connectivity**: ESP microcontrollers are equipped with integrated Wi-Fi and, in the case of the ESP32, also Bluetooth capabilities. These wireless interfaces enable seamless communication between devices over local networks or the internet, making them ideal for M2M communication.
- **Low Power Consumption**: ESP microcontrollers are designed to operate efficiently, which is crucial for battery-powered IoT devices. Their low power modes and sleep states allow for extended battery life, making them suitable for remote and energy-conscious applications.
- **High Processing Power**: ESP32, in particular, offers dual-core processors and higher clock speeds, providing the processing power required for data processing, encryption, and running complex applications.
- **Rich Set of I/O Interfaces**: These microcontrollers have a diverse range of digital and analog input/output pins, supporting various sensors and actuators, which are essential for collecting and acting on data in M2M scenarios.
- **Secure Communication**: ESP microcontrollers offer built-in security features, including secure boot, flash encryption, and support for secure sockets (SSL/TLS). This is vital for safeguarding data and communications in M2M applications.
- **Open-Source Ecosystem**: The ESP-IDF (Espressif IoT Development Framework) and Arduino IDE support these microcontrollers, making it easy for developers to create and deploy M2M applications. The large and active open-source community contributes to the rapid development of libraries and resources.
- **Affordability**: ESP microcontrollers are cost-effective solutions, making them accessible for a wide range of M2M applications, from hobbyist projects to commercial products.
- **Support for Multiple Protocols**: ESP-12/32 supports multiple communication protocols, including TCP/IP, HTTP, MQTT, and CoAP. This flexibility allows developers to choose the most suitable protocol for their specific applications, making it a versatile platform for various Wi-Fi-based projects.

Wi-Fi Modes in ESP devices

NodeMCU is an ESP8266-based development board that is commonly used in Internet of Things and Embedded Systems projects. The NodeMCU supports various operating modes that enable it to perform different tasks and functions. The main operating modes of the NodeMCU are as follows:

- **Station Mode (ST):**
  - **Description:** In Station mode, the NodeMCU connects to an existing Wi-Fi network as a client. This mode is commonly used when the NodeMCU needs to interact with other devices on the network or access the internet.
  - **Usage:** Ideal for scenarios where the NodeMCU needs to communicate with a central server or other devices on the same network.
- **Access Point Mode (AP):**
  - **Description:** In Access Point mode, the NodeMCU functions as a Wi-Fi hotspot and allows other devices to connect to it. The NodeMCU acts as a router, providing IP addresses to connected devices.
  - **Usage:** Useful when you want to create a local network where devices can communicate directly with the NodeMCU, such as in scenarios where the NodeMCU hosts a web server or acts as a gateway.
- **Station + Access Point Mode (ST+AP):**
  - **Description:** In this mode, the NodeMCU operates both as a Wi-Fi client (Station mode) and as an Access Point. It can connect to an existing Wi-Fi network while simultaneously providing a new network for other devices to connect to.
  - **Usage:** This mode is beneficial when you want the NodeMCU to connect to the internet via an existing Wi-Fi network and, at the same time, provide its own local network.
- **Mesh (Mesh):**
  - **Description:** The ESP8266 Mesh mode allows multiple ESP8266 devices to communicate with each other in a self-organizing mesh network. Devices in the network can act as both clients and access points.
  - **Usage:** Suitable for scenarios where multiple ESP8266 devices need to communicate with each other without a centralized router. Each device in the mesh can relay data to others, forming a dynamic and decentralized network.

- **Promiscuous Mode (Promisc):**
  - **Description:** In Promiscuous mode, the ESP8266 can capture and analyze all Wi-Fi packets in the vicinity, even those not intended for it. This mode is often used for network monitoring and packet sniffing.
  - **Usage:** Commonly employed for network security analysis, troubleshooting, or monitoring network traffic within a specific area.

These modes provide flexibility and versatility to NodeMCU, making it suitable for a wide range of applications. Depending on the project requirements, you can choose the appropriate mode or even switch between modes dynamically to adapt to changing conditions or user inputs.

Station Mode: Connecting ESP to Wi-Fi

Connecting an ESP-12 module to a Wi-Fi network involves several steps, including configuring the module, providing it with the network credentials, and initiating the connection. Transferring data over Wi-Fi is the most common method of M2M communication using ESP devices. In this section, we will focus on ESP devices, their working with Wi-Fi, and the process of data transmission over Wi-Fi using various protocols.

Connecting ESP to a Wi-Fi Network

Here is a code for connecting the ESP-12 to a Wi-Fi network using Arduino IDE:

```
#include <ESP8266WiFi.h>


const char* ssid = "YourWiFiSSID";

const char* password = "YourWiFiPassword";


void setup() {

  Serial.begin(115200);

  delay(10);

  Serial.println();


  WiFi.begin(ssid, password);
```

```
  while (WiFi.status() != WL_CONNECTED) {
    delay(500);
    Serial.print(".");
  }

  Serial.println("WiFi connected");
  Serial.print("IP address: ");
  Serial.println(WiFi.localIP());
}

void loop() {
  // Your code here
}
```

Code Explanation

```
#include <ESP8266WiFi.h>
```

- This line includes the necessary library for Wi-Fi communication. The code uses the **ESP8266WiFi** library to interact with the ESP8266 Wi-Fi module, which is embedded in the ESP-12 module.

```
const char* ssid = "YourWiFiSSID";
const char* password = "YourWiFiPassword";
```

- These lines define two variables, **ssid** and **password**, which store your Wi-Fi network credentials. Replace **"YourWiFiSSID"** with the name (SSID) of your Wi-Fi network and **"YourWiFiPassword"** with the password to connect to the network. These are the values that the ESP-12 module will use to join your Wi-Fi network.

```
void setup() {
  Serial.begin(115200);
  delay(10);
  Serial.println();
```

- The **setup()** function is where you initialize the code. It begins by setting up the serial communication with the ESP-12 module. The **Serial.begin(115200)** function initializes serial communication at a baud rate of 115200, allowing you to send and receive data between your computer and the ESP-12 module.

- **delay(10)** is a small delay to ensure that the serial communication is stable. **Serial.println()** prints a newline character, creating a clean separation in the serial monitor output.

```
WiFi.begin(ssid, password);

 while (WiFi.status() != WL_CONNECTED) {
   delay(500);
   Serial.print(".");
 }
```

- In this section, the code attempts to connect to the Wi-Fi network using the provided ssid and password. **WiFi.begin(ssid, password)** initiates the connection process. The code then enters a loop where it checks the connection status using **WiFi.status().**
- The loop waits for the connection to be established. During this time, the code prints a series of dots (.) in the serial monitor. This serves as a visual indicator to show that the ESP-12 module is attempting to connect to the Wi-Fi network.

```
Serial.println("WiFi connected");
Serial.print("IP address: ");
Serial.println(WiFi.localIP());
```

- After the ESP-12 module successfully connects to the Wi-Fi network, the code prints WiFi connected to the serial monitor. It then retrieves and prints the IP address assigned to the module using **WiFi.localIP().** This IP address is crucial for communicating with the module on the network.

```
void loop() {
  // Your code here
}
```

- The **setup()** function is followed by the **loop()** function. The **loop()** function is where you can include your own code to perform various tasks. It runs continuously once the ESP-12 module is connected to the Wi-Fi network.

The example provided does not include any specific tasks within the **loop()** function, as it is designed to demonstrate the Wi-Fi connection process. You can add your own code here to control devices, collect data, or perform any other desired actions in your Wi-Fi-based project.

This example is a simple demonstration of connecting an ESP-12 to a defined Wi-Fi network hardcoded in the program. There are multiple use cases and IoT applications where the user will not be able to define the Wi-Fi ssid and password in the code. Hence, there needs to be a way to provide the Wi-Fi credentials without hardcoding them into the sketch. The solution to that is WiFiManger library.

Wi-Fi Commissioning Using Wi-Fi Manager

The WiFiManager library is available for both ESP-12 and ESP-32-based microcontrollers and plays a very important part in the Wi-Fi commissioning process by providing the ssid and the password to the ESP devices remotely via smartphone or PC. It is particularly useful in IoT projects, as it allows devices to connect to different Wi-Fi networks without the need for reprogramming each time the network changes.

Here are the features of WiFiManager Library:

- **Dynamic Wi-Fi Configuration**: WiFiManager enables dynamic configuration of Wi-Fi network settings, eliminating the need to hardcode SSID and password into your ESP device's code. This feature is beneficial when the device needs to connect to various networks in different locations.
- **Captive Portal**: WiFiManager creates a captive portal that appears as a web page when the device is first powered on or unable to connect to a saved Wi-Fi network. Users can input network credentials via their web browser.
- **Auto-Connect**: WiFiManager attempts to connect to a saved network if the credentials have been previously configured. If successful, the captive portal does not appear. This is useful for devices that regularly connect to the same network.
- **Fallback AP Mode**: If the device cannot connect to a network and no credentials are saved, WiFiManager can switch to Access Point (AP) mode. The device acts as a hotspot, allowing you to configure it via a smartphone or computer.
- **Customization**: WiFiManager can be customized to match the look and feel of your application. You can modify the portal's appearance by adding your branding and changing the UI elements.

- **Configuration Persistence**: Once network credentials are entered and saved, WiFiManager stores them in the ESP device's non-volatile memory, ensuring that the device can automatically connect to known networks on subsequent power-ups.

Using WiFiManager Library in ESP Devices

Here are the steps to use the WiFiManager library in your ESP devices:

- **Install WiFiManager Library**:
  - In the Arduino IDE, go to **`Sketch -> Include Library -> Manage Libraries.`**
  - Search for WiFiManager and install the library.
- **Include WiFiManager Library in Your Sketch**:
  - In your Arduino sketch, include the WiFiManager library at the beginning of your code using the following line:

    ```
    #include <WiFiManager.h>
    ```
- **Initialize WiFiManager:**
  - Create a global instance of the WiFiManager class:

    ```
    WiFiManager wifiManager;
    ```
- **Configure WiFi Parameters:**
  - In your **`setup()`** function, you can configure WiFiManager with additional parameters. For example, you can set a custom hostname for the device:

    ```
    wifiManager.setHostname("MyESPDevice");
    ```
- **Connect to Wi-Fi Using WiFiManager:**
  - In your **`setup()`** function, use the **`autoConnect()`** method to initiate Wi-Fi configuration:

    ```
    if (!wifiManager.autoConnect("MyESPDevice-AP")) {
    // Failed to connect or configure, take appropriate action
    }
    ```

  The **`autoConnect()`** method will attempt to connect to a known network. If it fails, it will start an Access Point with the SSID **`MyESPDevice-AP`**. Users can connect to this hotspot and configure the Wi-Fi settings.

- **Save Wi-Fi Credentials:**

  After configuration, WiFiManager will save the SSID and password in the ESP device's flash memory. Subsequent reboots will attempt to connect to the saved network automatically.

- **Customize the Captive Portal (Optional):**

  You can customize the captive portal by adding custom HTML, CSS, and JavaScript. This step is optional but allows you to tailor the portal to your specific requirements.

- **Add Your Application Logic:**

  Incorporate your application's logic into the `loop()` function. WiFiManager handles the Wi-Fi configuration aspect, while your code can focus on the device's main functionality.

Sample Code for WiFiManager

```
#include <WiFiManager.h>


WiFiManager wifiManager;


void setup() {

  Serial.begin(115200);

  wifiManager.setHostname("MyESPDevice");


  if (!wifiManager.autoConnect("MyESPDevice-AP")) {

    Serial.println("Failed to connect to WiFi or configure.");

    // Add code to handle the failure, e.g., deep sleep or error recovery.

  }


  // WiFiManager handles connection and saves credentials, no need to
  code it.

}


void loop() {
```

```
  // Your application logic here.
}
```

In this example, WiFiManager is used to set up Wi-Fi configuration. If a saved network is available, the ESP device will connect to it. Otherwise, it will create an Access Point for configuration. Once configured, the device will automatically connect to the saved network on future boot-ups.

By using the WiFiManager library, you can make your ESP devices more user-friendly, allowing for easy and flexible Wi-Fi configuration, which is particularly valuable for IoT projects where devices may move between different networks or locations.

Access Point Mode

Access Point (AP) mode in NodeMCU allows the NodeMCU device to act as a Wi-Fi hotspot, enabling other devices to connect to it. This mode is particularly useful when you want the NodeMCU to host a local network, and connected devices can communicate with the NodeMCU directly.

Here's the code for using NodeMCU in Access point mode:

```
#include <ESP8266WiFi.h>

const char *apSSID = "NodeMCU_AP";
const char *apPassword = "password123";

void setup() {
    Serial.begin(115200);

    // Set up NodeMCU as an Access Point
    WiFi.softAP(apSSID, apPassword);

    // Obtain and print the Access Point's IP address
    IPAddress apIP = WiFi.softAPIP();
    Serial.print("Access Point IP address: ");
    Serial.println(apIP);
```

```
}

void loop() {
    // Check if there are clients connected to the Access Point
    if (WiFi.softAPgetStationNum() > 0) {
        Serial.println("Client connected to Access Point!");
    }

    // Your loop code
}
```

Code Explanation

```
#include <ESP8266WiFi.h>
```

- This line includes the necessary library for Wi-Fi communication. The code uses the ESP8266WiFi library to interact with the ESP8266 Wi-Fi module, which is embedded in the ESP-12 module.

```
const char* apSSID = "YourWiFiSSID";
const char* apPassword = "YourWiFiPassword";
```

- These lines define two variables, **apSSID** and **apPassword**. Set the SSID (network name) and password for your Access Point. This is the information that other devices will use to connect to the NodeMCU's network.

```
void setup() {
    Serial.begin(115200);

    // Set up NodeMCU as an Access Point
    WiFi.softAP(apSSID, apPassword);

    // Additional setup code
}
```

- In the **setup()** function, configure the NodeMCU to operate in Access Point mode using the **WiFi.softAP()** function.

- This code snippet initializes the NodeMCU as an Access Point with the specified SSID and password.

```
void setup() {
    Serial.begin(115200);

    // Set up NodeMCU as an Access Point
    WiFi.softAP(apSSID, apPassword);

    // Obtain and print the Access Point's IP address
    IPAddress apIP = WiFi.softAPIP();
    Serial.print("Access Point IP address: ");
    Serial.println(apIP);

    // Additional setup code
}
```

- Optionally, you can obtain the IP address assigned to the Access Point. This can be useful if you want to provide a web interface or other services hosted by the NodeMCU.

```
void loop() {
    // Check if there are clients connected to the Access Point
    if (WiFi.softAPgetStationNum() > 0) {
        Serial.println("Client connected to Access Point!");
    }

    // Your loop code
}
```

- In the **loop()** function, you can handle client connections. For example, you might want to check if any clients are connected

In this example, the NodeMCU is set up as an Access Point with the SSID "NodeMCU_AP" and password "password123." The IP address of the Access Point is printed to the serial monitor. The **loop()** function checks if any clients are connected to the Access Point and prints a message if so.

This Access Point mode is beneficial when you want devices to connect directly to the NodeMCU, creating a local network for communication. It's commonly used in scenarios where the NodeMCU hosts a web server, provides a user interface, or acts as a central hub for IoT devices.

Client-Server Communication Using ESP-12 Microcontroller

The ESP-12 microcontroller is capable of running in both station mode and access point mode. This allows the use of HTTP protocol, enabling ESP devices to function as both a client and a server. Here, the ESP-12 in station mode acts as a client, while the one in AP mode acts as a server, making communication and data transmission between them possible.

Let's consider one example using two different ESP-12 modules, one acting as a client and the other as a server. The client is a door sensor attached to the ESP-12, which detects the current state of the door (open/close) and transfers this data to server ESP-12. The server ESP-12 has an LED connected to it, which turns on when the door is opened. There are two sketches involved in this, one for the client and another for the server. Let's take a look at them one by one.

Server Side Code

```
#include <ESP8266WiFi.h>

#include <WiFiClient.h>

#include <ESP8266WebServer.h>

#include <ESP8266HTTPClient.h>


const char* ssid = "Nodemcu_AP";

const char* password = "11223344";

int max_connection = 8;



IPAddress staticIP(10,10,10,1); // IP address from Admin pannel

IPAddress gateway(10,10,10,1);

IPAddress subnet(255,255,255,0);
```

```
int httpCode;

HTTPClient http;

ESP8266WebServer server(80); //Server on port 80

void handleRoot() {
  server.send(200, «text/plain», «hello from esp8266!»);
}
void dro() {
  server.send(200, «text/plain», «Door Opened» );
  Serial.println(«Door Opened»);
  digitalWrite(D2, HIGH);
}
void drc() {
  server.send(200, «text/plain», «Door Closed» );
  Serial.println(«Door Closed»);
  digitalWrite(D2, LOW);;
}


void setup(void){

  Serial.begin(115200);
  Serial.println(«»);
  WiFi.mode(WIFI_AP);
  WiFi.softAP(ssid, password, 1, false, max_connection);
  WiFi.softAPConfig(staticIP, gateway, subnet
```

```
  Serial.printf(«Stations connected to soft-AP = %d\n»,    WiFi.
  softAPgetStationNum());


  IPAddress myIP = WiFi.softAPIP(); //Get IP address

  Serial.print(«HotSpt IP:»);

  Serial.println(myIP);

   pinMode(D2, OUTPUT);


   delay(1000);


   server.on(«/», handleRoot);

   server.on(«/dro», dro);

   server.on(«/drc», drc);

   server.begin();                  //Start server

   Serial.println(«HTTP server started»);

}


void loop(void){


      server.handleClient();          //Handle client requests

}
```

Code Explanation

```
#include <ESP8266WiFi.h>

#include <WiFiClient.h>

#include <ESP8266WebServer.h>

#include <ESP8266HTTPClient.h>
```

- These lines include the necessary libraries for Wi-Fi communication, handling client connections, managing a web server, and making HTTP requests using the ESP8266.

```
const char* ssid = "Nodemcu_AP";
const char* password = "11223344";
int max_connection = 8;
```

- Defines the credentials for the Access Point (AP). **ssid** and **password** represent the network name and password, respectively; **max_connection** specifies the maximum number of allowed connections to the AP.

```
IPAddress staticIP(10,10,10,1); // IP address from Admin panel
IPAddress gateway(10,10,10,1);
IPAddress subnet(255,255,255,0);
```

- Defines the static IP address, gateway, and subnet mask for the Access Point. These settings are used for configuring the network in static mode.

```
int httpCode;
HTTPClient http;
ESP8266WebServer server(80); // Server on port 80
```

- **httpCode** is declared as an integer for storing HTTP response codes. An **HTTPClient** object **http** is created for handling HTTP requests. An **ESP8266WebServer** object **server** is initialized on port 80 to handle web server functionalities.

```
void handleRoot() {
  server.send(200, "text/plain", "hello from esp8266!");
}

void dro() {
  server.send(200, "text/plain", "Door Opened" );
  Serial.println("Door Opened");
  digitalWrite(D2, HIGH);
}

void drc() {
  server.send(200, "text/plain", "Door Closed" );
  Serial.println("Door Closed");
  digitalWrite(D2, LOW);;
}
```

- These functions define the responses when specific URLs are accessed. **`handleRoot()`** sends a **`"hello from esp8266!"`** message when the root URL is accessed. **`dro()`** and **`drc()`** send **`"Door Opened"`** and **`"Door Closed"`** messages, respectively, when corresponding URLs are accessed. They also toggle the state of pin D2 and print status messages to the serial monitor.

```
void setup(void){
  Serial.begin(115200);
  Serial.println("");
  WiFi.mode(WIFI_AP);            // Only Access point
  WiFi.softAP(ssid, password, 1, false, max_connection);
  WiFi.softAPConfig(staticIP, gateway, subnet);
  Serial.printf("Stations connected to soft-AP = %d\n", WiFi.
  softAPgetStationNum());

  IPAddress myIP = WiFi.softAPIP(); // Get IP address
  Serial.print("HotSpot IP:");
  Serial.println(myIP);

  pinMode(D2, OUTPUT);
  delay(1000);

  server.on("/", handleRoot);
  server.on("/dro", dro);
  server.on("/drc", drc);
  server.begin();
  Serial.println("HTTP server started");
}
```

- In the **`setup()`** function:
  - Serial communication is initiated.
  - NodeMCU is set to Access Point mode (**`WIFI_AP`**) and the Access Point is configured with provided credentials.
  - The soft AP configuration (static IP, gateway, subnet) is set.

  - The number of connected stations to the soft AP is printed to the serial monitor.
  - The IP address of the Access Point is obtained and printed.
  - Pin D2 is set as an output.
  - The server is configured to handle specific URLs (**"/"**, **"/dro"**, **"/drc"**) with corresponding functions.
  - The HTTP server is started.

    ```
    void loop(void){
      server.handleClient();
    }
    ```

- In the **loop()** function, **server.handleClient()** is called to handle incoming client requests.

Overall, this sketch sets up the NodeMCU in Access Point mode, creates an HTTP server, and defines specific responses when accessing different URLs hosted by the NodeMCU. It toggles the state of pin D2 based on certain URL accesses and provides status messages on the serial monitor.

Client Side Code

```
#include <ESP8266WiFi.h>

#include <ESP8266HTTPClient.h>

#include <ESP8266WebServer.h>


const char* ssid ="jio";

const char* password ="Hi, I'm Door Sensor";

IPAddress ip(10,10,10,55);

IPAddress gateway(10,10,10,1);

IPAddress subnet(255,255,255,0);


String message = "10101010";


ESP8266WebServer server(80);

void handleRoot() {
```

```
server.send(200, "text/html", message);

}

void setup() {
server.on("/", handleRoot);
server.begin();
Serial.begin(115200);
delay(500);
WiFi.config(ip,gateway,subnet);
for(uint8_t t = 4; t > 0; t--) {
Serial.printf("[SETUP] WAIT ...\n", t);
Serial.flush();
delay(1000);
}
WiFi.mode(WIFI_STA);
WiFi.disconnect(true);
WiFi.begin(ssid,password);
if(WiFi.status() != WL_CONNECTED) {
delay(500);
Serial.print(".");

Serial.println("Connected");
}
pinMode(D2,INPUT);
}

void loop() {
```

```
server.handleClient();

if((WiFi.status() == WL_CONNECTED))
  {
HTTPClient http;
if(digitalRead(D2) == HIGH)
{

http.begin("http://10.10.10.1/dro");//HTTP
Serial.print("10.10.10.1/dro");
int httpCode = http.GET();
http.end();
}

else if(digitalRead(D2) == LOW)
{
http.begin("http://10.10.10.1/drc");
Serial.println("10.10.10.1/drc");
int httpCode= http.GET();
http.end();
}
   }
}
```

Code Explanation

```
#include <ESP8266WiFi.h>
#include <ESP8266HTTPClient.h>
#include <ESP8266WebServer.h>
```

```
const char* ssid = "jio";
const char* password = "11223344";
IPAddress ip(10,10,10,55);
IPAddress gateway(10,10,10,1);
IPAddress subnet(255,255,255,0);

String message = "Hi, I'm Door Sensor";

ESP8266WebServer server(80);

void handleRoot() {
  server.send(200, "text/html", message);
}
```

- These lines include the necessary libraries for Wi-Fi communication, handling HTTP requests, and managing a web server on the ESP8266. It also define the Wi-Fi credentials (ssid and password), as well as the IP address, gateway, and subnet mask for configuring the Wi-Fi connection.
- The message is initialized as a string containing **"Hi, I'm Door Sensor."**
- An ESP8266WebServer object named server is created to handle HTTP requests on port 80. The **handleRoot()** function is defined to respond to requests at the root URL **("/")** by sending a text/html response with the content of the message variable.

```
void setup() {
  server.on("/", handleRoot);
  server.begin();
  Serial.begin(115200);
  delay(500);
  WiFi.config(ip, gateway, subnet);
  for (uint8_t t = 4; t > 0; t--) {
```

```
    Serial.printf("[SETUP] WAIT ...\n", t);
    Serial.flush();
    delay(1000);
  }
  WiFi.mode(WIFI_STA);
  WiFi.disconnect(true);
  WiFi.begin(ssid, password);
  if (WiFi.status() != WL_CONNECTED) {
    delay(500);
    Serial.print(".");
    Serial.println("Connected");
  }
  pinMode(D2, INPUT);
}
```

In the setup() function:

- The root `("/")` URL is associated with the **`handleRoot()`** function in the server.
- The server begins listening for incoming HTTP requests.
- Serial communication is initiated.
- A delay is added for setup.
- Wi-Fi configuration is set to use a static IP address (ip, gateway, subnet).
- The ESP8266 is set to Station mode (**`WIFI_STA`**) and any existing WiFi connection is disconnected.
- An attempt to connect to the specified WiFi network (ssid and password) is made. If not connected, dots are printed to the serial monitor and "Connected" is printed.

```
void loop() {
  server.handleClient();
  if ((WiFi.status() == WL_CONNECTED)) {
```

```
    HTTPClient http;

    if (digitalRead(D2) == HIGH) {
      http.begin("http://10.10.10.1/dro");
      Serial.print("10.10.10.1/dro");
      int httpCode = http.GET();
      http.end();
    } else if (digitalRead(D2) == LOW) {
      http.begin("http://10.10.10.1/drc");
      Serial.println("10.10.10.1/drc");
      int httpCode = http.GET();
      http.end();
    }
  }
}
```

In the **loop()** function:

- **server.handleClient()** checks for and handles incoming HTTP client requests to the server.
- If the Wi-Fi connection is established (WL_CONNECTED), an HTTPClient object http is created.
- Depending on the state of pin D2 (input), an HTTP GET request is made to either **"http://10.10.10.1/dro"** or **"http://10.10.10.1/drc."**
- The URLs are accessed based on the state of pin D2 being HIGH or LOW, and the HTTP response code is stored in httpCode. The **http.end()** function is used to close the HTTP connection after the request.

This sketch essentially sets up an ESP8266 web server that responds with the message content when accessed at the root URL **("/")**. It also monitors the state of pin D2 and performs different HTTP GET requests based on its state when connected to the specified Wi-Fi network (Server).

Wireless Sensor Network Using Client-Server M2M

In the previous example, there was only one client and a server. However, there can be multiple cases where more than one client is required to transfer information to a single server. The previously mentioned method was suitable for one-to-one communication between the client and the server but is not suitable for multiple clients.

This example focuses on using multiple clients to transfer data to a central ESP-12 Server. However, a limitation of this method is that the ESP-12 only allows 8 connections, meaning that only 8 clients can connect to the ESP-12 server.

Server Side Code

```
#include <ESP8266WiFi.h>

#include <ESP8266WebServer.h>

#include <ESP8266HTTPClient.h>

#include <SoftwareSerial.h>


const char* ssid = "server1";

const char* password = "qwertyuiop";

int max_connection = 8;

String URL;

int httpCode;

String payload;

String ID;

String state;


ESP8266WebServer server(80);

HTTPClient http;


IPAddress ip (10, 10, 10, 1);
```

```
IPAddress gateway (10, 10, 10, 1);
IPAddress subnet (255, 255, 255, 0);

void setup() {
  Serial.begin(115200);
  WiFi.mode(WIFI_AP);
  Serial.println(«Setup Access point»);
  Serial.println(«Disconnect from any other modes»);
  WiFi.disconnect();
  Serial.println(«stating access point with SSID» +String(ssid));
  WiFi.softAP(ssid, password, 1, false, max_connection);
  WiFi.softAPConfig(ip, gateway, subnet);
  IPAddress myIP = WiFi.softAPIP();
  Serial.println(myIP);
  server.on(«/»,handleroot);
  server.on(«/feed»,feed);
  server.begin();
}

void handleroot(){

  server.send(200,»text/plain»,»hello»);
}

void feed(){
  String data2 = server.arg(«state»);
  String data1 = server.arg(«ID»);
  server.send(200,»text/plain»,»Response»);
```

```
  Serial.println(data1+»=»+data2);
}


void loop (){

      server.handleClient();
}
```

Code Explanation

```
#include <ESP8266WiFi.h>
#include <ESP8266WebServer.h>
#include <ESP8266HTTPClient.h>
#include <SoftwareSerial.h>
```

- These lines include necessary libraries for Wi-Fi communication, handling HTTP requests, and enabling a web server on the ESP8266.
- The **SoftwareSerial.h** library is included for potential use in serial communication with other devices.

```
const char* ssid = "server1";
const char* password = "qwertyuiop";
int max_connection = 8;

String URL;
int httpCode;
String payload;
String ID;
String state;

ESP8266WebServer server(80);
HTTPClient http;
```

```
IPAddress ip (10, 10, 10, 1);
IPAddress gateway (10, 10, 10, 1);
IPAddress subnet (255, 255, 255, 0);
```

Definitions and declarations are made here:

- **ssid** and **password** represent the Wi-Fi credentials (SSID and password).
- **max_connection** specifies the maximum number of allowed connections to the ESP8266 access point.
- Strings (URL, payload, ID, state) are initialized for potential use in the code.
- Objects server and http are created for the web server and HTTP client, respectively.
- ip, gateway, and subnet are specified for the IP address, gateway, and subnet mask configurations of the Access Point.

```
void setup() {
  Serial.begin(115200);
  WiFi.mode(WIFI_AP);
  WiFi.disconnect();
  WiFi.softAP(ssid, password, 1, false, max_connection);
  WiFi.softAPConfig(ip, gateway, subnet);
  IPAddress myIP = WiFi.softAPIP();
  Serial.println(myIP);
  server.on("/", handleroot);
  server.on("/feed", feed);
  server.begin();
}
```

In the **setup()** function:

- Serial communication is initialized at a baud rate of 115200.
- ESP8266 is set to Access Point mode (**WIFI_AP**).
- Any existing Wi-Fi connection is disconnected **(WiFi.disconnect()).**

- The ESP8266 is configured to act as an Access Point with the specified credentials and network parameters.
- The IP address of the Access Point is obtained and printed to the serial monitor.
- The **server** object sets handlers for specific paths (**"/"** and **"/feed"**) and starts the web server.

```
void handleroot() {
  server.send(200, "text/plain", "hello");
}


void feed() {
  String data2 = server.arg("state");
  String data1 = server.arg("ID");
  server.send(200, "text/plain", "Response");
  Serial.println(data1 + "=" + data2);
}
```

handleroot() and **feed()** functions are defined to handle different HTTP requests:

- **handleroot()** responds with **"hello"** when the root (**"/"**) path is accessed.
- **feed()** extracts data from HTTP parameters (with names **"state"** and **"ID"**), sends a "Response" back, and prints the received data to the serial monitor.

```
void loop() {
  server.handleClient();
}
```

In the **loop()** function:

- **server.handleClient()** continuously checks for and handles incoming HTTP client requests to the server.

Overall, this sketch sets up the ESP8266 as an Access Point, establishes a web server, and defines handlers for different HTTP requests. It responds with specific messages for different paths and processes received data from HTTP parameters.

Client Side Code

```
#include <ESP8266WiFi.h>

#include <ESP8266HTTPClient.h>


String id = "sensor 1";


int prevstate = LOW;

String d;

String data;


const char* ssid = "server1";

const char* password = "qwertyuiop";

String host = "http://10.10.10.1/feed?";


WiFiClient client;

HTTPClient http;


IPAddress ip (10, 10, 10, 32);

IPAddress gateway (10, 10, 10, 1);

IPAddress subnet (255, 255, 255, 0);



void setup() {

  pinMode(2, INPUT);

  Serial.begin(115200);

  ESP.eraseConfig();

  WiFi.persistent(false);
```

```
  Serial.println(«SET ESP IN STA MODE»);
  WiFi.mode(WIFI_STA);
  Serial.println(«- connecting to wifi»);
  WiFi.config(ip, gateway, subnet);
  WiFi.begin(ssid, password);
  Serial.println(«.»);
  Serial.println(«- wifi connected»);
  Serial.println(«»);
  Serial.print(«Connected to «);
  Serial.println(ssid);
  Serial.print(«IP address: «);
  Serial.println(WiFi.localIP());

}

void readdata(){

  int currentstate = digitalRead(2);
  if(prevstate != currentstate){
    if(currentstate == HIGH){
      d = «high»;
      data = «ID=»;
      data += String(id);
      data += «&state=»;
      data += String(d);
      http.begin(host);
      http.addHeader(«content-type»,»application/x-www-form-
      urlencoded»);
```

```
      http.POST(data);
      http.writeToStream(&Serial);
      http.end();
      Serial.println(«data stream: «+data);
    }else{
      d = «low»;
      data = «ID=»;
      data += String(id);
      data += «&state=»;
      data += String(d);
      http.begin(host);
      http.addHeader(«content-type»,»application/x-www-form-
      urlencoded»);
      http.POST(data);
      http.writeToStream(&Serial);
      http.end();
      Serial.println(«data stream: «+data);
    }
  }prevstate = currentstate;
}
void loop () {
  readdata();

}
```

Code Explanation

#include <ESP8266WiFi.h>

#include <ESP8266HTTPClient.h>

- These lines include necessary libraries for Wi-Fi communication and handling HTTP requests on the ESP8266.

```
String id = "sensor 1";

int prevstate = LOW;

String d;

String data;


const char* ssid = "server1";

const char* password = "qwertyuiop";

String host = "http://10.10.10.1/feed?";

WiFiClient client;

HTTPClient http;


IPAddress ip (10, 10, 10, 32);

IPAddress gateway (10, 10, 10, 1);

IPAddress subnet (255, 255, 255, 0);
```

Definitions and declarations are made here:

- **id** represents the unique identifier for the motion sensor device.
- **prevstate** stores the previous state of the motion sensor.
- Strings **d** and **data** are initialized for storing sensor states and data for HTTP requests.
- WiFi credentials (**ssid** and **password**) for the hub's network are defined.
- **host** represents the URL to which the sensor data will be sent.
- Objects **client** and **http** are created for WiFi communication and handling HTTP requests.
- **ip, gateway**, and **subnet** specify the IP address, gateway, and subnet mask for the sensor.

```
void setup() {

  pinMode(2, INPUT);

  Serial.begin(115200);
```

```
  ESP.eraseConfig();
  WiFi.persistent(false);
  Serial.println("SET ESP IN STA MODE");
  WiFi.mode(WIFI_STA);
  Serial.println("- connecting to wifi");
  WiFi.config(ip, gateway, subnet);
  WiFi.begin(ssid, password);
  Serial.println(".");
  Serial.println("- wifi connected");
  Serial.println("");
  Serial.print("Connected to ");
  Serial.println(ssid);
  Serial.print("IP address: ");
  Serial.println(WiFi.localIP());
}
```

In the **setup()** function:

- Pin 2 is set as an input pin for the motion sensor.
- Serial communication is initiated at a baud rate of 115200.
- Configuration settings are adjusted:
    - **ESP.eraseConfig()** clears any previously stored WiFi configuration.
    - **WiFi.persistent(false)** sets Wi-Fi configuration to non-persistent.
    - ESP8266 is set to Station mode (**WIFI_STA**).
    - WiFi parameters (IP, gateway, subnet) are configured.
- Wi-Fi connection to the specified network (ssid and password) is established, and the local IP address is printed to the serial monitor.

```
void readdata() {
  int currentstate = digitalRead(2);
  if (prevstate != currentstate) {
```

```
if (currentstate == HIGH) {
  // When motion is detected (HIGH state), prepare and send HTTP
  POST request
  d = "high";
  data = "ID=";
  data += String(id);
  data += "&state=";
  data += String(d);
  http.begin(host);
  http.addHeader("content-type", "application/x-www-form-
  urlencoded");
  http.POST(data);
  http.writeToStream(&Serial);
  http.end();
  Serial.println("data stream: " + data);
} else {
  // When no motion is detected (LOW state), prepare and send HTTP
  POST request
  d = "low";
  data = "ID=";
  data += String(id);
  data += "&state=";
  data += String(d);
  http.begin(host);
  http.addHeader("content-type", "application/x-www-form-
  urlencoded");
  http.POST(data);
```

```
      http.writeToStream(&Serial);

      http.end();

      Serial.println("data stream: " + data);

    }

  }

  prevstate = currentstate;

}
```

readdata() function:

- Reads the current state of the motion sensor.
- Compares the current state with the previous state to detect changes.
- When a change in state is detected:
  - Prepares data for an HTTP POST request based on the motion sensor state (HIGH or LOW).
  - Sends an HTTP POST request to the specified host with the sensor data (ID and state).
  - Writes the HTTP request data to the serial monitor for debugging purposes.

```
void loop() {

  readdata();

}
```

In the **loop()** function:

- **readdata()** function is called repeatedly to continuously monitor the motion sensor state and send data to the specified host when changes occur.

Here, in this sketch, the client acts as a motion sensor device. When motion is detected, it immediately updates the status to the server with the sensor ID and the current state of the sensor. Similarly, multiple sensors can be used, each with its specific ID.

ESP-NOW

In the world of Internet of Things and wireless communication, ESP-NOW is a powerful protocol that offers fast, dependable, and low-power communication between an ESP8266 or an ESP32. Developed by Espressif Systems, the makers of the world-renowned ESP microcontroller family, ESP-NOW serves as the dedicated protocol for direct communications between ESP devices, providing an alternative to conventional Wi-Fi and Bluetooth communication.

ESP-NOW works on the data link layer. This means that you do not need a Wi-Fi router or Access Point to communicate with an ESP8266 module or an ESP32 module. The primary focus of ESP-NOW is on speed and efficiency, making it perfect for applications where devices must exchange data quickly and in a power-efficient peer-to-peer mode.

Key Features of ESP-NOW

- **High Speed and Low Latency:** ESP-NOW operates at a significantly faster rate compared to traditional Wi-Fi communication. By bypassing the complexities of TCP/IP stacks, it achieves lower latency and faster data transmission, crucial for real-time applications.
- **Low Power Consumption:** One of the standout features of ESP-NOW is its optimization for low power consumption. Devices using this protocol can communicate efficiently while consuming minimal power, making it suitable for battery-operated IoT devices.
- **Peer-to-Peer Communication:** ESP-NOW facilitates direct communication between ESP devices without relying on an intermediary Access Point or router. This direct device-to-device communication eliminates network congestion and offers a more streamlined communication pathway.
- **Lightweight Protocol:** Designed to be lightweight, ESP-NOW operates on a simple and efficient protocol stack. This simplicity contributes to faster processing times and reduced overhead in data transmission.

Implementing ESP-NOW in ESP8266/ESP32

ESP-NOW can be leveraged in projects using the ESP8266 or ESP32 microcontrollers through the Arduino IDE. The Espressif ESP-IDF (Espressif IoT Development Framework) also provides APIs for utilizing ESP-NOW in ESP32-based projects.

To implement ESP-NOW in Arduino-based projects, developers need to include the **esp_now.h** library and follow the ESP-NOW API provided by Espressif. This API allows developers to establish communication between devices, define data structures to be exchanged, and handle callbacks for data transmission status.

Sample Sketch for ESP-NOW

```
#include <esp_now.h>

#include <WiFi.h>


// Define the MAC address of the receiver ESP8266/ESP32 module

uint8_t receiverMACAddress[] = {0x12, 0x34, 0x56, 0x78, 0x9A, 0xBC}; //
Replace with your receiver's MAC address


// Structure to hold the data to be sent

typedef struct struct_message {

  int sensorValue;

  // Add other data you want to send here

} struct_message;


// Create a variable of the struct_message type

struct_message message;


// Callback function that will be executed when data is sent

void OnDataSent(const uint8_t* mac_addr, esp_now_send_status_t status) {

  Serial.print("Packet to: ");

  for (int i = 0; i < 6; i++) {

    Serial.print(mac_addr[i], HEX);

    if (i < 5) Serial.print(':');

  }
```

```
  Serial.println(status == ESP_NOW_SEND_SUCCESS ? " Sent" : " Failed");
}

void setup() {
  Serial.begin(115200);

  // Initialize ESP-NOW
  if (esp_now_init() != ESP_OK) {
    Serial.println("Error initializing ESP-NOW");
    return;
  }

  // Register peer
  esp_now_peer_info_t peerInfo;
  memcpy(peerInfo.peer_addr, receiverMACAddress, 6);
  peerInfo.channel = 0;
  peerInfo.encrypt = false; // Set to true if encryption is needed

  if (esp_now_add_peer(&peerInfo) != ESP_OK) {
    Serial.println("Failed to add peer");
    return;
  }

  // Set callback for sending data
  esp_now_register_send_cb(OnDataSent);
}
```

```
void loop() {
  // Simulated sensor value, replace this with your sensor reading
  int sensorValue = random(0, 1024);

  // Update the message structure with sensor data
  message.sensorValue = sensorValue;

  // Send the message using ESP-NOW
  esp_err_t result = esp_now_send(receiverMACAddress, (uint8_t *)
  &message, sizeof(message));
  if (result != ESP_OK) {
    Serial.println("Error sending the data");
  }

  delay(1000); // Change the delay according to your requirements
}
```

Code Explanation

```
#include <esp_now.h>
#include <WiFi.h>
```

- These lines import the necessary libraries for using ESP-NOW and Wi-Fi functionalities in the Arduino sketch.

  ```
  uint8_t receiverMACAddress[] = {0x12, 0x34, 0x56, 0x78, 0x9A,
  0xBC};
  ```

- This line defines the MAC address of the receiving ESP8266/ESP32 module. You should replace these hexadecimal values with the MAC address of your specific receiver device.

  ```
  typedef struct struct_message {
  int sensorValue;
  // Add other data you want to send here
  } struct_message;
  ```

- This block defines a structure named **struct_message**, which will be used to hold the data to be sent. In this case, it contains an integer variable **sensorValue,** which represents a simulated sensor reading. You can add more variables to this structure for additional data if needed.

```
struct_message message;
```

- This line declares a variable named **message** of type **struct_message,** which will hold the actual data to be sent.

```
void OnDataSent(const uint8_t* mac_addr, esp_now_send_status_t status)
{ // Callback function executed when data is sent
// Prints the status of the sent packet to the serial monitor
}
```

- This function is a callback executed when the data is sent using ESP-NOW. It prints the status of the sent packet to the serial monitor.

```
void setup() {
pinMode(2, INPUT);
Serial.begin(115200);
ESP.eraseConfig();
WiFi.persistent(false); // WiFi and ESP-NOW initialization and setup code }
```

- The **setup()** function initializes the serial communication, erases the ESP configuration, and sets Wi-Fi configurations.

```
void loop() { // Sending data using ESP-NOW in a loop }
The loop() function contains the main code for sending data repeatedly using ESP-NOW.
```

```
int currentstate = digitalRead(2);
```

- This line reads the state of pin 2, assuming it is connected to a sensor. It stores the current state in the **currentstate** variable.

```
if (prevstate != currentstate) { // Check if the current state is different from the previous state }
```

- This condition checks if there's a change in the state of the pin since the last iteration of the loop.

```
if (currentstate == HIGH)
```

```
{ // Prepare and send data when the sensor state is HIGH (motion
detected) }
else { // Prepare and send data when the sensor state is LOW (no
motion detected) }
```

- These conditions check if the current state of the pin indicates motion detection (HIGH) or no motion (LOW). Based on this, the data is prepared and sent using ESP-NOW to the specified receiver's MAC address.

The sketch repetitively checks the sensor state in the loop, prepares data accordingly, and sends it using ESP-NOW to the specified receiver's MAC address whenever there's a change in the sensor state. Adjustments or modifications can be made based on your specific sensor readings and the nature of the data you want to send.

Conclusion

In the world of IoT, M2M communication is the foundation that allows devices to communicate with each other and exchange information. In this chapter, we have delved into the complex world of IoT, specifically focusing on the client-server communication that ESP-12 modules enable and the transformative power of the ESP-NOW protocol.

The journey began with an exploration of the importance of multifunctional communication (M2M) in IoT ecosystems, focusing on its role in allowing devices to independently communicate with each other to drive the productivity and intelligence of connected systems.

We explored the key features of the ESP microcontroller, ESP-12 in particular, and how it serves as a communication module that connects IoT devices to the Internet of Things.

One of the highlights was the exploration of ESP-NOW, a special mechanism developed by ESPressif Systems that allows for fast and efficient communication with ESP8266 and ESP32 devices, using detailed explanations and sketches. We deciphered its key features, such as unparalleled speed, low latency, power efficiency, and support for direct peer-to-peer communication.

In the upcoming chapter, we will provide a comprehensive overview of the ESP-IDF (Espressif IoT Development Framework), a powerful and widely used framework for developing applications on Espressif's ESP32 microcontrollers. We will delve into the key features, architecture, and programming model of the ESP-IDF, highlighting its flexibility and efficiency for building IoT solutions.

References

1. Yassein, M. B., Krunz, M., Nofal, H., & Krishnamurthy, N. (2018). Machine-to-Machine (M2M) Communication. In Enabling the Internet of Things (pp. 1-24). Springer.
2. Ni, K., Chen, Y., & Zhang, K. (2019). Industrial Internet of Things (IIoT) and Its Wireless Technologies. IEEE Communications Magazine, 57(1), 68-74
3. Espressif Systems. (n.d.). ESP8266. Retrieved from https://www.espressif.com/en/products/socs/esp8266
4. Espressif Systems. (n.d.). ESP32. Retrieved from https://www.espressif.com/en/products/socs/esp32
5. Espressif's ESP-NOW Documentation: ESP-NOW - Espressif Docs
6. Official ESP8266 Arduino Core Documentation: ESP8266 Arduino Core
7. Official ESP32 Arduino Core Documentation: ESP32 Arduino Core

CHAPTER 8
Shifting to ESP-IDF

Introduction

Espressif IoT Development Framework (ESP-IDF) is a complete framework for developing applications for Espressif's microcontrollers, with a primary focus on the ESP32 series. It provides a powerful and flexible environment that allows developers to develop IoT solutions quickly and easily. The framework includes a collection of tools, libraries, and APIs designed to simplify the development process, facilitating easy hardware, software, and network integration.

Whether you are a beginner or a seasoned developer, the ESP-IDF supports a wide range of skill levels, enabling you to innovate and accelerate the creation of various IoT projects.

ESP-IDF supports the full range of features and capabilities of the ESP32 family. It offers a wide range of libraries and modules related to IoT development, such as Wi-Fi support, Bluetooth support, peripheral interface support, multitasking support, and RTOS support. ESP-IDF provides documentation, examples, and tutorials to ease the learning curve for beginners and help seasoned developers explore advanced functionalities.

ESP-IDF is an open-source project that fosters community collaboration and innovation. It has an active community of contributors and enthusiasts who continually enhance its features and compatibility with various applications.

Structure

In this chapter, the following topics will be covered:

- ESP-IDF over Arduino
    - Arduino IDE
    - How ESP-IDF is Better
    - Features of ESP-IDF
- Setting up Environment for ESP-IDF
    - Mac OS
    - Windows
    - Installing VS Code
- ESP-32 Compilation System
    - File Structure
    - Components of a Project
    - Main Program File
    - Configuration File
    - Build Directory
    - Common idf.py Commands
- Coding with ESP-IDF
    - Blinking of LED
    - Complete Source Code
    - Compiling the Code
- Connecting ESP-32 to Wi-Fi
    - Complete Code

ESP-IDF over Arduino-IDE

The Arduino Integrated Development Environment (IDE) stands as the foundational tool for developers, hobbyists, and creators diving into the world of microcontroller programming. Initially introduced in 2005, Arduino IDE has been instrumental in simplifying the process of programming microcontrollers and nurturing a thriving community of enthusiasts, educators, and professionals. At its essence, Arduino IDE serves as a user-friendly interface, enabling users to write, compile, and upload code to Arduino-compatible boards. This platform's accessibility, versatility, and extensive library support have significantly contributed to its widespread adoption across various domains, from education to prototyping and beyond.

The user interface of Arduino IDE is intuitive and straightforward, catering to both beginners and experienced programmers. Its simplicity lies in the minimalist layout, featuring a text editor, a toolbar with basic functionalities, and a message console displaying feedback from the board. Users can effortlessly write code in the familiar C/C++ language, supported by a plethora of libraries and examples accessible through the platform. Additionally, Arduino IDE simplifies hardware configuration, providing a seamless way to select the board type and the communication port, crucial steps in establishing communication between the computer and the microcontroller board.

One of the key pillars of Arduino IDE's popularity is its extensive library support. The Arduino community has developed a vast repository of libraries, encapsulating pre-written code snippets and functionalities. These libraries cover an extensive range of tasks, from interfacing with sensors and actuators to handling communication protocols such as Wi-Fi, Bluetooth, and more. This library ecosystem significantly accelerates development, allowing users to leverage existing code rather than starting from scratch, thereby reducing development time and effort.

Moreover, Arduino IDE's compatibility with multiple hardware platforms contributes to its versatility. While Arduino originated with the ATmega series of microcontrollers, it has expanded to support various architectures and boards from different manufacturers. This flexibility means developers can choose from a wide array of boards based on their project requirements, ranging from the classic Arduino Uno to more advanced models like the Arduino Mega, Nano, or boards from other vendors like Adafruit, SparkFun, and more.

The simplicity of Arduino IDE extends beyond its interface and library support; it also offers a robust and supportive community. Arduino boasts a vast community of users, beginners, experts, educators, and hobbyists alike. This community-driven approach fosters an environment where individuals can seek assistance, share knowledge, and collaborate on projects. Online forums, social media groups, and official Arduino forums serve as hubs for troubleshooting, idea sharing, and project inspiration, making the learning curve smoother for newcomers and providing a platform for seasoned developers to exchange insights.

Furthermore, Arduino IDE's compatibility with different operating systems, including Windows, macOS, and Linux, enhances its accessibility, allowing users to work within their preferred environment. The platform's open-source nature encourages collaboration, allowing developers to contribute to the software's improvement and expansion continually. As a result, Arduino IDE remains a dynamic and evolving tool, continually adapting to meet the evolving needs of its diverse user base.

Advantages of ESP-IDF over Arduino IDE

ESP-IDF (Espressif IoT Development Framework) and Arduino IDE are two prominent platforms used for IoT (Internet of Things) development, each with its strengths and suitability for various projects. Differentiating between the two involves considering factors such as complexity, flexibility, hardware compatibility, library support, and development capabilities. Let's explore how ESP-IDF excels compared to Arduino IDE in the realm of IoT development:

- **Complexity and Flexibility:**

  ESP-IDF, tailored specifically for Espressif's ESP32 and ESP32-S series microcontrollers, offers a more complex yet powerful environment compared to the user-friendly and simplified interface of Arduino IDE. While Arduino IDE is renowned for its ease of use, especially for beginners, ESP-IDF provides deeper control over the hardware, making it more suitable for complex IoT projects that require precise handling of resources, low-level control, and real-time processing.

- **Hardware Compatibility and Capabilities:**

  Arduino IDE supports a broad range of hardware, including Arduino boards and other compatible microcontrollers, offering versatility in hardware choices. However, ESP-IDF's primary focus on Espressif's ESP32 and ESP32-S series allows for harnessing the full capabilities of these microcontrollers. The ESP32, for instance, offers built-in Wi-Fi and Bluetooth connectivity, advanced peripherals, low-power modes, and support for a wide range of protocols, making it a compelling choice for IoT applications requiring robust wireless connectivity and processing capabilities.

- **Low-Level Control and Customization:**

  ESP-IDF grants developers direct access to low-level functionalities of the ESP32 microcontroller, enabling precise control over hardware resources. This level of control allows for optimizations, real-time operation, and customized implementations tailored to specific IoT applications. Arduino IDE, while offering simplicity, abstracts many hardware intricacies, potentially limiting the degree of customization and fine-tuning available to developers.

- **Real-Time Operating System (RTOS) Support**:

  ESP-IDF incorporates an RTOS specifically optimized for the ESP32, allowing developers to create applications that require multitasking, task prioritization, and precise timing. This is particularly advantageous in IoT scenarios where multiple tasks need to run concurrently, such as sensor data acquisition, communication protocols, and control operations. Arduino IDE lacks built-in support for RTOS, although there are third-party libraries available for multitasking.

- **Performance and Resource Utilization:**

  ESP-IDF's deeper control over hardware resources can lead to more efficient utilization of the microcontroller's capabilities. This optimization can result in improved performance, reduced power consumption, and better overall efficiency compared to Arduino IDE, especially in scenarios where resource management and efficiency are critical, such as battery-powered IoT devices or applications with stringent performance requirements.

- **Library and Community Support**:

  Arduino IDE boasts a vast collection of libraries and a large, active community. These resources simplify development by providing pre-written code snippets, making it easier to interface with various sensors, actuators, and communication protocols. However, ESP-IDF's library ecosystem, while more focused on the ESP32 ecosystem, is also extensive and continually growing, catering specifically to the capabilities and features of Espressif's microcontrollers.

- **Learning Curve and Educational Resources:**

  Arduino IDE's user-friendly interface and extensive educational resources, including tutorials, projects, and guides, make it an excellent choice for beginners and educators. Its simplicity lowers the learning curve, allowing individuals to quickly start prototyping and experimenting with IoT concepts. In contrast, ESP-IDF, with its more complex environment and lower abstraction level, might pose a steeper learning curve, making it more suitable for users with some programming and embedded systems experience.

ESP-IDF and Arduino IDE each offer distinct advantages in IoT development. While Arduino IDE emphasizes simplicity, ease of use, and broad hardware compatibility, ESP-IDF excels in providing low-level control, advanced capabilities, and optimized performance specifically tailored for Espressif's powerful microcontrollers like the ESP32. The choice between the two depends on the project requirements, the need for low-level control, the complexity of the application, and the developer's familiarity with programming and embedded systems. For intricate IoT applications demanding precise hardware control, real-time capabilities, and optimized performance, ESP-IDF stands out as a powerful toolset. However, for beginners or projects with less stringent requirements, Arduino IDE's simplicity and extensive community support might be more appealing.

Features of ESP-IDF

The ESP-IDF (Espressif IoT Development Framework) is a powerful and comprehensive platform designed specifically for developing IoT applications on Espressif's ESP32 and ESP32-S series of microcontrollers. Packed with a range of features, ESP-IDF empowers developers to create sophisticated and efficient IoT solutions. Let's delve into some of its top features:

- **FreeRTOS-Based Multitasking:**

  ESP-IDF is built upon FreeRTOS, a popular open-source real-time operating system. This enables developers to create applications that can perform multiple tasks simultaneously, manage task priorities, and handle real-time operations efficiently. Multitasking capabilities are crucial in IoT scenarios where devices need to handle multiple functions concurrently, such as collecting sensor data, handling network communication, and managing user interfaces.

- **Abstraction Layer for Hardware Access:**

  ESP-IDF provides an abstraction layer that simplifies the interaction with hardware peripherals, making it easier for developers to access and control various components of the ESP32 microcontroller. This abstraction layer offers a consistent and intuitive API (Application Programming Interface) to interact with features like GPIO (General Purpose Input/Output), I2C, SPI, UART, ADC/DAC, and more. It streamlines the process of interfacing with hardware, allowing developers to focus on application logic rather than low-level hardware details.

- **Integrated Wi-Fi and Bluetooth Connectivity:**

  The ESP32 microcontroller, at the core of ESP-IDF, comes equipped with built-in Wi-Fi and Bluetooth capabilities. ESP-IDF harnesses these features seamlessly, providing APIs and libraries for configuring, managing, and utilizing Wi-Fi and Bluetooth connectivity. This integration enables IoT devices to connect to wireless networks, communicate with other devices, and leverage protocols like TCP/IP, HTTP, MQTT, and BLE (Bluetooth Low Energy).

- **Power Management and Low-Power Modes:**

  Efficient power management is critical in IoT devices, especially those running on battery power. ESP-IDF offers various power-saving features and low-power modes that enable developers to optimize energy consumption. This includes features like sleep modes, which allow the microcontroller to enter low-power states to conserve energy when not actively processing tasks. These power management capabilities are essential for extending the battery life of IoT devices and reducing overall power consumption.

- **Advanced Peripheral Support:**

  The ESP32 microcontroller boasts a wide array of advanced peripherals, and ESP-IDF provides comprehensive support for utilizing these peripherals effectively. This includes support for features like capacitive touch sensors, camera interfaces, cryptographic hardware acceleration (AES, RSA, and SHA), secure boot, secure storage, and more. This rich set of peripherals and functionalities extends the capabilities of IoT devices, enabling the development of diverse and feature-rich applications.

- **Over-the-Air (OTA) Updates:**

  ESP-IDF facilitates OTA updates, allowing firmware updates to be delivered and installed on devices remotely, without the need for physical access. This feature is crucial in IoT deployments, enabling devices to receive updates, patches, or new features seamlessly. OTA updates help in maintaining the security, performance, and functionality of IoT devices, reducing maintenance overhead and enhancing device reliability.

- **Development Tools and Debugging Support:**

  ESP-IDF provides a comprehensive set of development tools, including a robust command-line interface (CLI), build system, debugging tools, and support for various IDEs like Visual Studio Code and Eclipse. Additionally, the framework includes debugging features such as real-time logging, debugging over JTAG, and support for tracing tools, aiding developers in identifying and resolving issues efficiently during the development process.

- **Extensive Documentation and Community Support:**

  ESP-IDF offers thorough and well-organized documentation, including programming guides, API references, tutorials, and examples. This comprehensive documentation serves as a valuable resource for developers at all levels of expertise, facilitating learning, troubleshooting, and exploration of advanced functionalities. Furthermore, the ESP-IDF community is vibrant and active, comprising developers, contributors, and enthusiasts who actively participate in forums, discussions, and sharing knowledge, fostering collaboration and support within the community.

Hence, ESP-IDF stands out as a robust and feature-rich framework for IoT development, offering a wide range of capabilities that empower developers to create innovative and efficient IoT solutions. Its integration of FreeRTOS, comprehensive hardware support, wireless connectivity, power management features, and extensive documentation make it a compelling choice for building advanced IoT applications.

Setting up Environment for ESP-IDF

Setting up the ESP-IDF (Espressif IoT Development Framework) environment involves several steps to configure your system for developing applications for Espressif's ESP32 and ESP32-S series of microcontrollers. Here's a step-by-step guide for setting up ESP-IDF on both macOS and Windows:

To start using ESP-IDF on ESP32, install the following software:

- **Toolchain**: To compile code for ESP32
- **Build tools**: CMake and Ninja to build a full application for ESP32
- **ESP-IDF:** Contains software libraries, source code for ESP32, and scripts to operate the Toolchain

Please refer to the updated guidelines for setting up the environment for the ESP-IDF. The most updated (December 2023) guidelines were used while writing this chapter. For the latest guidelines and documentation, visit: https://docs.espressif.com/projects/esp-idf/en/latest/esp32/get-started/

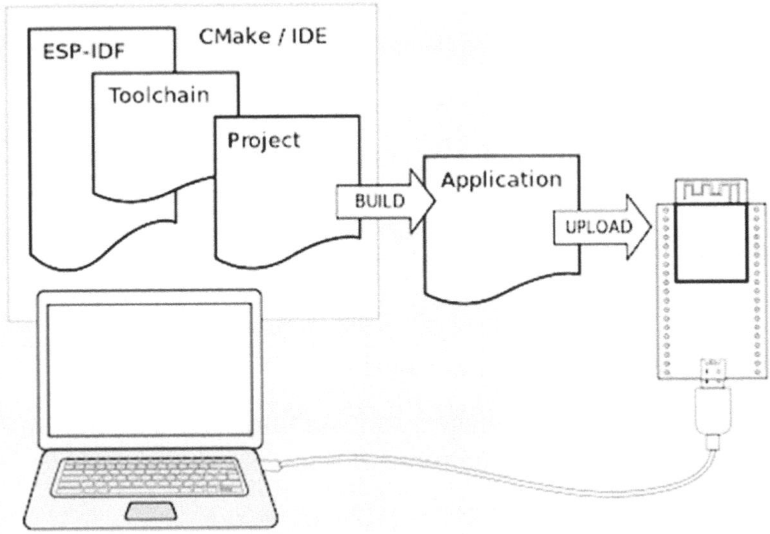

Figure 8.1: *Application Development for ESP32 using ESP-IDF*

macOS

Here are the steps to set up the ESP-IDF environment in macOS:

Step 1: Install Homebrew

Homebrew is a package manager for macOS, simplifying the installation of various software. To install Homebrew, open Terminal and paste the following command:

```
/bin/bash -c "$(curl -fsSL https://raw.githubusercontent.com/Homebrew/install/HEAD/install.sh)"
```

Step 2: Install Required Packages

Use Homebrew to install necessary tools and dependencies. In Terminal, execute the following command:

```
brew install cmake ninja dfu-util wget git python3
```

Step 3: Clone ESP-IDF Repository

Create a directory for ESP-IDF and clone the repository. Open Terminal and enter the following command:

```
mkdir -p ~/esp
```

```
cd ~/esp

git clone --recursive https://github.com/espressif/esp-idf.git
```

Step 4: Set Up Environment Variables

Define the **IDF_PATH** environment variable. In Terminal, enter the following command:

```
echo 'export IDF_PATH=~/esp/esp-idf' >> ~/.bash_profile

source ~/.bash_profile
```

Step 5: Install Required Python Packages

Utilize pip (Python package manager) to install necessary Python packages. In Terminal, execute the following command:

```
pip3 install --user -r $IDF_PATH/requirements.txt
```

Step 6: Toolchain Setup

Download and install the ESP-IDF Toolchain from the Espressif website. Follow the instructions provided in the ESP-IDF documentation for Toolchain installation.

Step 7: Verify Setup

Test the set up by building an example project. Open Terminal and navigate to the **hello_world** example:

```
cd $IDF_PATH/examples/get-started/hello_world
```

Build the project:

```
idf.py build
```

Windows

Here are the steps to set up the ESP-IDF environment in Windows:

Step 1: Install Git

Download and install Git for Windows from the official Git website.

Step 2: Install Python

Download and install Python 3 from the official Python website. During installation, ensure the option to add Python to the system PATH is selected.

Step 3: Install Required Packages

Use Command Prompt to install necessary tools and dependencies via pip. In Command Prompt, enter the following command:

```
pip install cmake ninja dfu-util wget
```

Step 4: Set up ESP-IDF

Create a directory for ESP-IDF and clone the repository. In Command Prompt, enter the following command:

```
mkdir C:\esp

cd C:\esp

git clone --recursive https://github.com/espressif/esp-idf.git
```

Step 5: Set Up Environment Variables

Add the **IDF_PATH** environment variable.

Right-click **This PC** or **My Computer** -> **Properties** -> **Advanced system settings** -> **Environment Variables.**

Add a new system variable named **IDF_PATH** and set its value to **C:\esp\esp-idf**.

Step 6: Install ESP-IDF Toolchain

Download and install the ESP-IDF Toolchain from the Espressif website.

Follow the instructions provided in the ESP-IDF documentation for Toolchain installation.

Step 7: Verify Setup

Open Command Prompt, navigate to the hello_world example, and build the project.

In Command Prompt, enter the following command:

```
cd C:\esp\esp-idf\examples\get-started\hello_world


idf.py build
```

Installing VS Code

ESP-IDF does not come with a code editor by default (although the most recent version of the installer for Windows does come with the option of installing ESP-IDF Eclipse). The code can be edited using any text editor of your choice and then compiled using terminal commands. In this chapter, we will be using VS code to edit our codes for the ESP32.

One of the most widely used code editing tools is Visual Studio Code (VS Code). VS Code is a free, high-quality code editor with an easy-to-use interface. It comes with a bunch of plugins that help you navigate through the code, highlight syntaxes, manage Git versions, and integrate with terminals. Espressif even has a plugin for VS Code that makes it easy to configure and debug your projects.

To open the current directory in VS Code, simply type the code command inside the terminal. To open the system's default terminal console inside VS Code, simply press *Ctrl+~*.

ESP32 Compilation System

ESP-IDF projects are a collection of a main program with an entry function and several independent functional parts. For instance, a project that controls LED switches is mainly composed of a main entry program with the main entry function and a driver component that controls GPIO. To realize LED remote control, you need to include the Wi-Fi/TCP/IP stack, and so on.

The compilation system can compile, link, and generate executable files (.bin) for the code through a set of building rules. The compilation system of ESP-IDF v4.0 and above versions is based on CMake by default, and the compilation script, `CMakeLists.txt`, can be used to control the compilation behavior of the code. In addition to supporting the basic syntax of CMake, the ESP-IDF compilation system also defines a set of default compilation rules and CMake functions, allowing you to write the compilation script with simple statements.

ESP-IDs compilation system provides a set of standard compilation rules as well as CMake functions.

File Structure

A project is a directory that contains the main entry program, user-defined components, and files needed to build the executable application, such as compilation script, configuration file, partition table, and more. Projects are copied and passed on, and the same executable file can also be compiled and generated on the same machine with the same ESP-IDF version. A typical project file structure in ESP-IDF is shown in *Figure* 8.2.

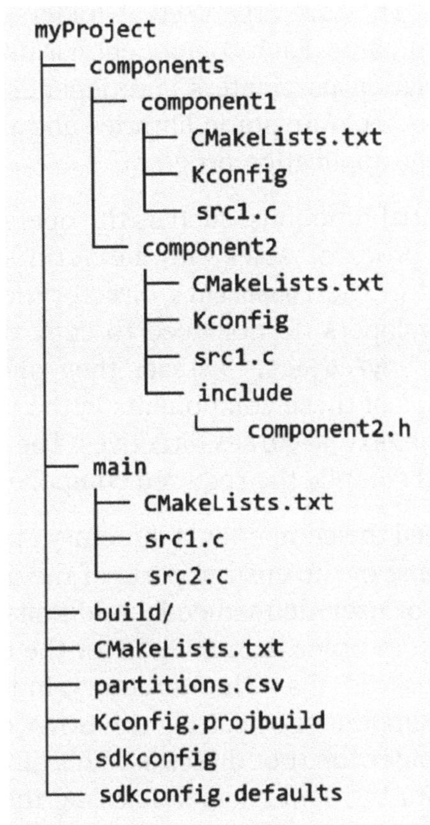

Figure 8.2: *Project File Structure in ESP-IDF*

The ESP-IDF supports multiple ESP32-based variants, such as ESP-32, ESP-32 C Series, ESP-32 S Series, and more. It is important to define the target hardware before compiling the complete project.

To define the target, use the following command:

```
idf.py set-target esp32c3
```

This command will compile the project for the ESP-32 C3 development board, loading the default parameters and compilation path for the defined hardware.

You can also use the set-target command to set a new target. The compilation system will clean up the target and reconfigure it after compilation. It can also be used to generate an executable program for your application.

Components of a Project

In ESP-IDF, components are modular and autonomous code units managed by the compilation system. They are organized as folders, where the folder name is the default component name. Each component has its own compilation script that defines the compilation parameters and dependencies. Components are compiled into their own separate static libraries and then merged with other components to create the application program.

ESP-IDF provides essential functions, such as the operating system, peripheral drivers, and network protocol stack, in the form of components. These components are stored in the **`components`** directory located within the ESP-IDF root directory. Developers do not need to copy these **`components`** to the **`components`** directory of **`myProject.`** Instead, they only need to specify the dependency relationships of these components in the project's **`CMakeLists.txt`** file using the **`REQUIRES`** or **`PRIV_REQUIRES`** directives. The compilation system will automatically locate and compile the required components.

This is why you don't need the components directory underneath **`myProject`**. It's only used to contain some of the custom parts of the project. These parts can be third-party libraries or user-defined code. Additionally, components can be sourced from any directory other than ESP-IDF or the current project, such as an open-source project saved in another directory. In this case, you only need to add the path of the component by setting the **`EXTRA_COMPONENT_DIRS`** variable in the **`CMakeLists.txt`** under the root directory. This directory will override any ESP-IDF component with the same name, ensuring the correct component is used.

Main Program File

In an ESP-IDF project, the main directory is the root directory that contains the project-specific files, configuration settings, source code, and build scripts. This directory serves as the starting point for organizing and managing the entire project structure.

Components of the Main Directory:

- **Project Configuration Files**: This includes files such as **`CMakeLists.txt,`** which define project-specific configurations, dependencies, build options, and settings required for the build system (**`idf.py`**) to compile the project.

- **Source Code**: The main directory typically contains the source code files (`.c`, `.cpp`, `.h`, and so on) that make up the application or firmware running on the ESP32/ESP8266 microcontroller.
- **Project-specific Configuration Files**: Any project-specific configuration files or resources needed for the application, such as device configurations, network settings, or custom configuration files, reside within this directory.
- **Build Scripts and Output Directories**: The build system generated by ESP-IDF (`idf.py`) generates build-related artifacts and intermediate files. These include the build output directory (`build/`) where compiled binaries, object files, and other build artifacts are stored.
- **Optional Directories**: Additional directories might be present for specific purposes, such as storing libraries, custom components, unit tests, documentation, or other project-related resources.

The main directory serves as the centralized location for all project-related files and resources. It allows developers to organize and structure their codebase, manage configurations, and collaborate effectively. This directory acts as the focal point for initiating builds, configuring the project, and managing dependencies using tools like idf.py and CMake.

Configuration Files

The project's root directory contains the essential `'sdkconfig'` file, which compiles configuration parameters for all project components. This file is autogenerated during compilation and can be modified or regenerated using the `'idf.py menuconfig'` command. The '`menuconfig`' options primarily stem from the project's `'Kconfig.projbuild'` and the components' '`Kconfig`'. Developers augment `Kconfig` with configuration items, fostering component flexibility and adjustability.

Build Directory

The project's `'build'` directory is the default location for intermediate files and the resulting executable programs produced by the `'idf.py build'` command. Typically, directly accessing the build directory isn't required. ESP-IDF offers specific commands to manage this directory. For instance, `'idf.py flash'` automatically locates the compiled binary file and flashes it to the designated flash address. Additionally, `'idf.py fullclean'` is available to thoroughly clean the entire build directory.

Common idf.py Commands

The ESP-IDF is a comprehensive platform for developing applications for Espressif's ESP32 and ESP8266 microcontrollers. The idf.py tool is the primary build system and command-line interface for managing ESP-IDF projects. Here are some commonly used idf.py commands:

- `idf.py build`: Compiles the project, generating firmware binaries.
- `idf.py flash`: Flashes the compiled firmware onto the ESP32/ESP8266 device connected via USB.
- `idf.py monitor`: Opens a serial monitor to view debug messages and logs from the device.
- `idf.py menuconfig`: Provides an interactive menu for configuring project settings, including device-specific configurations, components, and build options.
- `idf.py clean`: Removes build artifacts and temporary files, performing a clean build.
- `idf.py fullclean`: Cleans the entire project directory, including build artifacts, generated files, and the build directory.
- `idf.py erase_flash`: Erases the entire flash memory of the ESP32/ESP8266.
- `idf.py size`: Displays the size of the generated firmware binary.
- `idf.py help`: Shows help information, including a list of available commands and their descriptions.
- `idf.py set-target`: Sets the target device (ESP32/ESP8266) for the project.
- `idf.py set-idf-path`: Sets the path to the ESP-IDF framework.
- `idf.py set-project-path`: Sets the path to the project directory.
- `idf.py build-flash`: Builds and flashes the firmware to the device in one command.
- `idf.py apptrace`: Displays and manages application tracing data.
- `idf.py openocd`: Starts the OpenOCD debugger for ESP32/ESP8266.
- `idf.py gdb`: Starts the GDB (GNU Debugger) for debugging applications running on ESP32/ESP8266.
- `idf.py export`: Generates IDE project files (such as for VSCode, Eclipse, or others) for the ESP-IDF project.

These commands represent a subset of the functionalities provided by idf.py. The tool offers a wide range of capabilities for managing, building, flashing, debugging, and configuring ESP-IDF projects, catering to various development needs for IoT applications.

Coding with ESP-IDF

Espressif IoT Development Framework (ESP-IDF) is a robust and comprehensive platform designed for programming Espressif's ESP32 and ESP8266 microcontrollers. It empowers developers to craft embedded applications, IoT solutions, and connected devices using Espressif's powerful hardware.

Blinking of LED

Blinking the built-in LED on an ESP32 board using ESP-IDF involves setting up a project, configuring GPIO pins, and creating a simple program. Here are the steps:

Step 1: Create a new project

Use the **`idf.py create-project`** command to create a new project or navigate to an existing project directory.

Step 2: Write the program

- Open the project directory in your preferred code editor or IDE
- Navigate to the main source file (**`main.c`** or similar)
- Include necessary header files:

```
#include <stdio.h>
#include "freertos/FreeRTOS.h"
#include "freertos/task.h"
#include "driver/gpio.h"
```

Explanation:

- **`#include <stdio.h>`:** Includes the standard input/output header file for basic input/output operations.
- **`"freertos/FreeRTOS.h"`:** Includes the FreeRTOS header file, providing access to FreeRTOS functions and features.
- **`"freertos/task.h"`:** Includes the FreeRTOS task-related header file, essential for task management.

- **"driver/gpio.h"**: Includes the ESP-IDF GPIO driver header file, granting access to GPIO functionalities.

Define GPIO for the LED

```
#define LED_PIN GPIO_NUM_2 // Replace with the GPIO pin connected to the built-in LED
```

Explanation:

#define LED_PIN GPIO_NUM_2: Defines a macro **LED_PIN** and assigns it the value **GPIO_NUM_2.** This line specifies the GPIO pin number that will be used to control the LED. It is recommended to replace **GPIO_NUM_2** with the actual GPIO pin number connected to the built-in LED on the ESP32/ESP8266 board.

Create a task to blink the LED

```
void blink_task(void *pvParameter) {

    gpio_pad_select_gpio(LED_PIN);

    gpio_set_direction(LED_PIN, GPIO_MODE_OUTPUT);


    while (1) {

        gpio_set_level(LED_PIN, 1); // LED ON

        vTaskDelay(1000 / portTICK_PERIOD_MS); // Delay for 1 second


        gpio_set_level(LED_PIN, 0); // LED OFF

        vTaskDelay(1000 / portTICK_PERIOD_MS); // Delay for 1 second

    }

}
```

Explanation:

- **void blink_task(void *pvParameter) { ... }**: Defines a function named blink_task that takes a void pointer as a parameter. This function is a FreeRTOS task responsible for blinking the LED.
- **gpio_pad_select_gpio(LED_PIN);**: Configures the GPIO pin specified by LED_PIN for use as a GPIO pin.

- **`gpio_set_direction(LED_PIN, GPIO_MODE_OUTPUT);`:** Sets the direction of the GPIO pin specified by LED_PIN as an output pin.
- The subsequent **`while (1)`** loop toggles the LED on and off indefinitely:
  - **`gpio_set_level(LED_PIN, 1);`:** Sets the specified GPIO pin (LED_PIN) to a high level, turning the LED ON.
  - **`vTaskDelay(1000 / portTICK_PERIOD_MS);`:** Introduces a delay of 1 second using FreeRTOS, pausing the task for 1000 milliseconds.
  - **`gpio_set_level(LED_PIN, 0);`:** Sets the GPIO pin (LED_PIN) to a low level, turning the LED OFF.
  - **`vTaskDelay(1000 / portTICK_PERIOD_MS);`:** Creates another 1-second delay.

```
void app_main() {
    xTaskCreate(&blink_task, "blink_task", configMINIMAL_STACK_
    SIZE, NULL, 5, NULL);
}
```

Explanation:

- **`void app_main() { ... }`:** Defines the application's main entry point, required in ESP-IDF.
- **`xTaskCreate(&blink_task, "blink_task", configMINIMAL_STACK_SIZE, NULL, 5, NULL);`:** Creates a FreeRTOS task named "`blink_task`" using the `blink_task` function defined earlier. This line initializes a task that will continuously blink the LED.

Complete Source Code:

```
#include <stdio.h>

#include "freertos/FreeRTOS.h"

#include "freertos/task.h"

#include "driver/gpio.h"


#define LED_PIN GPIO_NUM_2 // Replace with the GPIO pin connected to the
built-in LED


void blink_task(void *pvParameter) {
```

```
    gpio_pad_select_gpio(LED_PIN);

    gpio_set_direction(LED_PIN, GPIO_MODE_OUTPUT);


    while (1) {

        gpio_set_level(LED_PIN, 1); // LED ON

        vTaskDelay(1000 / portTICK_PERIOD_MS); // Delay for 1 second


        gpio_set_level(LED_PIN, 0); // LED OFF

        vTaskDelay(1000 / portTICK_PERIOD_MS); // Delay for 1 second

    }

}


void app_main() {

    xTaskCreate(&blink_task, "blink_task", configMINIMAL_STACK_SIZE,
    NULL, 5, NULL);

}
```

Compiling the code

This section takes the Blink program as an example to demonstrate the compilation process of a simple ESP-IDF program. Here are the steps:

- **Set up the ESP-IDF environment:** Open the terminal and import the ESP-IDF environment variables. For Linux and Mac systems, use **`cd ~/esp/esp-idf`** to navigate to the ESP-IDF folder. Then, import the ESP-IDF environment variables using the command **`. ./export.sh`**. This process also performs a complete integrity check of the development environment.

  For Windows systems, you can directly find and open ESP-IDF 4.3 CMD or ESP-IDF 4.3 PowerShell in the program list. After the terminal is opened, the environment variables will be automatically added, as shown in *Figure* 8.3.

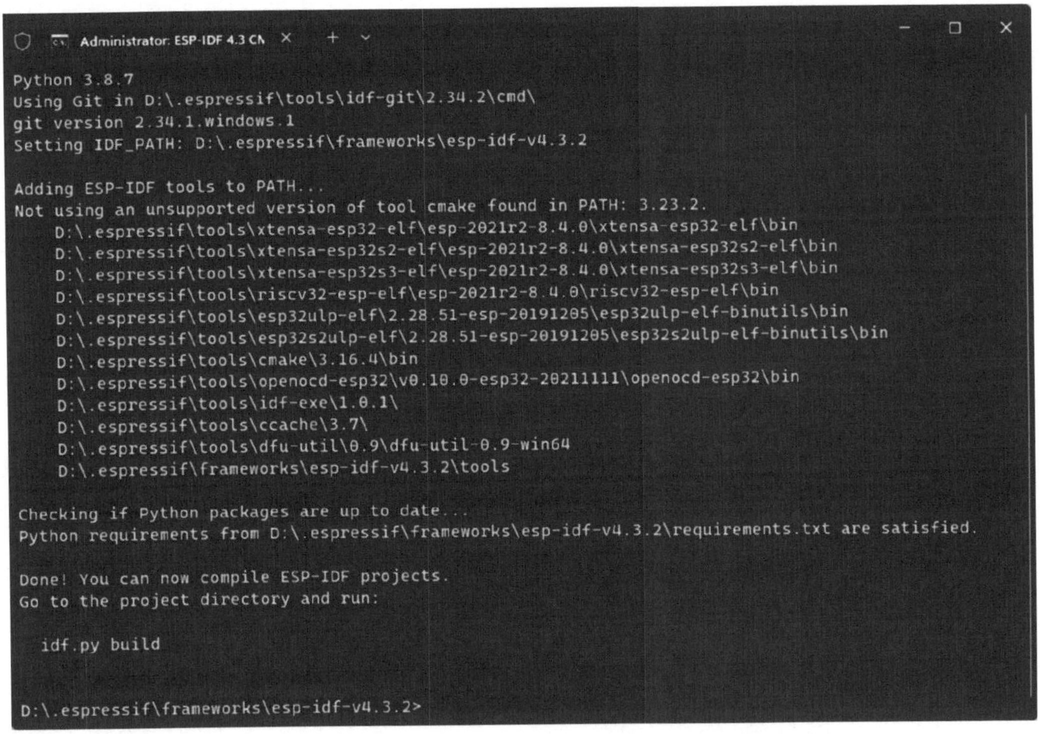

Figure 8.3: *Addition of environment variables in Windows*

- Navigate to the root directory of the project.
- Set the compilation target to ESP-32, use the following command to set the target:

  ```
  Idf.py set-target esp32
  ```

- **Configure the GPIOs**: Use idf.py menu config command to open the configuration interface for the device. Use the up/down keys to navigate and press the Enter key to select any specific configuration. Enter a number to update the GPIO to the given pin. Save the configuration, as shown in *Figure* 8.4.

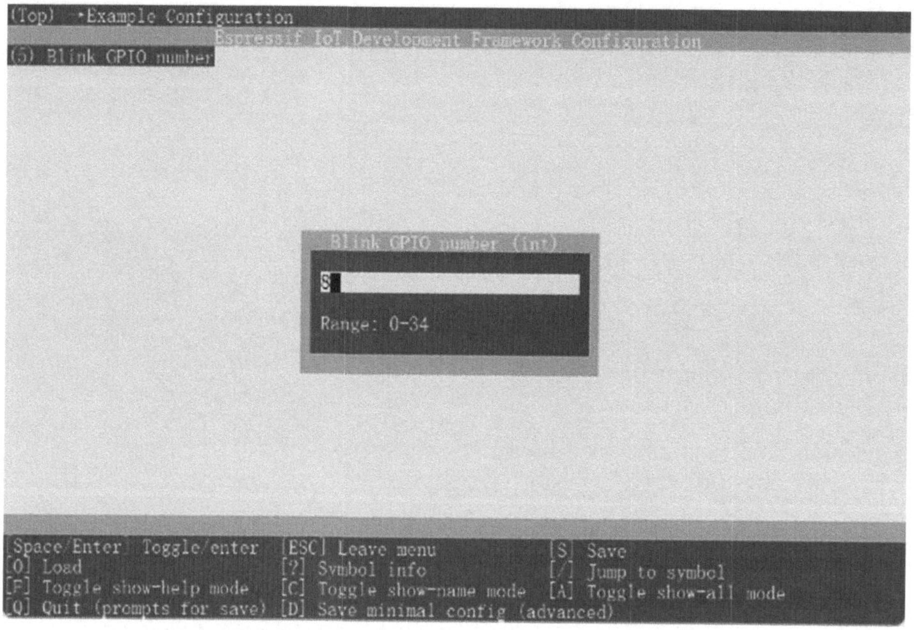

Figure 8.4: *GPIO configuration using menuconfig*

- **Build the code**: Use **`idf.py`** build to build the code. The building process will start (see *Figure* 8.5), and after the build is successful, a flash command will be prompted on the screen, as shown in *Figure* 8.6.

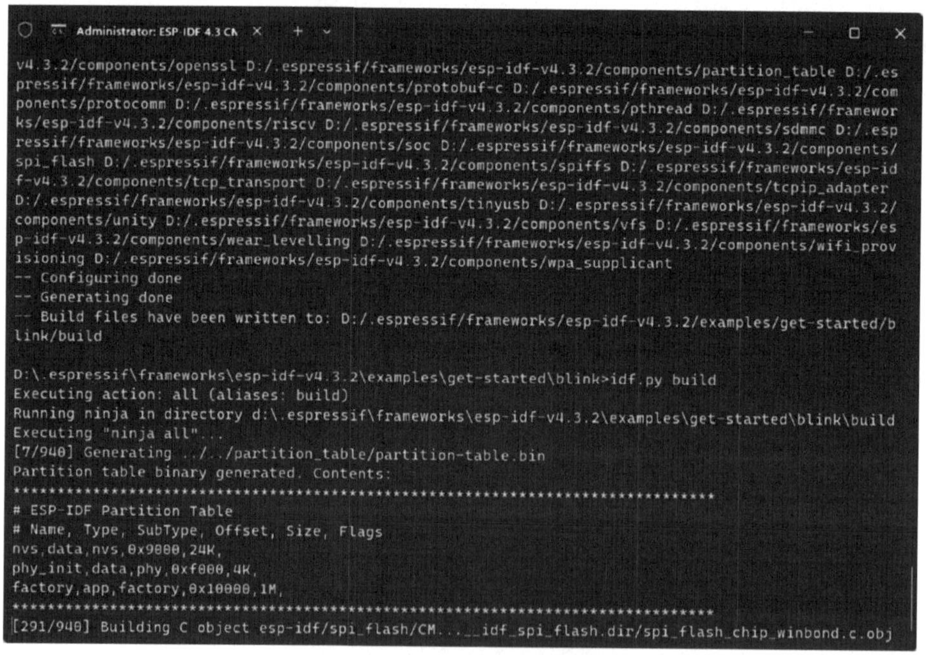

Figure 8.5: *Project Build process*

Figure 8.6 shows the screen after the build process is completed and is ready for flash.

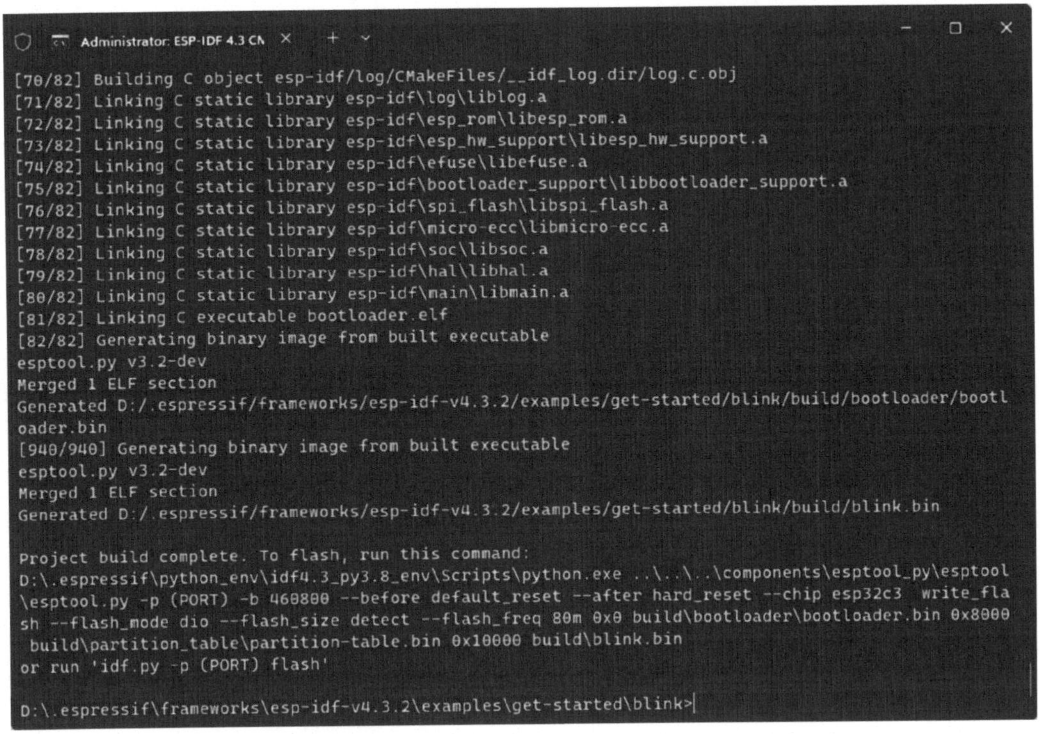

Figure 8.6: *After the Build process is finished*

Connecting ESP-32 to Wi-Fi

Connecting an ESP32 device to a Wi-Fi network using ESP-IDF involves configuring Wi-Fi settings and establishing a connection. Here are the steps:

- **Create a New Project:** Use the **`idf.py create-project`** command to create a new ESP-IDF project or navigate to an existing project directory.
- **Configure Wi-Fi Settings:** Include the header files:

```
#include <stdio.h>
#include "freertos/FreeRTOS.h"
#include "freertos/event_groups.h"
#include "esp_wifi.h"
#include "esp_event.h"
#include "esp_log.h"
```

Explanation:

- `#include <stdio.h>`: Standard input/output header.
- `#include "freertos/FreeRTOS.h"`: FreeRTOS header for task management.
- `#include "freertos/event_groups.h"`: FreeRTOS header for event group handling.
- `#include "esp_wifi.h"`: ESP-IDF header for Wi-Fi functionality.
- `#include "esp_event.h"`: ESP-IDF header for event loop handling.
- `#include "esp_log.h"`: ESP-IDF header for logging functionality.

- **Define the Wi-Fi Configuration Parameters**

```
#define WIFI_SSID "Your_WiFi_SSID"
#define WIFI_PASS "Your_WiFi_Password"
```

Explanation:

- `#define WIFI_SSID "Your_WiFi_SSID"`: Define Wi-Fi SSID as a macro.
- `#define WIFI_PASS "Your_WiFi_Password"`: Define Wi-Fi password as a macro.

- **Event Group to Handle Wi-Fi Events**

```
static EventGroupHandle_t wifi_event_group;
const int CONNECTED_BIT = BIT0;
```

Explanation:

- `wifi_event_group`: An event group handle for Wi-Fi events.
- `CONNECTED_BIT`: A constant bit flag indicating a successful Wi-Fi connection.

- **Wi-Fi Handler Function**

```
static esp_err_t wifi_event_handler(void *ctx, system_event_t *event) {
    switch(event->event_id) {
        case SYSTEM_EVENT_STA_START:
            esp_wifi_connect();
            break;
        case SYSTEM_EVENT_STA_CONNECTED:
            break;
        case SYSTEM_EVENT_STA_GOT_IP:
```

```
            xEventGroupSetBits(wifi_event_group, CONNECTED_BIT);
            break;
        case SYSTEM_EVENT_STA_DISCONNECTED:
            esp_wifi_connect();
            xEventGroupClearBits(wifi_event_group, CONNECTED_BIT);
            break;
        default:
            break;
    }
    return ESP_OK;
}
```

Explanation:

- **`wifi_event_handler`**: Function handling Wi-Fi events like start, connection, IP obtained, and disconnection.

- **Initialize Wi-Fi Connection**

```
void wifi_init_sta() {
    wifi_event_group = xEventGroupCreate();
    tcpip_adapter_init();
    esp_event_loop_init(wifi_event_handler, NULL);
    wifi_init_config_t cfg = WIFI_INIT_CONFIG_DEFAULT();
    esp_wifi_init(&cfg);
    esp_wifi_set_storage(WIFI_STORAGE_RAM);
    wifi_config_t wifi_config = {
        .sta = {
            .ssid = WIFI_SSID,
            .password = WIFI_PASS
        }
    };
    esp_wifi_set_mode(WIFI_MODE_STA);
    esp_wifi_set_config(ESP_IF_WIFI_STA, &wifi_config);
    esp_wifi_start();
    xEventGroupWaitBits(wifi_event_group, CONNECTED_BIT, false,
```

```
    true, portMAX_DELAY);
}
```

Explanation:

`wifi_init_sta()`:

- Function to initialize Wi-Fi in station (STA) mode.
- Create the event group for Wi-Fi events.
- Initialize TCP/IP stack adapter.
- Initialize the event loop for Wi-Fi event handling.
- Configure Wi-Fi initialization settings using the default configuration.
- Initialize Wi-Fi with the configuration.
- Set Wi-Fi storage to RAM.
- Set Wi-Fi mode to station (STA) mode.
- Set Wi-Fi configuration with SSID and password.
- Start Wi-Fi.
- Wait until the connection is established `(CONNECTED_BIT)` or indefinitely `(portMAX_DELAY)`.

- **Connect to Wi-Fi in the main function**

```
void app_main() {
    ESP_ERROR_CHECK(nvs_flash_init());
    ESP_ERROR_CHECK(esp_netif_init());
    ESP_ERROR_CHECK(esp_event_loop_create_default());
    wifi_init_sta();
}
```

Explanation:

- **`app_main()`:** Entry point of the application.

Complete Code

```
#include <stdio.h>

#include "freertos/FreeRTOS.h"

#include "freertos/event_groups.h"

#include "esp_wifi.h"

#include "esp_event.h"
```

```
#include "esp_log.h"

#define WIFI_SSID "Your_WiFi_SSID"
#define WIFI_PASS "Your_WiFi_Password"

static EventGroupHandle_t wifi_event_group;
const int CONNECTED_BIT = BIT0;

static esp_err_t wifi_event_handler(void *ctx, system_event_t *event) {
    switch(event->event_id) {
        case SYSTEM_EVENT_STA_START:
            esp_wifi_connect();
            break;
        case SYSTEM_EVENT_STA_CONNECTED:
            break;
        case SYSTEM_EVENT_STA_GOT_IP:
            xEventGroupSetBits(wifi_event_group, CONNECTED_BIT);
            break;
        case SYSTEM_EVENT_STA_DISCONNECTED:
            esp_wifi_connect();
            xEventGroupClearBits(wifi_event_group, CONNECTED_BIT);
            break;
        default:
            break;
    }
    return ESP_OK;
}
```

```
void wifi_init_sta() {
    wifi_event_group = xEventGroupCreate();
    tcpip_adapter_init();
    esp_event_loop_init(wifi_event_handler, NULL);
    wifi_init_config_t cfg = WIFI_INIT_CONFIG_DEFAULT();
    esp_wifi_init(&cfg);
    esp_wifi_set_storage(WIFI_STORAGE_RAM);
    wifi_config_t wifi_config = {
        .sta = {
            .ssid = WIFI_SSID,
            .password = WIFI_PASS
        }
    };
    esp_wifi_set_mode(WIFI_MODE_STA);
    esp_wifi_set_config(ESP_IF_WIFI_STA, &wifi_config);
    esp_wifi_start();
    xEventGroupWaitBits(wifi_event_group, CONNECTED_BIT, false, true,
    portMAX_DELAY);
}

void app_main() {
    ESP_ERROR_CHECK(nvs_flash_init());
    ESP_ERROR_CHECK(esp_netif_init());
    ESP_ERROR_CHECK(esp_event_loop_create_default());
    wifi_init_sta();
}
```

Conclusion

The ESP-IDF (Espressif IoT Development Framework) serves as a robust platform for developing applications for Espressif's ESP32 and ESP8266 microcontrollers, empowering developers to create efficient and feature-rich IoT solutions. Throughout this chapter, we have explored the fundamentals of ESP-IDF, understanding its architecture, project structure, and the creation of basic example programs tailored for ESP32 devices. We have delved into essential functionalities, including GPIO control, task management with FreeRTOS, and Wi-Fi connectivity setup.

ESP-IDF provides a comprehensive set of tools, libraries, and APIs that enable seamless development for IoT applications. The project structure includes essential components such as header files (`#include`), configuration settings, source code files, and build scripts managed by the `idf.py` build system. This structure streamlines project organization and management, facilitating the development process.

Further exploration of ESP-IDF can involve diving deeper into advanced functionalities like Bluetooth, sensor interfacing, web server implementation, OTA (Over-the-Air) updates, and MQTT (Message Queuing Telemetry Transport) protocol integration. These advanced features enhance the capabilities of ESP-IDF, enabling the creation of more sophisticated and versatile IoT applications.

In the upcoming chapter, we will take a look at the practical application of IoT in industries and compare Industry 3.0 with Industry 4.0. We will study the MODBUS Serial Communication protocol, which is still widely known in industries, and examine how IoT facilitates the data transmission process by capturing data from existing Modbus assets and using communication protocols to transfer it to the cloud for remote controlling and monitoring.

References

1. https://docs.espressif.com/projects/esp-idf/en/latest/esp32/get-started/
2. Ni, K., Chen, Y., & Zhang, K. (2019). Industrial Internet of Things (IIoT) and Its Wireless Technologies. IEEE Communications Magazine, 57(1), 68-74
3. Espressif Systems. (n.d.). ESP8266. Retrieved from https://www.espressif.com/en/products/socs/esp8266
4. Espressif Systems. (n.d.). ESP32. Retrieved from https://www.espressif.com/en/products/socs/esp32

5. Espressif's ESP-NOW Documentation: ESP-NOW - Espressif Docs
6. Official ESP8266 Arduino Core Documentation: ESP8266 Arduino Core
7. Official ESP32 Arduino Core Documentation: ESP32 Arduino Core
8. https://espressif.github.io/esp32-c3-book-en/chapter_7/7.4/7.4.2.html

CHAPTER 9

IoT in Industry 4.0

Introduction

The Fourth Industrial Revolution marks the convergence of the physical, digital, and biological realms of technology. At the core of this new era is the Internet of Things (IoT), a network of interconnected devices that communicate with each other and exchange information. IoT is shaking up industries, redefining how we think about connectivity and productivity. This chapter explores the deep implications of IoT in the context of Industrial Revolution 4.0.

The Fourth Industrial Revolution signifies a convergence of technologies, blurring the lines between physical, digital, and biological spheres. Driven by advancements in artificial intelligence (AI), robotics, big data analytics, and IoT, this era marks a pivotal shift in the way we live, work, and interact with technology. Klaus Schwab, in his seminal work, elucidates the fusion of technologies and its impact on socio-economic paradigms, highlighting the pivotal role of IoT in orchestrating this paradigm shift.

IoT in Industry 4.0

The Internet of Things (IoT) is the foundation of connectivity in the Fourth Industrial Revolution, enabling devices to communicate, gather, and analyze real-time data. From smart sensors built into machines to smart home devices that are connected, IoT enables seamless connectivity, transforming everyday objects into smart, data-driven beings. The term **Internet of Things** was coined by the father of the IoT, Kevin Ashton, to describe a network in which everyday objects have internet connectivity, allowing them to transmit and receive data.

The Industrial Internet of Things has revolutionized the manufacturing landscape, transforming traditional manufacturing processes and supply chain management as well as operational efficiency. Today's industrial systems are characterized by real-time monitoring, predictive maintenance, and autonomous systems. These features improve productivity while reducing downtime and operational costs. The integration of IoT into the industrial environment has been a game-changer, with many researchers and industry leaders examining the ways in which IoT can transform manufacturing.

Structure

In this chapter, the following topics will be covered:

- Industry 3.0 versus Industry 4.0: A Paradigm Shift in Manufacturing
  - Industry 3.0: The Era of Automation
  - The Sudden Shift in Industry 4.0
- Implications of the Shift: Transformation in Manufacturing
- Top Technologies in Industry 3.0
- Networking Technologies in Industry 3.0
- Introduction to Serial Communication
  - MODBUS – the Protocol for Industry 3.0
  - Importance of MODBUS in Industry 3.0
- RS-232
  - Understanding RS-232
  - Technical Specifications
  - Benefits
  - Industrial Application of RS-232
- RS-485
  - Understanding RS-485
  - Technical Specifications

- o Benefits
- o Industrial Application of RS-485
- Digitizing MODBUS
  - o IoT Gateway as a Solution
  - o Benefits of MODBUS Digitization with IoT Gateways
  - o Challenges and Considerations
  - o Case Studies and Success Stories
- MODBUS and NODEMCU
  - o Code for NODEMCU
  - o Code Explanation
  - o Hardware Connection
- OneM2M Communication
  - o Importance of OneM2M Communication in Industry 4.0
  - o Benefits of OneM2M
- Matter: The Next Big Thing in IoT Smart Home
  - o Beyond the Hype: MATTER in Action
  - o Benefits to the End User

Industry 3.0 versus Industry 4.0: A Paradigm Shift in Manufacturing

The evolution from Industry 3.0 to Industry 4.0 represents a significant shift in manufacturing and industrial processes, driven by technological advancements and the integration of digital technologies.

Industry 3.0: The Era of Automation

Industry 3.0 marked a pivotal phase in manufacturing, characterized by the introduction of automation and computerization into industrial processes. Key features of Industry 3.0 included the adoption of programmable logic controllers (PLCs), early robotics, and the use of computers for basic automation tasks. This era witnessed the optimization of production lines, leading to increased efficiency and precision in manufacturing.

The advent of Industry 3.0 brought forth notable improvements in productivity, enabling mass production and assembly line manufacturing. However, the systems were largely siloed, operating in isolated environments with limited connectivity between machines and systems. Automation was predominantly rule-based and lacked the flexibility and adaptability necessary for rapid changes in production requirements.

The Emergence of Industry 4.0: The Fourth Industrial Revolution

Industry 4.0 signifies a paradigm shift in manufacturing, propelled by the convergence of digital technologies, data analytics, and connectivity. Unlike its predecessor, Industry 4.0 integrates cyber-physical systems (CPS), the Internet of Things (IoT), artificial intelligence (AI), big data, and cloud computing to create interconnected and intelligent manufacturing environments.

The Sudden Shift in Industry 4.0

The shift represents a significant transformation in the way businesses operate, leveraging advanced technologies to enhance efficiency, productivity, and flexibility. Several factors contribute to the sudden shift in the Industry 4.0 landscape, such as:

- **Connectivity and Interoperability**: Industry 4.0 thrives on connectivity, enabling seamless communication between devices, machines, and systems. IoT serves as the backbone of this interconnected ecosystem, facilitating the exchange of real-time data. Machines and sensors are equipped with connectivity features, allowing them to share information and collaborate autonomously (Lee, 2015).
- **Cyber-Physical Systems (CPS)**: CPS forms the foundation of Industry 4.0, integrating physical machinery with digital systems. These systems are embedded with sensors, actuators, and control systems that facilitate real-time monitoring, analysis, and decision-making. This fusion of physical and digital realms enables autonomous and adaptive operations.
- **Advanced Analytics and AI**: Industry 4.0 harnesses the power of big data analytics and AI to derive actionable insights from the massive volumes of data generated by connected devices. AI algorithms enable predictive maintenance, intelligent decision-making, and optimization of manufacturing processes based on analyzed data.

- **Customization and Flexibility**: Unlike the standardized and rigid processes of Industry 3.0, Industry 4.0 emphasizes customization and flexibility. The ability to swiftly adapt production processes to changing demands and individualized customer requirements is a hallmark feature. This is achieved through modular production, where systems and components can be reconfigured quickly and efficiently.
- **Human-Machine Collaboration**: Industry 4.0 acknowledges the importance of human involvement in manufacturing. Rather than replacing human labor, it emphasizes human-machine collaboration. Workers are empowered with augmented reality (AR), virtual reality (VR), and wearable devices that enhance their capabilities and provide real-time information for decision-making.

Implications of the Shift: Transformation in Manufacturing

The sudden shift from Industry 3.0 to Industry 4.0 has far-reaching implications across various aspects of manufacturing:

- **Enhanced Efficiency and Productivity**: Industry 4.0 technologies optimize processes, minimize downtime through predictive maintenance, and improve resource utilization. This leads to increased efficiency and productivity across manufacturing operations.
- **Agility and Innovation**: The flexibility and adaptability of Industry 4.0 allow for rapid innovation and agile responses to market demands. Manufacturers can swiftly adjust production lines and introduce new products, responding to changing consumer preferences.
- **Data-Driven Decision-Making**: The abundance of data generated by interconnected devices enables data-driven decision-making. Real-time analytics empower manufacturers with valuable insights for optimizing processes, reducing waste, and improving quality.
- **Transformation of Business Models**: Industry 4.0 facilitates new business models centered around services, customization, and predictive maintenance. Companies are transitioning from traditional product-centric models to service-oriented approaches, offering value-added services and personalized experiences.

Top Technologies in Industry 3.0

Industry 3.0, marked by the introduction of automation and computerization into industrial processes, saw the emergence and adoption of several key technologies that transformed manufacturing and automation. Here are some of the top technologies that defined Industry 3.0:

- **Programmable Logic Controllers (PLCs):** PLCs revolutionized industrial automation by replacing hardwired relay systems with programmable controllers. These devices could be programmed to control machinery and perform various tasks, enhancing flexibility and efficiency in manufacturing processes.
- **Supervisory Control and Data Acquisition (SCADA):** SCADA systems facilitated real-time monitoring and control of industrial processes across vast areas. They allowed operators to remotely monitor and manage different components of a system through graphical interfaces, enhancing operational visibility and control.
- **Computer Numerical Control (CNC) Machines:** CNC machines automated manufacturing processes by using computerized controls to operate machinery, such as lathes, mills, and routers. These machines offered precision, repeatability, and the ability to produce complex shapes and parts.
- **Human-Machine Interface (HMI)**: HMIs provided a graphical interface between operators and machines, allowing for intuitive interaction and control. They displayed real-time data, enabling operators to monitor processes and make informed decisions.
- **Robotics and Automated Assembly Lines:** Industry 3.0 saw the introduction of robots in manufacturing processes. These robots were employed for tasks like welding, assembly, and material handling, leading to increased efficiency and precision in production lines.
- **CAD/CAM Software:** Computer-Aided Design (CAD) and Computer-Aided Manufacturing (CAM) software enabled the design and manufacturing of products with greater accuracy and efficiency. They allowed engineers to create designs digitally and convert them into manufacturing instructions for CNC machines.
- **Barcodes and RFID Technology:** Barcodes and Radio-Frequency Identification (RFID) tags were used for inventory management, tracking products, and managing supply chains. They enabled automated

identification and tracking of items, streamlining logistics and inventory processes.

- **Process Control Systems:** Advanced process control systems were developed to regulate and optimize industrial processes. These systems utilized algorithms and sensors to maintain optimal conditions, ensuring consistent quality and efficiency.
- **Data Acquisition and Control Systems:** Systems for data acquisition and control collected data from various sensors and devices, allowing for monitoring and adjustment of parameters in real-time. They formed the basis for process optimization and predictive maintenance.

These technologies formed the backbone of Industry 3.0, driving automation, efficiency, and productivity in manufacturing and industrial processes.

Please note that while Industry 3.0 was defined by these technologies, the subsequent phases, including Industry 4.0, built upon these foundations, incorporating newer technologies like IoT, AI, and cloud computing for further advancements in industrial automation and connectivity.

Networking Technologies in Industry 3.0

The adoption of networking technologies such as Ethernet, serial communication (RS-232/485), and fieldbuses facilitated communication between devices and systems, enabling data exchange and control across industrial environments. Serial communication and MODBUS played pivotal roles in Industry 3.0, forming the backbone of networking in industrial settings. Exploring their importance involves understanding their functionalities, adoption, and impact on industrial communication during that era.

Serial communication and MODBUS provided a standardized method for devices from different manufacturers to communicate seamlessly. They offered a common language for devices in industrial environments, allowing for interoperability and compatibility among diverse equipment.

Serial communication, particularly RS-485, served as the backbone of networking in Industry 3.0. RS-485's multidrop capability enabled the creation of robust networks connecting multiple devices across industrial facilities. MODBUS, utilizing serial communication, facilitated data exchange between devices, PLCs, sensors, and other industrial equipment.

The use of serial communication and MODBUS allowed for real-time monitoring and control of industrial processes. SCADA systems, PLCs, and other control devices utilized MODBUS for data acquisition, enabling operators to monitor processes and make informed decisions based on real-time data.

RS-485 offered reliability in industrial environments characterized by electrical noise and harsh conditions. Its differential signaling and multidrop capability made it resilient to interferences, ensuring robust communication across factory floors and industrial settings.

Despite advancements in communication protocols in subsequent industrial eras, the legacy of serial communication and MODBUS persists in many industrial systems. Their widespread adoption during Industry 3.0 led to the establishment of communication standards that continue to be utilized in numerous industrial applications.

Serial communication, particularly RS-485, coupled with the MODBUS protocol, served as a cornerstone in Industry 3.0, providing a standardized and reliable method for devices to communicate in industrial settings. Their impact on industrial communication, networking, and real-time control remains evident, even as newer communication protocols evolve in Industry 4.0 and beyond.

Introduction to Serial Communication

Serial communication is a method of sending data one bit at a time over a communication channel. It involves the sequential transmission of data through a single wire or pair of wires, enabling devices to communicate and exchange information.

In Industry 3.0, two primary types of serial communication were prevalent: RS-232 and RS-485. RS-232, a common standard for serial communication, allowed devices to communicate over short distances. RS-485, known for its multidrop capability and longer range, enabled communication over longer distances and in noisy industrial environments.

MODBUS: The Protocol for Industry 3.0

The MODBUS protocol stands as a foundational communication protocol used extensively in industrial automation and control systems. Developed by Modicon (now Schneider Electric) in the late 1970s, MODBUS was designed to enable communication between devices and systems in industrial environments, facilitating data exchange, monitoring, and control.

Operating on a master-slave architecture, MODBUS employs a simple and structured messaging system, allowing a master device, typically a supervisory control system or a programmable logic controller (PLC), to communicate with one or multiple slave devices.

This protocol utilizes various communication methods, including serial communication (such as RS-232/485) and TCP/IP for Ethernet-based networks, to facilitate communication over short and long distances. MODBUS uses a request-response mechanism, where the master device initiates communication by sending a query to the slave devices, prompting them to respond with the requested data or perform specific actions.

Its simplicity, versatility, and reliability have made MODBUS widely adopted in industrial automation, offering a standardized method for devices from different manufacturers to communicate seamlessly, fostering interoperability and compatibility among diverse industrial equipment.

The protocol's structured format, ease of implementation, and ability to support various data formats make it suitable for real-time monitoring, control, and data exchange in industrial settings, cementing its legacy as a fundamental communication protocol in the realm of industrial automation and control systems.

Importance of MODBUS in Industry 3.0

The MODBUS protocol became the industrial standard, and soon, every industrial device became MODBUS compatible. Here are the important factors to consider when choosing MODBUS as the protocol for Industry 3.0:

- **Interoperability and Compatibility:** During the Industry 3.0 era, MODBUS played a crucial role in fostering interoperability among devices and systems from different manufacturers. It provided a standardized communication protocol that allowed diverse industrial equipment to communicate seamlessly, regardless of their origins.
- **Integration of Devices:** In Industry 3.0, manufacturing plants and industrial facilities comprised various devices and systems from different vendors. MODBUS facilitated the integration of these heterogeneous systems, enabling data exchange for monitoring, control, and automation purposes.
- **SCADA and PLC Communication:** SCADA systems and PLCs, fundamental components of Industry 3.0, heavily relied on the MODBUS protocol for data transmission. It enabled SCADA systems to gather real-time data from remote devices and control processes, while PLCs utilized MODBUS to communicate with sensors, actuators, and other industrial devices.

- **Cost-Effectiveness and Simplicity:** One of the key strengths of MODBUS in Industry 3.0 was its simplicity and cost-effectiveness. Its straightforward implementation and minimal overhead made it an attractive choice for industrial applications, especially in environments where complex communication protocols were unnecessary.

The MODBUS protocol was at the core of Industry 3.0. It enabled the interoperability, integration, and exchange of data between various industrial equipment and systems. Because of its simplicity, compatibility, and affordability, MODBUS was widely used in SCADA and PLCs, as well as various industrial automation applications at the time.

As Industry 4.0 advances with more sophisticated communication protocols and technologies, the continued use and legacy of MODBUS demonstrate its importance in industrial communication.

Even as technology progresses toward Industry 4.0 and beyond, the legacy of MODBUS persists in many industrial applications. Despite its limitations in speed, security, and complexity compared to newer protocols, many existing systems still rely on MODBUS due to its widespread adoption, simplicity, and compatibility with legacy devices.

RS-232

RS232, or Recommended Standard 232, is a communication protocol that has been a cornerstone in serial data transmission for decades. Its development by the Electronic Industries Association (EIA) in the 1960s laid the foundation for serial communication between devices, forming the backbone of numerous industrial, commercial, and personal applications.

Understanding RS232 Protocol

Let us take a look at the working of RS-232 Protocol. When a device initiates communication, it sends a start bit, followed by the data bits, parity bit (if used), and stop bit(s). The receiving device decodes this serial data and reconstructs the original parallel data. Handshaking signals like RTS/CTS or XON/XOFF are utilized for flow control to prevent data loss due to buffer overflow.

- **Working Principle:** At its core, RS232 is a serial communication protocol defining the electrical characteristics and signaling for the exchange of data between devices. It uses a simple asynchronous transmission method, where data is sent one bit at a time over a single wire or a pair of wires.

- **Physical Interface:** The RS232 standard specifies the physical interface, including voltage levels, signal timing, and connector pin assignments. It commonly uses a 9-pin or 25-pin connector, with each pin serving specific functions such as data transmission (TX), data reception (RX), ground (GND), and control signals (such as RTS/CTS for flow control).
- **Data Transmission:** RS232 operates by converting parallel data from a device into a serial format for transmission. It uses a start bit, data bits (typically 7 or 8), optional parity bit for error detection, and stop bit(s) to indicate the end of a data frame. This asynchronous nature allows devices to communicate without a synchronized clock signal.

Technical Specifications

Technical Specifications for RS232 Protocol are as follows:

- **Electrical Characteristics:**
    - **Voltage Levels**: Typically uses voltage levels between -15V and -3V for logical 1 and +3V and +15V for logical 0.
    - **Signal Levels**: Single-ended signaling with a ground reference.
    - **Data Rate**: Commonly supports data rates up to 115.2 kbps (kilobits per second) over short distances (up to 15 meters).
- **Physical Interface:**
    - **Connectors**: Uses either a 9-pin or 25-pin connector, with pin assignments for data transmission (TX), data reception (RX), ground (GND), control signals (RTS/CTS, DTR/DSR), and others.
    - **Cable**: Typically uses shielded or unshielded twisted pair cables for transmission.
- **Data Transmission:**
    - **Frame Structure**: Start bit, data bits (7 or 8), optional parity bit (even, odd, or none), stop bit(s).
    - **Transmission Mode**: Asynchronous transmission without a synchronized clock signal.
- **Flow Control:**
    - **Handshaking**: Supports hardware flow control using RTS/CTS (Ready To Send/Clear To Send) or software-based XON/XOFF protocols for flow control.

Benefits of RS232

Here are a few benefits of using RS232 protocol:

- **Universal Compatibility:** RS232 has been widely adopted across industries, ensuring compatibility among various devices regardless of the manufacturer.
- **Simple Implementation**: Its relatively straightforward implementation makes it accessible for basic communication needs without complex hardware or software requirements.
- **Reliability**: In many industrial settings, RS232 is favored for its robustness in noisy environments due to its voltage signaling.

Industrial Applications

Some of the most common applications of RS232 are as follows:

- **Automation and Control Systems:** RS232 has been integral in industrial automation, connecting PLCs (Programmable Logic Controllers), sensors, and control devices. Its reliability and simplicity make it suitable for various manufacturing processes and machinery control.
- **Data Acquisition:** In scientific and industrial settings, RS232 interfaces with instruments and data acquisition systems for real-time data collection, allowing efficient monitoring and analysis.
- **Legacy Systems:** Many legacy devices and equipment still utilize RS232, necessitating its use in industries where upgrading or replacing existing machinery may not be feasible due to cost or technical limitations.

While RS232 remains prevalent, newer technologies like USB, Ethernet, and wireless protocols are increasingly replacing it in modern devices due to faster data rates, easier connectivity, and higher versatility. RS232, despite its age, remains an integral part of industrial and commercial applications due to its reliability, simplicity, and widespread adoption. Its legacy continues to be felt across various sectors, although newer technologies are gradually taking its place.

RS-485

RS485, an evolution of RS232, stands as a robust communication protocol known for its versatility and reliability in industrial applications. Its development, building upon the foundation of RS232, brought about improvements in long-distance data transmission and noise immunity, making it a go-to solution for various industrial communication needs.

Understanding RS485 Protocol

Devices on an RS485 network are connected in a daisy-chain or bus topology. Each device has a unique address, allowing targeted communication. Differential signaling ensures that the receiver detects the voltage difference between the A and B wires, enabling data transmission even in the presence of noise.

- **Working Principle:** RS485, similar to RS232, facilitates serial data transmission but excels in enabling communication over longer distances and in noisy environments. It's a differential signaling standard, meaning it transmits data as voltage differences between two wires (A and B), providing better noise immunity compared to the single-ended signaling of RS232.
- **Physical Interface:** RS485 typically employs a 2-wire or 4-wire configuration. In the 2-wire setup, one pair of twisted wires (A and B) transmits data bidirectionally, while the 4-wire configuration includes an additional pair for full-duplex communication, enabling simultaneous transmission and reception.
- **Data Transmission:** Similar to RS232, RS485 utilizes a start bit, data bits (commonly 8), optional parity bit for error checking, and stop bit(s). However, its differential signaling allows it to achieve higher data rates over longer distances (up to 1200 meters) with improved noise immunity.

Technical Specifications

Technical specifications for RS485 Protocol are as follows:

- **Electrical Characteristics:**
    - **Voltage Levels**: Utilizes differential signaling, typically around 2V to 6V (differential) for logical 1 and inverted levels for logical 0.
    - **Signal Levels**: Differential signaling with better noise immunity compared to RS232.
    - **Data Rate**: Supports higher data rates up to 10 Mbps (megabits per second) over longer distances (up to 1200 meters).
- **Physical Interface:**
    - **Configuration**: 2-wire or 4-wire setup (2-wire for half-duplex, 4-wire for full-duplex communication).

  - **Connectors**: Utilizes standard connectors similar to RS232, often with twisted pair cables for better noise immunity.
- **Data Transmission:**
  - **Frame Structure**: Start bit, data bits (usually 8), optional parity bit, stop bit(s).
  - **Transmission Mode**: Asynchronous or synchronous transmission with better noise immunity due to differential signaling.
- **Multi-drop Capability:**
  - Allows multiple devices to be connected on the same bus, each with a unique address, facilitating multi-drop communication.

Benefits of RS485

Here are a few benefits of using RS485 protocol:

- **Longer Distance Communication:** RS485 excels in transmitting data over extended distances, making it suitable for applications spread across large industrial environments.
- **Noise Immunity:** Its differential signaling reduces susceptibility to electromagnetic interference (EMI) and noise, ensuring reliable data transmission in electrically noisy settings.
- **Multi-Drop Capability:** RS485 supports multi-drop configurations, enabling multiple devices to communicate on the same bus, thereby reducing wiring complexity in industrial setups.

Industrial Applications

Some of the most common applications of RS232 are as follows:

- **Building Automation:** RS485 finds extensive use in building automation systems, linking various components like HVAC (Heating, Ventilation, and Air Conditioning), access control systems, and lighting controls due to its ability to cover large distances and handle multiple devices.
- **Industrial Control Systems:** In industrial settings, RS485 is integral to control systems, connecting PLCs, motor drives, sensors, and HMI (Human-Machine Interface) devices, ensuring efficient and reliable communication among different components.
- **Transportation and Traffic Management:** RS485 is utilized in traffic signal control systems, toll booth management, and transportation networks

due to its long-distance capabilities and resistance to interference, enabling seamless communication across wide areas.

RS485 remains a cornerstone in industrial communication due to its robustness, long-distance capabilities, and noise immunity. Its prevalence across various sectors highlights its importance, although advancements in technology continue to shape the landscape of industrial communication. While RS485 continues to be extensively used in industries, the advent of Ethernet-based protocols, wireless technologies, and IoT (Internet of Things) devices is gradually expanding communication options, offering higher speeds and greater flexibility.

Serial Quick Reference Guide

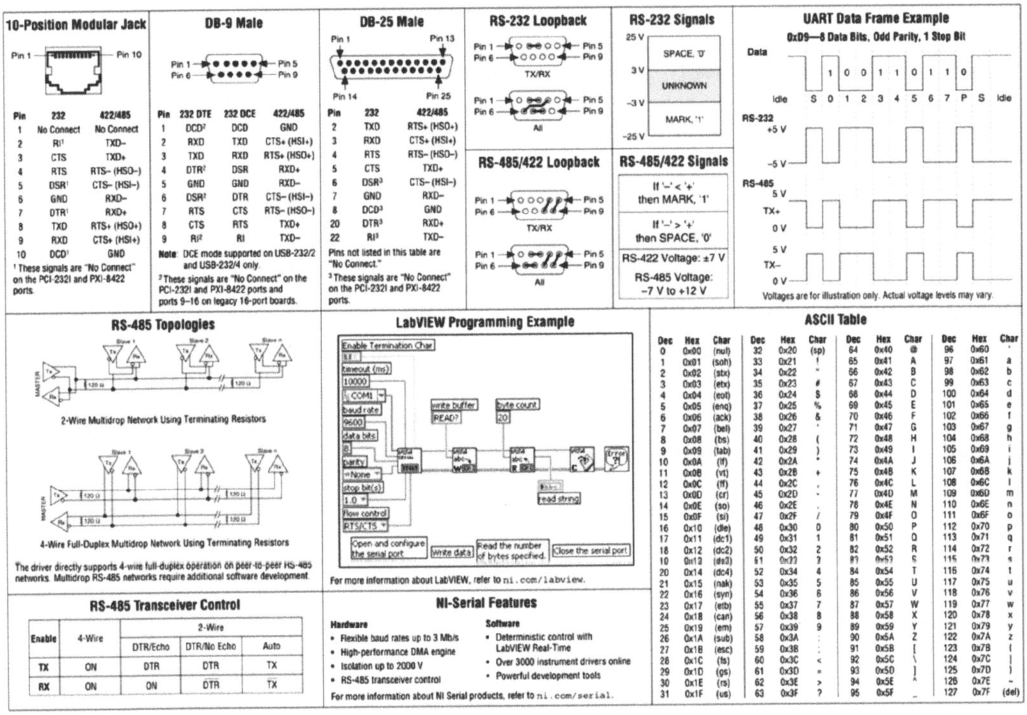

Figure 9.1: *RS232/485 quick reference guide*

Digitizing MODBUS

In the era of Industry 4.0, the integration of legacy systems with modern technologies has become imperative for efficient and intelligent industrial operations. One such integration is the digitization of Modbus protocols through the use of Internet of Things gateways. Modbus, a widely used communication protocol in industrial automation, is known for its simplicity and reliability.

By leveraging IoT gateways, organizations can bridge the gap between legacy Modbus-enabled devices and the Internet, unlocking new possibilities for real-time monitoring, analytics, and enhanced decision-making. This chapter explores the intricacies of digitizing Modbus protocols with IoT gateways, the benefits it offers, and the challenges involved.

Modbus operates in a master-slave architecture, where a master device initiates communication with one or more slave devices. The master sends requests for data, and the slaves respond accordingly. This simplicity and efficiency have contributed to the widespread adoption of Modbus in industries such as manufacturing, energy, and transportation.

Challenges in Traditional Modbus Systems

While Modbus has proven its reliability over the years, traditional Modbus systems face limitations when it comes to connectivity, scalability, and data accessibility. These challenges include:

- **Limited Connectivity:** Traditional Modbus networks often rely on serial communication, which has limitations in terms of distance and speed. Ethernet-based Modbus solutions exist, but the integration of legacy devices can be challenging.
- **Scalability Issues:** As industrial systems expand, the scalability of traditional Modbus networks becomes a concern. Adding new devices and expanding the network may require significant modifications and result in downtime.
- **Data Accessibility:** Extracting data from Modbus-enabled devices for analysis and decision-making can be cumbersome. Real-time monitoring and remote access to Modbus data are crucial for modern industrial processes but are not inherently supported by traditional Modbus setups.

IoT Gateway as a Solution

The advent of IoT gateways offers a viable solution to overcome the limitations of traditional Modbus systems. An IoT gateway serves as a bridge between legacy devices and the Internet, enabling seamless communication, data collection, and integration with cloud-based platforms. Here's how IoT gateways facilitate the digitization of Modbus protocols:

- **Protocol Translation:** IoT gateways are equipped to translate Modbus protocols into more modern and universally accepted communication protocols such as MQTT (Message Queuing Telemetry Transport) or

HTTP. This translation allows Modbus-enabled devices to communicate with cloud services and other IoT devices.

- **Connectivity Options:** IoT gateways support various connectivity options, including wired (Ethernet) and wireless (Wi-Fi, cellular) connections. This flexibility addresses the connectivity limitations of traditional Modbus networks, especially in scenarios where devices are geographically dispersed.
- **Edge Computing Capabilities:** Many IoT gateways are equipped with edge computing capabilities, allowing them to process data locally before transmitting it to the cloud. This is particularly beneficial in applications where real-time analytics and low-latency communication are critical.
- **Security Features:** Security is a paramount concern in industrial environments. IoT gateways come with robust security features, including encryption, authentication, and secure boot mechanisms, ensuring the integrity and confidentiality of Modbus data during transmission.

Implementation Steps

Implementing the digitization of Modbus protocols using IoT gateways involves several key steps:

1. **Device Assessment:** Begin by assessing the existing Modbus-enabled devices in the industrial environment. Identify their communication protocols, physical interfaces, and data types.
2. **Gateway Selection:** Choose an IoT gateway that aligns with the specific requirements of the Modbus-enabled devices. Consider factors such as protocol support, connectivity options, and security features.
3. **Configuration and Integration:** Configure the IoT gateway to communicate with Modbus-enabled devices. This involves specifying the communication parameters, addressing schemes, and data types. Integrate the gateway into the existing network infrastructure.
4. **Protocol Translation:** Set up the IoT gateway to translate Modbus protocols into a format compatible with cloud platforms or other IoT devices. This step ensures seamless communication between legacy devices and modern systems.
5. **Connectivity Setup:** Establish the desired connectivity for the IoT gateway. This may involve connecting the gateway to the local network via Ethernet or configuring wireless connectivity options such as Wi-Fi or cellular.

6. **Security Configuration:** Implement robust security measures on the IoT gateway to safeguard against unauthorized access and data breaches. This includes configuring encryption, authentication, and access control settings.
7. **Testing and Validation:** Thoroughly test the integration of IoT gateways with Modbus-enabled devices. Validate data transmission, protocol translation, and security features to ensure the reliability and integrity of the system.

Benefits of Modbus Digitization with IoT Gateways

The digitization of Modbus protocols using IoT gateways brings forth a multitude of benefits for industrial processes:

- **Enhanced Connectivity:** IoT gateways overcome the limitations of traditional Modbus networks by providing versatile connectivity options, including Ethernet, Wi-Fi, and cellular. This ensures seamless communication between devices, regardless of their physical location.
- **Real-time Monitoring:** With IoT gateways, organizations can achieve real-time monitoring of Modbus-enabled devices. This capability is crucial for proactive maintenance, performance optimization, and early detection of anomalies.
- **Scalability:** The flexibility of IoT gateways facilitates the seamless integration of new Modbus-enabled devices as industrial systems expand. This scalability is essential for accommodating the dynamic nature of modern industrial environments.
- **Remote Access and Control:** IoT gateways enable remote access to Modbus data, allowing operators and engineers to monitor and control industrial processes from anywhere with an internet connection. This remote accessibility enhances operational efficiency and reduces the need for on-site presence.
- **Data Analytics and Insights:** By integrating Modbus data into cloud-based platforms, organizations can leverage advanced analytics and machine learning algorithms to derive actionable insights. This data-driven approach enables informed decision-making and predictive maintenance strategies.
- **Cost-effectiveness:** The digitization of Modbus protocols using IoT gateways eliminates the need for extensive infrastructure upgrades.

Organizations can leverage existing Modbus-enabled devices while enhancing their capabilities with modern IoT technologies, resulting in a cost-effective solution.

Challenges and Considerations

While the benefits of Modbus digitization with IoT gateways are substantial, certain challenges and considerations need to be addressed:

- **Legacy Device Compatibility:** Some legacy Modbus-enabled devices may have limitations in terms of compatibility with IoT gateways. In such cases, additional hardware or firmware updates may be required to ensure seamless integration.
- **Security Concerns:** Connecting industrial systems to the internet introduces cybersecurity risks. Organizations must implement robust security measures on both the IoT gateways and cloud platforms to protect against unauthorized access, data breaches, and malicious attacks.
- **Data Privacy Compliance:** Industries operating in regulated environments must adhere to data privacy and compliance standards. Ensure that the digitization process complies with relevant regulations to avoid legal and regulatory consequences.
- **Reliability and Redundancy:** Industrial processes demand high levels of reliability. Implementing redundancy measures and backup systems is crucial to minimize downtime in the event of IoT gateway failures or communication disruptions.
- **Integration with Existing Systems:** The digitization process should seamlessly integrate with existing SCADA systems, control systems, and other components of the industrial infrastructure. Compatibility and interoperability are key considerations during the implementation phase.

Case Studies and Success Stories

Several industries have successfully implemented the digitization of Modbus protocols using IoT gateways, leading to improved efficiency, reduced operational costs, and enhanced decision-making capabilities. Here are a few notable case studies:

- **Manufacturing Industry:** A leading automotive manufacturer implemented IoT gateways to digitize Modbus protocols across its production lines. This enabled real-time monitoring of machine health, predictive maintenance, and streamlined production processes, resulting in a significant reduction in downtime and increased overall equipment effectiveness (OEE).

- **Energy Sector:** A power plant integrated IoT gateways to connect Modbus-enabled sensors and actuators to a cloud-based platform. This allowed for centralized monitoring of energy consumption, optimization of power generation, and the implementation of energy-efficient strategies, leading to cost savings and sustainability improvements.
- **Water Treatment Facilities:** Municipal water treatment facilities adopted IoT gateways to digitize Modbus protocols from legacy SCADA systems. This resulted in remote monitoring of water quality, timely detection of equipment failures, and improved compliance with water quality standards.

MODBUS and NODEMCU

Nodemcu's Wi-Fi and microcontroller capabilities make it an all-powerful tool for connecting with industrial giants and Modbus RS485 devices. Let's take a look at how to use this powerful duo to gain valuable insights from your Modbus RS485 machines.

Think of Modbus as a language your devices speak. RS485, on the other hand, is the communication channel, a robust serial interface for long-distance data exchange. Combining these two, Modbus RS485 allows for intelligent communication between multiple devices on a single bus, like a bustling marketplace buzzing with information.

The Nodemcu, an ESP8266-based microcontroller, acts as your interpreter and data courier. Its built-in Wi-Fi lets you wirelessly access the data acquired from Modbus devices, opening doors to remote monitoring, control, and analysis.

Hardware Handshake:

To bridge the gap between Nodemcu and Modbus RS485 device, you will need some handy hardware:

- **Nodemcu:** The Wi-Fi micro-controller.
- **Level Converter:** Modbus RS485 uses differential signals (A and B), unlike Nodemcu's logic levels. A level converter translates this voltage language, ensuring smooth communication. Popular options include MAX3485 and ADM2483.

- **Resistors:** Depending on your level converter, you might need pull-up and pull-down resistors for stable signal transmission.
- **Wires:** Connect the level converter's A and B pins to the Modbus RS485 device's corresponding terminals. The Nodemcu connects to the level converter's RX and TX pins.

Code for NODEMCU

Here is the code for Nodemcu:

```
//ESP8266 with MFM meter


#include <ModbusRTU.h>

#include <SoftwareSerial.h>




float InttoFloat(uint16_t Data0,uint16_t Data1) {

  float x;

  unsigned long *p;

  p = (unsigned long*)&x;

  *p = (unsigned long)Data0 << 16 | Data1; //Big-endian

  return(x);

}

SoftwareSerial S(D3, D2);




ModbusRTU mb;


bool  cbWrite(Modbus::ResultCode  event,  uint16_t  transactionId,  void*
data) {
```

```
  Serial.printf_P("Request result: 0x%02X, Mem: %d\n", event, ESP.
  getFreeHeap());

  return true;

}


void setup() {

pinMode(D4, OUTPUT);

  Serial.begin(9600);

  S.begin(9600, SWSERIAL_8N1);

  mb.begin(&S,D4); // RE/DE connected to D0 of ESP8266

  mb.master();

}


uint16_t val[2];

void loop() {


  if (!mb.slave()) {

      digitalWrite(D4, HIGH);  // Enable RS485 transmitter for sending
      request

    mb.readHreg(10, 400133, val, 2, cbWrite); // Slave id is 1 and
    register address is 3926 and

      digitalWrite(D4, LOW);

    //we are reading 2 bytes from the register and saving in val

    while(mb.slave()) { // Check if transaction is active

      mb.task();

      delay(100);

    }

    Serial.println("Register Values ");
```

```
    Serial.println(val[0]);

    Serial.println(val[1]);

  float voltage= InttoFloat(val[1],val[0]);

  Serial.println("Voltage= ");

  Serial.print(voltage);

  Serial.println("V");


      }

  delay(500);


}
```

Code Explanation

Here's a line-by-line explanation of the code:

1. **Header Files:**
   a. **`#include <ModbusRTU.h>`:** Includes the ModbusRTU library for communicating with Modbus devices.
   b. **`#include <SoftwareSerial.h>`:** Includes the SoftwareSerial library for creating serial communication on arbitrary pins.
2. **Function Definition:**
   a. **`float InttoFloat(uint16_t Data0, uint16_t Data1)`:** This function converts two 16-bit integers (**`Data0`** and **`Data1`**) into a floating-point value. It assumes a big-endian byte order, which might need adjustment for your meter.
3. **Software Serial:**
   a. **`SoftwareSerial S(D3, D2);`:** Creates a software serial object named **`"S"`** using pins **`D3`** as RX and **`D2`** as TX. This will be used for Modbus communication.
4. **Modbus Object:**
   a. **`ModbusRTU mb;`:** Creates a **`ModbusRTU`** object named **`"mb"`** for managing Modbus communication.

5. **Callback Function:**
   a. **`bool cbWrite(Modbus::ResultCode event, uint16_t transactionId, void* data)`:** This function is called when a Modbus write request completes. It prints the request result and available memory to the serial monitor.
6. **Setup Function:**
   a. **`pinMode(D4, OUTPUT);`:** Sets pin D4 as an output, likely used to control RS485 transmission.
   b. **`Serial.begin(9600);`:** Starts serial communication on the hardware serial port for debugging.
   c. **`S.begin(9600, SWSERIAL_8N1);`:** Starts software serial communication with 9600 baud rate and 8N1 settings for Modbus.
   d. **`mb.begin(&S, D4);`:** Initializes the Modbus object using the software serial port and pin D4 for RS485 control.
   e. **`mb.master();`:** Sets the ESP8266 as the Modbus master, initiating communication with devices.
7. **Loop Function:**
   a. **`if (!mb.slave()) { ... }`:** Checks if the ESP8266 is not currently in a slave transaction.
   b. **`digitalWrite(D4, HIGH);`:** Enables the RS485 transmitter.
   c. **`mb.readHreg(10, 40133, val, 2, cbWrite);`:** Reads two 16-bit registers (4 bytes) from the device with slave ID 10, starting at address 400133, and stores the values in the val array. The cbWrite function is called when the transaction completes.
   d. **`digitalWrite(D4, LOW);`:** Disables the RS485 transmitter.
   e. **`while(mb.slave()) { ... }`:** Waits for the transaction to complete.
   f. **`mb.task();`:** Processes Modbus tasks.
   g. **`delay(100);`:** Delays 100 milliseconds.
   h. **`Serial.println("Register Values ");`** and subsequent lines: Print the read register values and convert them to a floating-point voltage value using the InttoFloat function.
   i. **`delay(500);`:** Delays 500 milliseconds before starting the next loop iteration.

Hardware Connection

The connections between the Nodemcu and the MAX485 Module are shown in *Figure* 9.2.

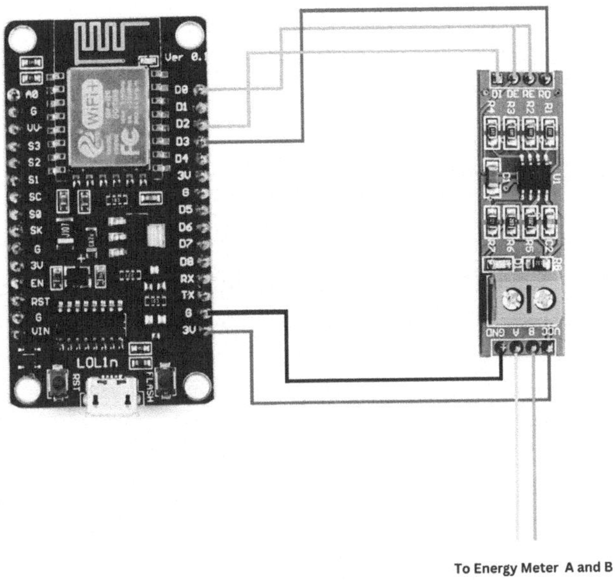

Figure 9.2: *Connection Diagram*

You can connect the Energy meter to the Module with the help of wires, as shown in *Figure* 9.3.

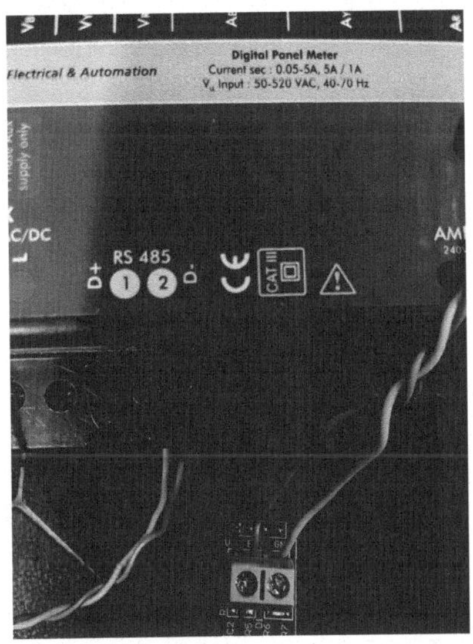

Figure 9.3: *Meter Connections with Module*

A few important things to understand while programming are the Slave ID of the MFM meter, its Baud Rate, Parity, and register addresses. Refer to the user manual of the meter to obtain this information.

The user must take care of all these details before programming the Nodemcu. To do this, refer to the programming mode section in the MFM meter's user manual. Enter programming mode and note down all these important details for data transmission.

OneM2M Communication

OneM2M represents a global standard for Machine-to-Machine (M2M) and Internet of Things (IoT) communications, designed to foster interoperability and harmonization across various IoT applications and devices. Established by leading ICT standards development organizations, OneM2M aims to unify disparate IoT technologies, enabling seamless data exchange and communication.

It stands as a pivotal standard in the realm of IoT communication, embodying a comprehensive framework crafted to foster seamless interoperability and harmonization across diverse IoT devices and applications.

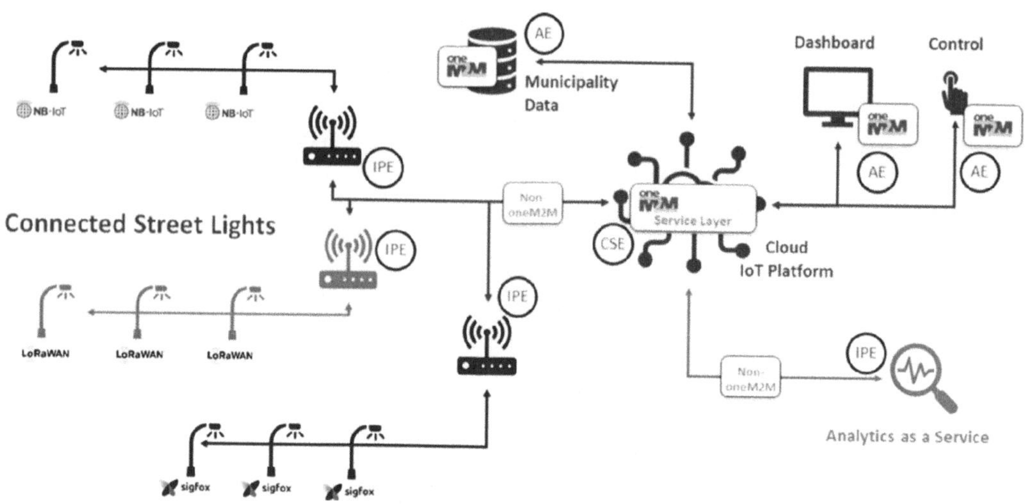

Figure 9.4: OneM2M Protocol

At its core, OneM2M establishes a standardized service layer architecture, encompassing multiple hierarchical levels from Application to Connectivity, aimed at facilitating robust communication and data exchange among heterogeneous IoT entities. Its Common Services Entity (CSE) acts as the linchpin, orchestrating data management, enabling device discovery, and delivering cross-domain interoperability. This protocol embraces diverse communication technologies, including wireless and wired solutions, and provides a universal interface for seamless integration, irrespective of the underlying network or device heterogeneity.

OneM2M's emphasis on scalability, security, and flexibility propels its relevance in facilitating global connectivity, enabling real-time data aggregation and analytics, thus empowering industries to derive actionable insights and make informed decisions in the context of smart manufacturing, smart cities, and beyond. The protocol's standardized approach not only ensures interoperability but also fosters innovation, laying the foundation for a connected, adaptive, and efficient IoT ecosystem across various domains and industries.

Importance of OneM2M Communication in Industry 4.0

Here are some important factors to consider when using OneM2M for industrial applications:

- **Interoperability and Standardization:** In the Industry 4.0 landscape, where diverse IoT devices and technologies coexist, OneM2M plays a crucial role in establishing standardized communication protocols. Its framework ensures interoperability among devices from different manufacturers and technology domains, promoting a unified ecosystem that allows seamless integration and interaction.
- **Scalability and Flexibility:** OneM2M's standardized architecture enables scalable and flexible deployment of IoT solutions. It supports various communication protocols and networks, allowing devices to communicate regardless of their underlying technologies. This flexibility accommodates diverse use cases, ranging from smart manufacturing to smart cities, by providing a common platform for data sharing and management.
- **Security and Data Management:** Security is paramount in Industry 4.0, and OneM2M addresses this by implementing robust security measures. It offers secure authentication, authorization, and encryption mechanisms to safeguard sensitive data transmitted between IoT devices, ensuring data integrity and privacy in interconnected environments.
- **Real-time Monitoring and Decision-making:** OneM2M's standardized approach facilitates real-time data collection, processing, and analysis from various IoT devices. This capability empowers industries with

actionable insights, enabling data-driven decision-making and enhancing operational efficiency across manufacturing, logistics, energy management, and more.

- **Global Connectivity and Integration:** As an international standard, OneM2M fosters global connectivity by harmonizing IoT deployments worldwide. It enables seamless integration across borders and industries, promoting collaboration and innovation on a global scale.
- **Ecosystem Development and Innovation:** By providing a common framework for IoT devices and applications, OneM2M fosters an ecosystem conducive to innovation. It encourages the development of new IoT solutions, services, and applications, driving advancements in technology and enhancing the overall efficiency and effectiveness of Industry 4.0 initiatives.

OneM2M stands as a foundational element in the evolution of IoT technologies within Industry 4.0, offering a standardized and interoperable framework that enables the seamless integration, security, scalability, and innovation required in modern industrial landscapes. Its role as a unifying force in IoT communication lays the groundwork for a connected, efficient, and adaptable industrial ecosystem that fuels the transformative potential of the Fourth Industrial Revolution.

Benefits of OneM2M

OneM2M stands as a standardized communication protocol designed specifically for the IoT ecosystem. It aims to create a common platform for various IoT devices and applications, ensuring interoperability, scalability, and seamless communication across diverse IoT deployments. Let's take a look into the benefits of OneM2M in detail:

- **Interoperability:** OneM2M enables interoperability among different IoT devices, networks, and applications, regardless of the underlying technology or vendor. By providing a common framework and standardized interfaces, it facilitates communication and data exchange between heterogeneous devices and systems.
- **Standardization:** OneM2M offers a standardized architecture, data models, and interfaces. This uniformity simplifies development, integration, and deployment processes for IoT solutions. It ensures consistency across various IoT deployments, promoting compatibility and ease of adoption.

- **Scalability:** The protocol supports scalable solutions, accommodating a vast number of devices and applications within an IoT ecosystem. It allows seamless expansion by handling large volumes of data and managing numerous connected devices efficiently.
- **Flexibility and Adaptability:** OneM2M's flexible architecture enables the integration of diverse devices, services, and applications. It supports various communication technologies, allowing IoT deployments to adapt and evolve with emerging technologies and changing requirements.
- **Security and Privacy:** OneM2M incorporates robust security measures to protect IoT networks and data. It provides authentication, access control, encryption, and privacy mechanisms, ensuring data integrity and confidentiality across the IoT infrastructure.
- **Resource Optimization:** The protocol optimizes network and device resources by efficiently managing data transmission, reducing bandwidth consumption, and minimizing power usage. It employs smart data handling techniques, enabling more efficient utilization of IoT resources.
- **Service Enabling Features:** OneM2M facilitates the creation of advanced IoT services by offering features like service discovery, event handling, notifications, and remote management. These capabilities empower developers to build innovative and value-added services on top of the IoT platform.
- **Cross-Domain Applications:** OneM2M supports cross-domain applications, enabling seamless integration and collaboration between different IoT domains, such as smart cities, healthcare, transportation, and industrial automation. It fosters the creation of comprehensive and interconnected IoT ecosystems.
- **Ecosystem Integration:** The protocol allows integration with other existing IoT standards and initiatives, promoting collaboration and convergence within the IoT landscape. It facilitates harmonization with protocols like MQTT, CoAP, and LwM2M, expanding its applicability and reach.
- **Global Adoption and Support**: OneM2M enjoys global recognition and support from various standardization bodies, industry alliances, and stakeholders. This widespread acceptance fosters a vibrant ecosystem of products and solutions compliant with OneM2M standards.

Matter: The Next Big Thing in IoT Smart Home

For years, the smart home market has been plagued by a fragmented landscape. Imagine a tower of Babel where smart devices whisper instructions in incompatible languages, refusing to cooperate unless under the command of their native app. This frustrating reality has held back the true potential of the smart home, leaving the average consumer in a state of bewildered paralysis. Fortunately, a beacon of hope shines on the horizon in the form of the Matter Protocol.

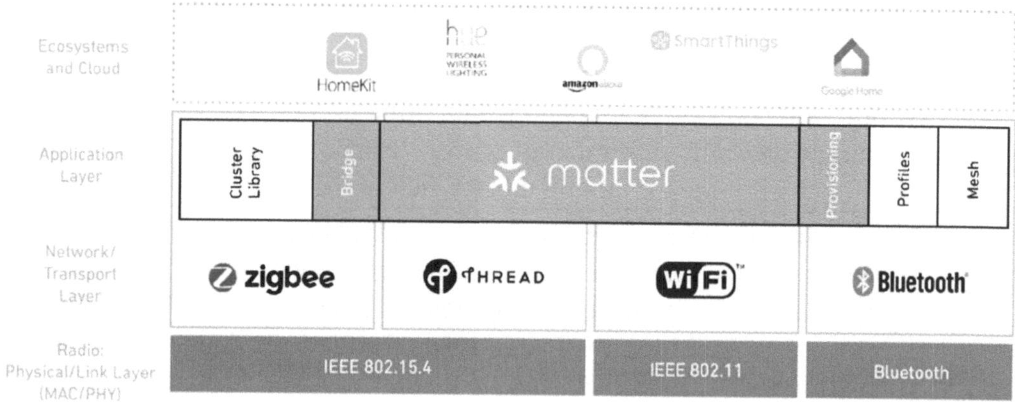

***Figure 9.5**: Matter Protocol*

Matter, born from the ashes of Project Connected Home over IP (CHIP), is an open-source communication standard that aims to unify the smart home ecosystem. Developed by a consortium of industry giants including Amazon, Apple, Google, Samsung, and Zigbee Alliance, Matter speaks the universal language of interoperability. No longer will your Google Assistant be a stranger to your Philips Hue lights, or your Samsung smart lock remain aloof from your Alexa commands. Matter promises seamless communication, allowing different brands and platforms to play happily together in the sandbox of your smart home.

What Makes Matter Magical?

The secret sauce lies in Matter's core principles:

- **IP-Based Communication:** Matter ditches the proprietary protocols of the past and embraces the ubiquitous language of the internet - Internet

Protocol (IP). This means your smart devices connect like your laptop or phone, leveraging the existing infrastructure of your Wi-Fi network for reliable and secure communication.

- **Threading the Future:** While Wi-Fi reigns supreme for long-range connections, Thread shines for low-power devices and multi-hop communication. Matter utilizes Thread mesh networks, where devices act as relays, extending the reach and redundancy of your smart home. Imagine turning on your smart light switch even in the furthest corner of your basement; that's the power of Thread.
- **Commissioning Made Easy:** Eliminate the need for wrestling with obscure manuals and cryptic codes. Matter simplifies device setup using Bluetooth Low Energy (BLE). Simply hold your phone near a device, and it magically enters your smart home ecosystem.
- **Rock-Solid Security:** Security is paramount in a world where even your toaster is connected. Matter prioritizes data encryption and secure device authentication, ensuring your smart home is not vulnerable to prying eyes and malicious hackers.
- **Local Control Reigns Supreme:** While cloud-based control offers convenience, it also creates dependence on remote servers. Matter champions local control, allowing you to control your devices directly without relying on the internet, a crucial point for privacy-conscious individuals.

Beyond the Hype: Matter in Action

So, how will Matter change our lives? Imagine waking up to the gentle sunrise hues cast by your smart lights, triggered by a sensor detecting the first rays of dawn. Your coffee machine preheats, courtesy of a seamlessly interconnected routine between your smart plug and phone calendar. As you leave for work, your smart lock automatically secures the door, while your thermostat adjusts to an energy-efficient setting. Throughout the day, your Matter-enabled devices orchestrate a symphony of comfort and convenience, anticipating your needs and adapting to your lifestyle.

Latest Updates about Matter

The Matter revolution is still in its early stages, but the momentum is undeniable. Here's a snapshot of the latest developments:

- **Official Launch (November 2022):** After years of anticipation, the Matter 1.0 specification was officially released in November 2022, marking a new era in smart home interoperability.
- **Device Certification Begins:** The Connectivity Standards Alliance (CSA) has initiated the Matter certification program, paving the way for the first Matter-certified devices to hit the market in 2023.
- **Ecosystem Expansion:** Major players like Google, Amazon, and Apple are actively integrating Matter into their platforms and devices. With each new addition, the Matter ecosystem gains strength and ubiquity.
- **Future Roadmap:** The CSA actively plans for future Matter iterations, with ambitions to expand supported device types and functionalities, further solidifying its role as the lingua franca of the smart home.

Benefits for the End User

For consumers, Matter presents a future free from the shackles of proprietary ecosystems. Here's why it matters:

- **Freedom of Choice:** No longer are you restricted to a single brand or platform. Matter empowers you to mix and match devices from different manufacturers, creating a smart home tailored to your specific needs and preferences.
- **Simplified Setup and Control:** Say goodbye to complex configuration processes and app overload. Matter promises a seamless, unified experience, where all your devices can be controlled through a single app or even voice commands.
- **Enhanced Security and Reliability:** Matter's robust security features and mesh network technology ensure your smart home is not only secure but also reliable, minimizing the risk of outages and disruptions.

Conclusion

This chapter has explored the paradigm shift from Industry 3.0 to Industry 4.0, focusing on the transformative implications of this shift for the manufacturing sector. We began by providing an overview of Industry 3.0, characterized by automation and the use of programmable logic controllers (PLCs). We then delved into the defining features of Industry 4.0, including the integration of cyber-physical systems (CPS), the Industrial Internet of Things (IIoT), and artificial intelligence (AI).

We discussed the top technologies shaping Industry 4.0, highlighting the significance of networking technologies, serial communication protocols like MODBUS, RS-232, and RS-485, and the role of IoT gateways in digitizing MODBUS communication. We also examined the importance of OneM2M communication and Matter, the next big thing in smart home technology.

By showcasing real-world examples, we aimed to demonstrate the tangible benefits and potential of this transformative industrial revolution.

In closing, it is evident that Industry 4.0 represents a significant leap forward in manufacturing. By embracing the power of interconnectedness, intelligence, and automation, Industry 4.0 promises to revolutionize production processes, enhance efficiency, and drive innovation across the entire manufacturing landscape. As we move forward, it is crucial to continue investing in research and development, fostering collaboration between industry and academia, and developing the skilled workforce necessary to navigate this exciting new era of industrial production.

References

1. Schwab, K. (2017). The Fourth Industrial Revolution. Crown Business.
2. Ashton, K. (2009). That 'Internet of Things' Thing. RFID Journal.
3. Porter, M. E., & Heppelmann, J. E. (2014). How Smart, Connected Products Are Transforming Companies. Harvard Business Review.
4. Lee, I. (2015). The Internet of Things (IoT): Applications, investments, and challenges for enterprises. Business Horizons, 58(4), 431-440.
5. Lee, J., & Lee, K. (2015). The Internet of Things (IoT): Applications, investments, and challenges for enterprises. Business Horizons, 58(4), 431-440.
6. Schuh, G., Anderl, R., & Gausemeier, J. (2017). Industrie 4.0 Maturity Index–Managing the Digital Transformation of Companies. In Advances in Production Technology (pp. 43-53). Springer.
7. Lu, Y., Xu, X., Lu, Y., & Fu, Y. (2017). Industry 4.0: State of the art and future trends. International Journal of Production Research, 55(12), 3609-3629.
8. Kagermann, H., Lukas, W. D., & Wahlster, W. (2013). Industrie 4.0: Mit dem Internet der Dinge auf dem Weg zur 4. industriellen Revolution. VDI nachrichten, 22, 23-24.
9. Rinaldi, A. (2004). MODBUS Messaging on TCP/IP Implementation Guide v1.0b.

10. Hopkins, M. (2006). Industrial Network Basics: Practical Guides for the Industrial Technician. Pearson Prentice Hall.
11. Covington, J. W. (2004). Industrial Automation: Hands-On. McGraw-Hill Education.
12. Ludwig, W. (2004). The Basics of MODBUS. Saelig Company, Inc.
13. EIA/TIA RS-232 Standard Documentation.
14. EIA/TIA RS-485 Standard Documentation.
15. https://www.ni.com/docs/en-US/bundle/serial-feature/resource/371253g.pdf
16. Marconi, A., & Bucciarelli, E. (2019). Industrial Internet of Things (IIoT): Challenges, Opportunities, and Directions. Sensors, 19(17), 3791. https://www.mdpi.com/1424-8220/19/17/3791
17. Sherali, Z., Ahmed, F., & Habib, M. A. (2020). IoT-Based Communication Protocols for Industry 4.0: A Review. IEEE Access, 8, 194409-194429. https://ieeexplore.ieee.org/document/9200659
18. Yang, C., Kim, J., & Kim, J. H. (2020). Industrial IoT Gateway for Process Monitoring Based on MQTT Protocol. Electronics, 9(3), 545. https://www.mdpi.com/2079-9292/9/3/545
19. Lee, J., Bagheri, B., & Kao, H. A. (2015). A Cyber-Physical Systems architecture for Industry 4.0-based manufacturing systems. Manufacturing Letters, 3, 18-23. https://www.sciencedirect.com/science/article/pii/S221282711400091X
20. Connectivity Standards Alliance (CSA): https://csa-iot.org/
21. Build With Matter - Smart Home Device Solution (CSA-IOT): https://csa-iot.org/
22. Matter Protocol - IoT Device Development - Silicon Labs: https://www.silabs.com/wireless/matter
23. Figure 9.4 Reference - https://www.onem2m.org/images/using-onem2m/image1.png
24. Figure 9.5 Reference - https://lh5.googleusercontent.com/FmZ59ivO-etKf-WPT2AGEp0WNdTa7bhoAi-eCeWDutoPfk34g9XSPo-czvL3mfW-Po45kjgMCUINPDAdyffFI9Lf_vsz7splFhyb_AlrSCVs4YW2A79zDCRu-vAPkFoxAjqhjeF_GcCl1YfgBJ6wgbMmarU8Cu5W-3Mw0m_Hk5hcY5iB-CxvVwc-XNdo9Q

Index

F

G

H

I

L

M